CRITICAL
MANAGEMENT
RESEARCH

SAGE was founded in 1965 by Sara Miller McCune to support the dissemination of usable knowledge by publishing innovative and high-quality research and teaching content. Today, we publish more than 750 journals, including those of more than 300 learned societies, more than 800 new books per year, and a growing range of library products including archives, data, case studies, reports, conference highlights, and video. SAGE remains majority-owned by our founder, and on her passing will become owned by a charitable trust that secures our continued independence.

Los Angeles | London | Washington DC | New Delhi | Singapore

edited by Emma Jeanes & Tony Huzzard

CRITICAL MANAGEMENT RESEARCH

Reflections from the Field

Los Angeles | London | New Delhi
Singapore | Washington DC

Los Angeles | London | New Delhi
Singapore | Washington DC

SAGE Publications Ltd
1 Oliver's Yard
55 City Road
London EC1Y 1SP

SAGE Publications Inc.
2455 Teller Road
Thousand Oaks, California 91320

SAGE Publications India Pvt Ltd
B 1/I 1 Mohan Cooperative Industrial Area
Mathura Road
New Delhi 110 044

SAGE Publications Asia-Pacific Pte Ltd
3 Church Street
#10-04 Samsung Hub
Singapore 049483

Editor: Jai Seaman
Assistant editor: Lily Mehrbod
Production editor: Ian Antcliff
Copyeditor: Richard Leigh
Proofreader: Clare Weaver
Indexer: David Rudeforth
Marketing manager: Catherine Slinn
Cover design: Francis Kenney
Typeset by: C&M Digitals (P) Ltd, Chennai, India
Printed in Great Britain by Henry Ling Limited at
The Dorset Press, Dorchester, DT1 1HD

Chapter 1 © Emma Jeanes and Tony Huzzard 2014
Chapter 2 © Mats Alvesson and Jörgen Sandberg 2014
Chapter 3 © Emma Jeanes, Bernadette Loacker and
Martyna Śliwa 2014
Chapter 4 © Daniel Nyberg and Helen Delaney 2014
Chapter 5 © Tony Huzzard and Yvonne Johansson 2014
Chapter 6 © Mathias Skrutkowski 2014
Chapter 7 © Susanne Ekman 2014
Chapter 8 © Jon Bertilsson 2014
Chapter 9 © Karen Lee Ashcraft and Catherine S. Ashcraft 2014
Chapter 10 © Peter Svensson 2014
Chapter 11 © Hugh Willmott 2014
Chapter 12 © Martin Parker 2014
Chapter 13 © Emma Jeanes and Tony Huzzard 2014

First published 2014

Library of Congress Control Number: 2014935430

British Library Cataloguing in Publication data

A catalogue record for this book is available from
the British Library

ISBN 978-1-4462-5742-5
ISBN 978-1-4462-5743-2 (pbk)

Contents

List of contributors

Mats Alvesson is Professor of Business Administration at the University of Lund, Sweden and at University of Queensland Business School, Australia. Research interests include critical theory, gender, power, management of professional service (knowledge intensive) organizations, leadership, identity, organizational image, organizational culture and symbolism, qualitative methods and philosophy of science. Recent books include *The Triumph of Emptiness* (Oxford University Press 2013), *Qualitative Research and Theory Development* (Sage 2011, with Dan Kärreman), *Constructing Research Questions* (Sage 2013, with J Sandberg) and *Interpreting Interviews* (Sage 2011).

Karen Lee Ashcraft (karen.ashcraft@colorado.edu) is Professor of Organizational Communication at the University of Colorado Boulder. Her research examines organizational forms, occupational and professional identities, and relations of difference such as gender and race through qualitative methodologies, and has appeared in such venues as *Academy of Management Review, Academy of Management Journal, Administrative Science Quarterly*, and *Communication Theory*.

Catherine S. Ashcraft is a Senior Research Scientist with the National Center for Women & Information Technology at the University of Colorado Boulder. Her research examines new technologies, diversity, youth sexualities, and critical multicultural pedagogies, and has appeared in venues such as the *American Educational Research Journal, Teachers College Record, International Journal of Qualitative Studies in Education, Anthropology & Education, and Journal of Applied Communication.*

Jon Bertilsson, PhD, is a lecturer and consumer researcher at the Department of Business Administration, Lund University, Sweden. He conducts consumer cultural studies of consumption practices, with a particular interest in brands. His research also involves critical studies of firms' branding practices and their effects on people and society.

Helen Delaney is a research fellow in the Department of Business Administration at Lund University, Sweden and a lecturer in the Department of Management and International Business at the University of Auckland. Her research and teaching focuses primarily on the sociology of work and critical perspectives towards organizations. Helen is a member of the editorial collective of the journal *ephemera: theory & politics in organization*.

Susanne Ekman is Assistant Professor at Department of Organization, Copenhagen Business School. Her research interest lies mainly within the field of knowledge intensive companies. On a more theoretical level, she has explored the ambiguous consequences of freedom fantasies and authority relations in numerous contexts. Being a dedicated empirical researcher, she is also engaged in the discussion of how best to establish fruitful methodologies for critical research. She has published with Palgrave Macmillan and Oxford University Press, and has journal publications in *Human Relations* and *Organization*, in addition to a number of Danish publications.

Tony Huzzard is Professor of Organisation Studies at the Department of Business Administration, Lund University and is also Visiting Professor at the Chalmers University of Technology in Gothenburg. He has researched and published widely on organizational development, work organization and industrial relations. His current research interests are diverse, including corporate governance and work organization, process organizing in health care and the branding of business schools.

Emma Jeanes is based at Exeter University, and is affiliated to Lund University. Her research interests include the experiences of work, gender, discrimination, ethics, reflexivity, and the distinctions between work and life 'outside' of (paid) work. She takes an historical, sociological and philosophical approach to her research.

Yvonne Johansson is a senior lecturer at the School of Social Work at Lund University in Sweden. Her main research interest is in health and social care sectors with a particular focus on evaluation and knowledge development.

Bernadette Loacker works as a post-doctoral researcher and lecturer at the Department of Business Administration at the University of Lund, Sweden. Her research interests include contemporary modes and practices of work organization, institutional and organizational forms of power and control, subjectivities and identities at work, and poststructuralist organization theories. She is a member of the editorial collective of the journal *Ephemera: Theory and Politics in Organization*.

Daniel Nyberg is Professor of Sustainability in the International Centre for Corporate Social Responsibility (ICCSR) at the University of Nottingham. His research focuses on political activities in and by organizations.

Martin Parker works in the School of Management at Leicester University. His last books were *Alternative Business: Outlaws, Crime and Culture* (Routledge 2012) and the co-edited *Companion to Alternative Organization* (Routledge 2013). He writes about things that have happened to him, or that he has seen on TV.

Jörgen Sandberg is Professor in the School of Business at the University of Queensland, Australia. His research interests include competence and learning in organizations, leadership, practice-based research, qualitative research methods, and philosophy of science. His work has appeared in several journals, including *Academy of Management Review*, *Academy of Management Journal*, *Harvard Business Review*, *Journal of Management Studies*, *Organisational Research Methods* and *Organization Studies*. His most recent book (co-authored with Mats Alvesson) is *Constructing Research Questions: Doing Interesting Research* (Sage 2013).

Mathias Skrutkowski is a PhD student in Business Administration at Lund University. The research for his PhD thesis explores internal reactions to managerial change projects in organizations that suffer crises of confidence.

Martyna Śliwa is a Professor of Management and Organization Studies at Essex Business School, University of Essex. Her research interests include migration and transnationalism, intersectionality in organizations, critical management education and the use of literary fiction as a vehicle for organizational inquiry. She is a member of the editorial collective of the journal *Ephemera: Theory and Politics in Organization*.

Peter Svensson, PhD, is a lecturer and researcher at the Department of Business Administration, Lund University, Sweden. His current research interests include knowledge production in business life, workplace democracy, employee voice, marketing management discourse and the use of natural language in financial reporting.

Hugh Willmott is Professor of Management at Cass Business School and Research Professor in Organization Studies, Cardiff Business School. He co-founded the International Labour Process Conference and the International Critical Management Studies Conference. He has contributed to leading management and social science journals and has published numerous books. Full details can be found on his homepage: https://sites.google.com/site/hughwillmottshomepage

ONE

Introduction

Emma Jeanes and Tony Huzzard

The idea for this book emerged from a number of conversations among colleagues[1] in which meetings ostensibly arranged to discuss research projects were overtaken by the often unspoken questions, frustrations and anxieties about the processes and expectations surrounding critical research and research collaboration. 'Being critical' has become an increasingly common way of describing oneself as an organization or management scholar. As we will go on to explore, what started as a small nascent group of scholars has become a substantial community – in terms of size and impact – particularly in Europe. With the 'critical' label come certain expectations as to how the scholar approaches the field of study. In practice, however, these expectations are usually evident in the types of research questions and the writing up of research. Arguably less attention is given to the other aspects of accessing, researching and leaving the research site, and the negotiations around the collective nature of research. In some cases the critical label is something of a casually worn badge – perhaps one that was once chosen because it meant something but has now become more of a habit to wear, where its symbolism has become less significant over time and is no longer discussed.

---

[1] That these ideas should emerge in such a context is no surprise, given some of its characteristics. The discussions were held in the Lund University Management and Organisation Studies (LUMOS) group, which is an internationally diverse group of mostly 'critical' scholars, with many of its members having come to Lund from as far afield as Australia, New Zealand and the US and – perhaps even more importantly – from different academic cultures. The group also has close collaborative relations with colleagues in the field internationally. As a consequence, questions of 'the way we do things around here' (to adopt the phrase of Deal and Kennedy, 1982) were often present.

The casualization of critical research, in which some scholars partially engage with its tenets, lay at the heart of our conversations and the concern of this text. In a community in which ethics, fairness and giving voice to those who are marginalized (see below for a more detailed introduction) should be at the core of the research endeavour, we instead often find piecemeal engagement, conflicting interpretations, and the challenges of the critical project in practice. This is not to suggest that these issues are not of concern to scholars (though the degree of reflexivity in the community is by no means all that we might hope) but that the theory of doing critical research is a challenge to realize in practice. These are important concerns, and are not easily addressed by texts on research design that focus on an abstract and idealized approach to research. The purpose of this text is to explore the various stages of research, reflecting on what it means to be a critical researcher and the problems, challenges and negotiations of these events by engaging with experiences of critical researchers.

In our discussions, what became interesting was how, for some, their research practices were taken-for-granted, commonsensical ways of undertaking research (and thus not worthy of much discussion), and for others they were confronting, challenging and counterproductive (and a constant topic of conversation). Notions such as those of equity, ethics, autonomy, and collective responsibility remain at the margins of collegial discourse; and texts on methodology and research design tend to underplay their significance and, in doing so, limit the possibility of reflexivity in relation to them (but see, for example, Alvesson et al., 2008; Brewis and Wray-Bliss, 2008; Cunliffe, 2003; Wray-Bliss, 2003). Reflexivity, whilst manifest in many forms and thus something of a heterogeneous concept, argues in broad terms for researchers to position themselves in relation to their object of study in order that their impact on the object, the subject, and on the nature of their knowledge claims can be assessed. Its practice, as will be explored, can be enacted in a variety of ways. Yet textbooks on methodology and research design tend to have short sections or brief mentions of reflexivity in otherwise substantial volumes. Ethics in research usually fares better, and often warrants a dedicated chapter. But, like reflexivity, ethics is a situated concern and is best understood in context. The challenges of navigating ethics and reflexivity are thus usefully explored in relation to researchers' practice. Many of the issues around being and what it means to be an ethical, reflexive, critical and ultimately scholarly researcher are left unsaid. This text seeks to put these notions at the heart of the research process, and adopt a more comprehensive, though not exhaustive, approach: from thinking through the initial question, fieldwork, analysis and writing up, and including – importantly – the relationships within the academic community as a part of that process. Our aim is to ensure critical research practice is explored and questioned so that other researchers may in turn become more reflexive in their own practice.

In a text of this kind it helps to have a number of voices and influences (or 'reflections'). As well as enjoying contributions from many scholars, the process of writing this book has been to some extent a collaborative one, with contributors commenting on each other's chapters as well as the editors, and many co-authored chapters. As a result the book hopes to capture some of the critical spirit, and ensure that no perspective dominates (with the usual caveat that the editors take responsibility for the final text). As intimated in the title, our particular focus in the book is that of exploring some of the methodological issues and implications of doing Critical Management Studies (CMS). The book was conceived from the belief that the methodological aspects of CMS have been relatively neglected to date. But the book is not just another methods book; we are not presenting a 'how to do it' text for critical management scholars. Rather, it focuses (mostly) on contemporary accounts of those engaged in fieldwork and managing the challenges posed before, during and after entering the field. In this sense it has been put together in the spirit of John Van Maanen's *Tales of the Field* (1988/2011). The idea has been to cover different types of research projects and approaches in different contexts, encouraging our contributors to be reflexive in their explorations of their experiences and practices, and to draw out the ethical issues where appropriate. But first, what do we mean by critical management studies and critical management research?

The what and why of critical management studies

In the recent *Oxford Handbook of Critical Management Studies*, Alvesson et al. (2009: 1) define the field as 'a movement that questions the authority and relevance of mainstream [management] thinking and practice'. This field or movement emerged during the 1990s out of a disenchantment with management studies as it was taught in business schools and represented in research outputs in the leading business and management journals. The source of this disenchantment was a belief that what Alvesson et al. describe as the 'mainstream' was overly instrumental in its objectives. This was reflected in an unreflective ambition of serving certain interests within the domain of practice, notably the interests of elite groups such as owners and/or senior managers at the expense of those who are disadvantaged by such groups. In the domain of knowledge creation or social science, again, certain interests were being more or less privileged over others, namely technocratic knowledge interests with an overwhelming belief in the scientific virtues of the positivist ideal and rational instruments for pursuing 'shared goals'. The aims of the CMS scholar, rather, are generally aligned with what Jürgen Habermas has termed emancipatory knowledge interests whereby the researcher seeks to pursue critical reflection and change in social relations to reduce subordination and enhance self-actualization (Alvesson and Willmott, 1996).

To be more precise, critical scholars increasingly questioned a central domain assumption of the mainstream, namely that management is 'a neutral and value free activity that concerns attaining the instrumental goals of organizations that serve a common good' (Voronov et al., 2009 following Adler et al., 2007). An alternative, critical approach to the study of management and its various sub-fields requires the 'questioning of taken-for-granteds, both about practice and its social and institutional context ... Identifying and questioning both purposes and conflicts of power and interest' (Reynolds, 1998: 192). The broad aim here is that of a radical critique of management theory and practice and a distancing from the knowledge interests and practitioner interests that dominate mainstream scholarship and the practice that such scholarship both informs and is informed by. In a broad statement on the premises, practices, problems and prospects of CMS authored by Adler et al., the term 'radical' signals an 'attentiveness to the socially divisive and ecologically destructive broader patterns and structures – such as capitalism, patriarchy, neo-imperialism etc. – that condition local action and conventional wisdom' (2007: 120). The term 'critique' is not just a problematization of specific practices or beliefs but also 'aims to show how such beliefs and practices are nurtured by, and serve to sustain, divisive and destructive patterns and structures; and also how their reproduction is contingent and changeable, neither necessary nor unavoidable' (2007: 120).

In a relatively early paper, Fournier and Grey (2000), proposed three core unifying elements in CMS. First, it has a commitment to some form of denaturalization. This in essence is a matter of destabilizing that which is taken for granted in dominant accounts of management knowledge. The naturalization of a social order comes into being when members of the social order uncritically accept 'that's how things are' or that 'there is no alternative' (Alvesson et al., 2009: 9). This, for example, might entail not questioning the necessity of the ideology or discourse of shareholder value in much of UK and US capitalism (Lazonick and O'Sullivan, 2000). Secondly, it entails a non-performative stance. Performativity here is that which sees the pursuit of efficiency as the guiding objective towards which both management practice and management knowledge are directed. A critical approach, on the contrary, would not seek to align knowledge, truth and efficiency. Rather, it 'is concerned with performativity only in that it seeks to uncover what is being done in its name' (Fournier and Grey, 2000: 17). Finally, reflexivity on the part of the researcher is necessarily also a core characteristic of CMS. This acknowledges that our accounts of the social world are influenced by our positions in such a world. Accordingly, a core requirement in the conduct of critical management research is the capacity to reflect on how the processes of our own knowledge production are shaped by our values, experiences and pre-understandings (Adler et al., 2007: 128–9; Alvesson and Sköldberg, 2008; Thompson and McHugh, 2009: 13–14).

Much of the early work in the field originated in the UK where disenchantment against the mainstream was particularly strongly felt. This first expressed itself in the publication of an anthology titled *Critical Management Studies* in 1992 by Alvesson and Willmott and was followed up by various activities including conference streams, research networks and the first biennial Critical Management Studies Conference held at Manchester in 1999 (see Fournier and Grey, 2000, for an account of the early emergence of the field). However, it is important to acknowledge that although this period first saw the emergence of the CMS label or brand (Thompson, 2004), critical scholarship on management and organization did not of course start here. Fournier and Grey, for example, cite the earlier works of Burnham (1945), Mills (1956) and Enteman (1993) as texts that broadly sought to 'problematize the growing social power of management as a practice and as a social grouping' (2000: 6). To this we can add, from the domain of industrial sociology, works such as Bendix (1956), Braverman (1974), Benson (1977), Nichols and Beynon (1977), and Clegg and Dunkerley (1980). Accordingly, the emergence of the domain of CMS in the 1990s was by no means the first engagement by critical scholars in the broad fields of management, work and employment. Indeed, we can trace elements of radical critique – in the sense defined here by Adler et al. – in the founding fathers of sociology, Marx, Weber and to a lesser extent Durkheim (Alvesson et al., 2009: 4).

A further antecedent of CMS is critical theory itself. The central concern of critical theory is to analyse social conditions with a particular emphasis on exploitation, repression, asymmetrical power relations and distorted communication (Alvesson and Deetz, 2000). As well as critiquing the unwarranted use of power, it also seeks to change established social relations so that 'human beings are freed from dependency, subordination and repression' (Scherer, 2009: 30). In terms of conducting social science, critical theorists reject positivism as the established benchmark for developing objective and thereby 'true' knowledge in both the natural and social sciences. It is thereby a technology for domination that has entailed a one-sided instrumental conception of reason (Horkheimer and Adorno, 1947/1972). This scepticism towards the positivist ideal was a key foundation for the later work in critical theory by Jürgen Habermas who saw the role of communication as a central aspect of social relations, and communicative distortion as being broadly concomitant with structures of domination (Habermas, 1984/1987). The work of Habermas and other critical theorists has had a major influence on the evolution of CMS in the past two decades (see, for example, Alvesson and Willmott, 1996; Rasche and Scherer, 2014).

Critical management studies as a contested terrain

However, although there are broad elements that define and delineate CMS as a shared domain of scholarship, there are also elements of difference. Fournier and Grey (2000: 26) describe these differences in terms of 'CMS as a fragmented and slippery domain, fractured by multiple lines of division which to a large extent reproduce divisions in the social sciences more generally'. Whilst CMS scholars can be said to be broadly united in rejecting the epistemological ideals of positivism (cf. Donaldson, 1996), epistemology nevertheless delineates clear contours of difference in other respects. Adler et al. (2007) set out three distinct but in some respects overlapping epistemological views that characterize the CMS movement: standpoint theory, poststructuralism and critical realism. We will briefly describe these in turn.

Standpoint theorists reject any notion that an objective, value-free social science is possible. The production of all research accounts of the social world is inseparable from the political standpoint of their author (Lukacs, 1923/1971). CMS scholars typically approach the study of management and organizations from the standpoint of the disadvantaged or underprivileged in a world of asymmetrical power relations and structures of domination. In essence standpoint theorists take the perspective of such groups who are explicitly excluded from mainstream approaches that privilege a managerial perspective. This includes, for example, the perspectives of women (implying feminism), ethnic minorities (perhaps implying post-colonialism) and workers (often implying labour process analysis).

Poststructuralists, although sharing this critique of the mainstream, nevertheless are sceptical of the assumption in standpoint theory that individuals sharing the same position in the social order have similar objective interests. Moreover, poststructuralists also argue, in line with postmodernism more generally, that our knowledge of the social world is always contingent on the discursive practices through which we interrogate it and that there is no objective value-free language for capturing social phenomena empirically (Jones, 2009). This casts doubt on whether the structures of domination we as researchers wish to study can be separated from the linguistic practices through which we constitute them. The epistemological assumptions here turn the attention of the CMS scholar to the study of language in the constitution of managerial knowledge. It also calls for a focus on the role of power in fixing a particular or dominant way of understanding the world. This clearly connects with the centrality of (de)naturalization in the domain description of CMS proposed by Fournier and Grey (2000).

The third epistemological sub-domain of CMS identified by Adler et al. (2007) is that of critical realism. Critical realists have a more optimistic view than poststructuralists on the possibilities of the social scientist to make truth claims about social structures or 'generative mechanisms'. Although these are deemed by the critical realist to be real, the knowledge that we have of them is nevertheless socially constructed (Duberley and Johnson, 2009). The analytical focus of critical realists is on underlying shifts in structures of domination that perpetuate the position of elites within the social order (Reed, 2009). Critical realists typically start out their research endeavours by trying to explain outcomes in terms of tracing back, through the technique of retroduction, to tease out the generative mechanisms of central explanatory potential. Whilst such mechanisms may be observable or unobservable, they nevertheless signal an objectivist ontology, albeit one which is multilayered in that there is an empirical layer (which is observable), an actual layer (existing in time and space) and a real layer (a set of structures that have causal powers from which observable events emerge).

Perhaps the most fundamental debates within CMS have tended to revolve around the competing epistemological stances of the second and third of these sub-domains. Moreover, such debates are replicated elsewhere in the social sciences and arguably pre-date the coining of the CMS 'brand' in the 1990s. For example, the argument over subjectivism versus objectivism is traceable back at least to Burrell and Morgan's *Sociological Paradigms and Organizational Analysis* (1979), if not further. The core of their argument was that research in management and organizational studies could be mapped as being in one of four distinct paradigms, what they termed as being functionalist sociology, interpretivism, radical structuralism and radical humanism. Together, these formed a 2 × 2 matrix defined along two axes: first, that of the dichotomy between subjectivist and objectivist metatheory; and second, that between the sociology of regulation and the sociology of radical change (Burrell and Morgan, 1979).

Subsequently, the inherent dualism between subject and object in their matrix was trenchantly critiqued by those broadly embracing a poststructuralist stance in what became euphemistically known as the paradigm wars in organization studies (Jackson and Carter, 1991; Willmott, 1993). This division was also reflected in another arena – the labour process tradition whereby broadly poststructuralist approaches (e.g. Knights and Willmott, 1989) were counterposed by the work of more materialist authors who subsequently acknowledged a broad commitment to critical realism (e.g. Thompson and Ackroyd, 1995). The upshot of these divisions is that a precise definition and boundary for CMS has been a contested terrain. Some seek to define CMS as being delineated by one of the positions. For example, Keleman and Rumens (2008) see CMS as being broadly coterminous with postmodernism in organization studies, whereas, for example, Adler et al. (2007) see CMS as more broadly embracing the multiple epistemologies described here.

Doing critical management studies

Our discussion of the broad outlines of CMS so far suggests that a considerable literature now exists on the what and why of CMS, and perhaps too on the who and when of the field. In our view, however, rather less has been written on the how of CMS. Rectifying this shortcoming by focusing on methodological reflections from the field is the primary motivation for this book. One notable exception is the volume *Doing Critical Management Research* by Alvesson and Deetz (2000). Whilst acknowledging that all social science is critical in the sense that critical scholarship must guard against poor argumentation, doubtful sources and internal coherency, critical social science and CMS go considerably beyond this. Critical research in the latter sense also entails creating 'a balance between a critical basic orientation, [that is,] being informed by specific theoretical ideas and a political agenda' (see also Parker, 1995) and 'an open, empirically sensitive interest in discovering themes of oppression' (Alvesson and Deetz, 2000: 9).

Alvesson and Deetz broadly delineate CMS in terms of embracing both critical theory and postmodernism, although these terms are by no means coterminous. Meeting some of the earlier objections to Burrell and Morgan's paradigm framework, not least from postmodernists, Alvesson and Deetz suggest alternative dimensions for structuring what they call a metatheory of representational practices (2000: 24). The two dimensions in their model are firstly the origin of concepts and problems (dichotomized along the axis local/emergent and elite/a priori), and secondly the relation to dominant social discourse (dichotomized along the axis dissensus to consensus). This produces a 2 × 2 matrix depicting four types of studies: normative studies (seen as modern or progressive), interpretive studies (seen as premodern or traditional), critical studies (seen as late modern or reformist) and dialogic studies (seen as postmodern or deconstructionist). The term 'paradigm' preferred by Burrell and Morgan is eschewed here. Instead, the four basic positions identified entail particular assumptions and understandings which guide empirical work and which 'develop mobile but specifiable relations to each other and position particular types of conflicts and contradictions internal to them' (Alvesson and Deetz, 2000: 25). Clearly the latter two types of study have been of most interest within the field of CMS.

Qualitative methods have generally been preferred by CMS scholars. This is because quantitative methods have traditionally been associated with and serve the epistemologies of cause and effect that normally characterize scholarly endeavour in the natural sciences. For the critical social scientist, however, quantitative work entails a thinness of data, a predilection to a control orientation on the part of the researcher and a tendency to suppress variety (Alvesson and Deetz, 2000). Yet Alvesson and Deetz go further than the straightforward critique of quantitative methods that can be found in most standard textbooks on social science research methods. They also propose a number of specific practices for the critically inspired researcher. Firstly, they suggest a more intense effort at undertaking interpretations of, for example, interviews. This should recognize that interviews are a politically charged product which confers an obligation on the researcher to engage in reflexive practice on his or her role in the generation of the data. Another practice is that of reflexively evaluating language use. This is particularly pertinent in that language is seen as being central in how social relations are constructed, often in metaphorical or ambiguous ways. Thirdly, critical researchers may usefully seek to relate their interview or other material to the identity constructions both of those with whom they are engaging in the field and themselves. Fourthly, research practice should recognize the context within which the research setting is embedded. This acknowledges that meanings elicited in the field are contingent on the historical and cultural setting in which they are embedded. Overall, Alvesson and Deetz suggest that the practices proposed here set up a framework for a critical methodology that produces insight, critique and transformative redefinition.

Arguably, however, it less clear how there might be an explicitly 'critical' element to conducting research for the critical realist beyond the obvious and distinct metatheoretical points of departure of the approach. In general, the critical realist has a more sanguine standpoint on our capacity to access the field and draw inferences from our material that are not infected or strongly shaped by the discourses through which we attain such access. Language matters for the critical realist, but only in so far as it can in itself be a generative mechanism of specific discernible outcomes. Indeed, a recent lucid account by a proponent of critical realism outlined approaches to realist research designs by generally dispensing with the term 'critical' altogether (Ackroyd, 2009).

More recently, a further line of debate within CMS has been opened up on whether, and if so, how, CMS might engage more explicitly with practice. At issue here is Fournier and Grey's (2000) argument that CMS should be essentially non-performative in character. Those broadly supportive of this standpoint see CMS solely in terms of radical critique (see Parker, 2002, as an exemplar of this view). Others, however, in singling out the challenging of structures of domination in working life as a core theme of CMS, more closely align themselves with the previous arguments of authors such as Alvesson and Willmott (1992, 1996) in their call for studies of organizations to embrace the ambition of what they call micro-emancipation (Duberley and Johnson, 2009: 353–4). This they see as occurring in either the means or ends of an intervention and/or the onset of new social relations. This necessarily entails a more open stance on performativity than that envisaged by Fournier and Grey (2000). This is exemplified by a more recent critique by Spicer et al., who argue that CMS should be seen as a 'profoundly performative project' (2009: 537). These authors sought, rather, to identify ways in which CMS scholars might purposely engage with practice. Clearly rejected in their account, however, is any notion of means–ends calculation for converting inputs into outputs, particularly when the interests of employers or capital are privileged. Rather, a performative CMS should have an affirmative stance, have an ethic of care, be pragmatic, explore potentialities and have normative elements.

One way of acknowledging this debate is to argue that Adler et al.'s (2007) three sub-domains of epistemology within CMS (see earlier discussion) should be extended to include a fourth sub-domain, namely that of a critically informed pragmatism (see Keleman and Rumens, 2008: Chapter 4, for a discussion of the inheritance from American pragmatism in CMS). This argument has also in effect been embraced by other CMS scholars such as Voronov (2008) in his broad advocacy of an 'engaged critical management studies' and in a recently edited volume exploring the tensions between theory and practice in the work of CMS scholars (Wolfram Cox et al., 2009). These recent calls to engage with practice tend to revolve around the relative merits of theoretical or practical knowledge, or in the words of others, mode 1 or mode 2 knowledge (Gibbons et al., 2000). Again, we can see an approximate replication within CMS of debates around the nature of knowledge that are detectable elsewhere in the broader social sciences.

This section has broadly presented a very concise overview of some of the main proposals and debates on methods in CMS. However, much of the work covered here tends to be in the form of armchair theorizing. Whilst useful, the literature to date lacks work that reflects on concrete experiences from conducting CMS in the field. It is this shortcoming that this book seeks to redress. In the chapters to follow we report on various topics that our authors have encountered. Some of these encounters concern reflections prior to entering the field, some concern reflections from within the field, and others concern subsequent reflections away from the field. In the contributions we have discerned three central themes which we see of overarching saliency in the conduct of CMS research, namely reflexivity, ethics and researcher identity. We now turn to a brief discussion of these and the CMS research process prior to presenting short summaries of the chapters to follow.

Reflections on the research process

This book aims to inform those interested in research (particularly critical research) without becoming a text on research methodology, and seeks to explore various aspects of the research process without promising to provide a comprehensive account of the various so-called stages. One of the challenges of writing a text of this kind is meeting the needs of the novice researcher, who may be looking for a structured guide before undertaking research, while retaining the core focus of 'reflections from the field' – that is, accounts of research, the challenges and how these were or could be navigated, which will necessarily be personal and partial, but hopefully also rich and informative. Locating the ethical and political concerns of this text in researchers' accounts necessarily means that particular experiences are favoured over abstract possibilities. More fundamentally, the critical, reflexive, situated and subjectivist stance taken here rejects notions of neatly planned and executed research processes and questions the validity of such a claim. At the same time, the text seeks to proffer some insight and, consequentially, some guidance.

In this section a brief exploration of the research process, with appropriate references to sources for further guidance, will be given, and how this text relates to or complements this literature. The difficulty faced when writing about the stages of research is that you are writing about something that does not often occur in practice, and sometimes is not even sought in the first place. Many research projects emerge from other activities, develop serendipitously, or just fail to conform to the conventions set out in textbooks. Broadly, however, the research journey starts with a problem, area of interest or gap in knowledge, which is developed into a research question. Having developed the question, the researcher then contemplates how best to go about answering it, taking into account ontological, epistemological and practical concerns. To put it another way, the researcher considers what is known, how we know it, and the logistical and resource-based limitations of particular research designs.

There are already excellent texts that give researchers a grounding in ontological and epistemological concerns, such as Burrell and Morgan's (1979) *Sociological Paradigms and Organizational Analysis* and latterly Alvesson and Deetz 's (2000) *Doing Critical Management Research* (see the discussion in the previous section). The typologies presented in these texts help researchers locate their approach to research, and reflect on the nature, purpose and types of questions being asked and the appropriate methods of data collection. This text does not seek to replicate this work, though in several of the accounts presented in this text the ways in which the researchers see the world, and how this shapes the study, will be apparent. Nor does this text seek to provide a comprehensive overview of all possible techniques of data collection, or guide researchers in which technique to choose, when to choose them, for what purpose, and why. Volumes such Alan Bryman's (2012) *Social Research Methods* and, for less commonly used qualitative techniques, Denzin and Lincoln's (2011) *Handbook of Qualitative Research* provide good introductions to the range of techniques and when they might be suitable. In this book we focus on the most frequently used techniques in organization and management research, and consider them from a critical perspective. In response to the question 'which methods should I use?' we suggest that a number of factors could be considered, including: the type and nature of questions being asked; the level or unit of analysis presupposed in the research question; practical considerations; advice from collaborators, colleagues and superiors; instinct and personal preference/comfort; and ethical considerations. Further, what marks out a critical approach is reflexivity that recognizes the need to be responsive and sensitive to the field of study and what is proving to be insightful, interesting and, conversely, responding to unanticipated harm or distress caused. In short, we wish to stress the need to remain open to the field of study, and use a more emergent, responsive, and sensitive research design. Slavishly following a well-defined strategy forecloses the possibility of learning whilst 'in the field'.

All of the methods discussed have a qualitative orientation, which allows for in-depth, inductive and exploratory approaches to studying phenomena (see Silverman, 2011, for a good overview of qualitative methods). They also raise some of the more complex professional and ethical challenges. The volume is far from exhaustive in its treatment of the topic: there are also notable gaps in the range of methods discussed, such as diary methods, archival research and life histories, and design strategies, such as case study research (although many of its methodological components are discussed) to name a few examples. Their exclusion does not suggest they are not important and valuable methods for organizational analysis and critical management research (CMR). Nevertheless the majority of the book is devoted to the various methods, and the experiences, critiques and reflections on using these techniques in CMR. The chapters do not analyse in detail the nature of the methods, but instead focus on their application in CMR. The chapters also seek to demonstrate reflexivity in their use. As highlighted at the start of this introduction, one of the motivations behind this text was the feeling that CMR was not sufficiently critical of its own research practice. By taking a critical approach to the use of these methods it is hoped that these chapters will help other researchers develop their own scholarly, reflexive practice. Understanding and accounting for one's impact on the field of study can lead not only to more credible and reflexive outcomes, but also and relatedly to more ethical research both in terms of actions in the field, and the accounts of it when out.

Finally, the process of analysis and writing is core to the research process, though often receives less attention, ethically speaking, than the moments of face-to-face data collection. The process of analysis plays a crucial role in CMR and it is arguably the point at which it diverges most markedly from 'traditional' (non-critical) research (Fournier and Grey, 2000). Reflexive engagement with the process of knowledge production is demonstrated at this stage.

The book therefore follows, loosely speaking, a traditional research trajectory: initial idea, development of research question, selection of methods (and site of study), analysis, writing up the research, with reflexivity and ethics thematically present at all times. However, it does not outline a stage-by-stage guide, as this would merely duplicate the already useful resources available. Instead it focuses on the reflections, experiences and analysis of the various stages within CMR, and – where appropriate – highlights the particular challenges faced in CMR. It also brings to the fore intra-community issues, such as how we work with fellow scholars, introducing what could be considered a 'collaborative ethic' alongside an individual one. Implied, though not often articulated explicitly in the chapters, is the identity of the researcher in the research process. Who we are, what we want to achieve, what 'being critical' means to us, and our desire for recognition as critical researchers are just some of the factors that inform our construction of knowledge. By attending to what it means to do critical research, how we navigate the research process, our relationships with our field of study and our community, the book seeks to surface many of the factors that shape who we are and encourage us to be reflexive about its consequences. The book is divided into four main sections – approaching the field, in the field, out of the field, and reflections on the field – which are introduced below.

Introducing the chapters

Approaching the field

Chapters 2 and 3 take up reflections by researchers regarding what to study, and how to go about researching it. Mats Alvesson and Jörgen Sandberg start out in Chapter 2 by recognizing that what makes a theory or a study interesting and influential is that it challenges our assumptions in some significant way. However, established ways for arriving at research questions mean spotting or constructing 'gaps' in existing theories and studies and tend to reinforce rather than challenge their assumptions. Both what they call 'gap-spotting' as well as inductive studies assume the taken-for-grantedness of the existing literature and for the most part fail to say something really of interest to the reader. As an alternative, the authors argue for a problematization approach that surfaces and challenges the underlying assumptions held by various research audiences. Secondly, the chapter also advocates the practice of mystery creation whereby empirical material is used as a source for constructing breakdowns and mysteries in organizational life. The chapter then suggests how these two approaches might be fruitfully combined. It also offers ways of invoking some of the increasing number of research orientations that directly or indirectly encourage problematization, such as certain versions of social constructionism, postmodernism, feminism, and critical theory, in the research process. These approaches are less frequently used to guide empirical work than they are to prevent a reproduction of assumptions in the research process. These practices of problematization and mystery creation need to be undertaken, it is argued, in the initial literature review and gradually developed in the empirical work. Problematization calls for reflexivity that questions knowledge, its assumptions and the effects of these assumptions on shaping research. Their call for interesting research can also be seen as an ethical question – ensuring that research funds are well spent, and the time of research subjects is not used carelessly.

Chapter 3, authored by Emma Jeanes, Bernadette Loacker and Martyna Śliwa, is based on a series of interviews discussing issues arising from collaboration within research teams and negotiating working relationships, as well as exploring other challenges in attempting to research in a more open style. The chapter provides insight into the range of issues arising from the research process, the types of challenges faced and advice sought, and the management of the working relationship. Several themes are developed in the chapter: (1) the meanings of collaboration, data sharing, ownership of data, authorship etc., and moments of 'disidentification' with(in) a group; (2) the intentions and reasons for collaboration; (3) experiences of collaboration; (4) the challenges of collaboration; and (5) the evaluation of collaboration and reflections on the manner by which a community of scholars can engage and reflect on working practices, shared learning and so on. They draw attention to the manner in which the immediate working environment, such as the expectations, relationships with and preferences of collaborators, impacts the process of knowledge production as well as the researcher and ongoing researcher relationships. In doing so they also remind us that ethical relations are of concern within the community as well as beyond. Intriguingly, the findings also show that CMS scholars, whilst reflective on their collaborations, do not always demonstrate reflexivity in their intra-scholarly collaboration.

In the field

In Chapter 4, authored by Daniel Nyberg and Helen Delaney, the book takes the reader into the field. The specific topic covered in the chapter is critical ethnography. It addresses the challenges of undertaking an ethnographic research project, reflecting on all stages of the process: gaining access, negotiating access within the organization, collecting the data, writing up the findings and managing the process of exit from the organization. Throughout, the chapter reflects on ethical challenges facing the critical ethnographer and how these were negotiated in a particular project, and how the researcher's reflexivity informed and influenced the research process. Increasingly, not least due to the growing pressures for journal publications, researchers focus on short-term, interview-based studies (in qualitative research) rather than in-depth, ethnographic studies. The chapter presents contemporary examples of the latter, drawing on a critical perspective, to explore the challenges of being a critical researcher in these contexts. Ethnography often requires the researcher to develop a closeness to the phenomenon of interest, and the people connected to it. At the same time, the researcher is often seeking to expose taken-for-granted assumptions and exploitative working practices. This can involve placing the researcher in an uncomfortable, ethically challenging position. This chapter examines these challenges with reference to case studies of a leadership development programme in New Zealand and work at a call centre in Australia, as well as the extant literature. It also reflects on the ways of negotiating these challenges and the consequences for the research and researcher.

Chapter 5, written by Tony Huzzard and Yvonne Johansson, has action research as its particular focus. What distinguishes action research from other forms of engagement with the field is its concomitant interest in the intervention practices of the researcher acting as a change agent. At issue here is how action research from a critical perspective might differ from other approaches to action research. Inevitably, action research entails an explicitly performative stance to the field for the CMS researcher, and, as the chapter explains, this is no easy task in the notionally anti-performative tradition of CMS. The chapter traces the evolution of action research historically, noting that certain versions, especially what has been termed participatory action research, have close alignment with the core aims of CMS. There are, however, many difficulties faced when taking a critical perspective, given that action that achieves desired performative effects usually entails agreement not only between researcher and practitioners but also among practitioners engaged in the change effort. The chapter explores the issues at stake here from one of the author's own experiences from in field, with reference to experiences from an action research project in Swedish health care. The chapter highlights how critical researchers can alternate between nearness and distance from the field as an iterative process of reflexive knowledge production.

In Chapter 6, Mathias Skrutkowski discusses the topic of doing covert research in one's own organization and the moral and existential aspects related to doing this type of work, a research methodology often referred to as auto-ethnography (Ellis, 2004) or at-home ethnography (Alvesson, 2009). The discussion of these aspects draws on the author's personal experiences from working and researching in his own organization and thereby doing ethnographic study as an insider. The issues related to covert research include the slippery moral slope of covert ethnography, where the researcher notes down observations about people's behaviour and reactions, without having sought their prior consent, but also the more existential, identity-related aspects of maintaining the façade or persona, and carrying out the (often hard) work, of a loyal, conscientious employee, whilst having a secondary, ulterior agenda. The latter can be seen as a variation on age-old themes in ethnographic research: the tension between the virtues and pitfalls of going native. Who are you and who do you become, when you spend your days doing work under false pretences? Compared to your research, the non-covert duties you carry out as an employee at work also have a firmer ontological basis, in many ways feeling more real than your covert agenda. In situating himself in the research, Skrutkowski demonstrates a reflexive approach in the process of knowledge production.

Interviewing is the topic explored by Susanne Ekman in Chapter 7. She aims to develop and describe a form of critically inspired interviewing which at the same time commits itself to remedying what she sees as recurrent problematic tendencies within CMS: its moral condescension, its polarized opposition to mainstream research, and an unreflexive tendency for CMS scholars to predefine subject positions for many of the key research subjects. Yet at the same time, in order to maintain some of the strengths of CMS as a critical endeavour, she proposes the idea of compassion interviewing as a means of transcending both much of CMS practice and the prescriptive instrumentalism in mainstream research. Through a reading of various classical texts on compassion, the author argues that compassion allows the researcher to make sense of all actors in the field while at the same time retaining the ability to point out injustice and suffering – retaining ethics in the moment of researching the subject and in the subsequent emancipatory account. A number of concrete interview techniques are outlined in the chapter, which allow the researcher to carry out this intention in practice. These are illustrated with reference to the author's own engagement with the field.

In Chapter 8, Jon Bertilsson acknowledges the increasing role of social media in organizational life and reflects on the possibilities this offers as a means of conducting research. He starts out by acknowledging the method of netnography developed by the consumer researcher Robert Kozinets at the end of the 1990s to investigate the consumer behaviour of cultures and communities existing on the internet. He argues, however, that the method has far greater potential than this and proposes its usage to explore research topics within the social sciences such as social interaction, hierarchies, power, status, identity and discourse – phenomena that are more commonly associated with the domain of critical management studies. Accordingly, he describes and illustrates what he terms 'critical netnography' which directs its attention in particular to uncovering and conceptualizing the various forms of domination, asymmetry, hierarchy, conflicts, discourses and status positions prevalent in such types of internet-based communications. The chapter also includes an empirical example of how a critical netnography may be conducted, which involves the analysis of text-based interactions of an online forum centring on interest in fashion and clothing.

Out of the field

In the next chapter, Chapter 9, Karen Lee Ashcraft and Catherine Ashcraft take a step back from the field and examine a ritual endemic to qualitative research in organization studies: composing the methods section of a paper that presents empirical material, a topic that is rarely the subject of collective reflection. They begin by identifying the crucial features of a 'scholarly' methods section that have come to be expected by the leading journals in organization studies commonly regarded as friendly to interpretive and critical work. They then unpack the implications of what they argue has become a common recipe. Reflexively, they then acknowledge the likelihood of contradictory readings and suggest ways we might celebrate, debate, censure and transform what they call the methods section ritual. Accordingly, the chapter proposes tangible tactics whereby authors, reviewers, and editors might expose and navigate the struggle over the 'good' methods section, in the admittedly ambitious hope that – together – they might render this academic ritual a more open, productive, humane, and even playful site of contest.

The analysis of empirical material is addressed in Chapter 10 by Peter Svensson. In this chapter Svensson tackles the interpretive and constructed nature of knowledge in ethnography. The aim of the chapter is to explore and argue for overinterpretations in critical organizational ethnographies as a means to attend to the silent and hidden forms of power that contribute to the structural stability of organizational culture. With reference to Geertz's (1973) notion of thick description, he argues that far from being a weakness in critical ethnography, overinterpretation – or thickening thick description – is necessary for the production of interpretations that go beyond the visible empirical evidence. With reference to two studies, he explores two forms of overinterpretation: the overwriting of the natives' experience and the illumination of organizational silence. In concluding, he explores the consequences of this 'violence' to the empirical material, and its challenge to 'reasonable interpretations'. He makes the case that working within these limits risks reproducing naturalized and hegemonic representations of our world, what he describes as 'underinterpretation'. By engaging in overinterpretations he argues we are better placed to engage in the emancipatory ambitions of the critical project. Such an approach necessarily requires researchers to be reflexive in their approach, and also raises challenging ethical questions not least in the nature of 'giving voice' to participants. It brings to the fore the tension between the construction of a collective voice or speaking on behalf of others as part of an emancipatory project, and giving voice to the natives' experiences.

Chapter 11 discusses empirical analysis. The focus of the author, Hugh Willmott, is on the role that theory plays in informing research. This may at first glance seem out of place in a book focused on fieldwork, but, as Willmott argues, theory is integral to practice. He explores the theory-dependent nature of data collection (or data construction) and interpretation: how a topic is approached and studied is informed by the ontological commitments of the researcher. Willmott explores the role of theory in his own work, reflecting first on his doctoral studies and then his subsequent career. He points not only to the role that theory plays in empirical work and how data is constructed and given meaning, but also to the consequences of this for knowledge production. Our focus on empirical data as in some way separate from theory means we are insufficiently reflexive about the role theory has played. Willmott also points to the hegemonic tendencies in the field, where certain concepts are taken for granted and enjoy what he describes as a 'mundane legitimacy' that encourages their unreflexive adoption. To move beyond these commonsensical notions in constructing meaning and interpreting data (which is precisely what you would anticipate in CMR) requires reflexivity in our research.

Reflections on the field

Writing and dissemination is the topic discussed by Martin Parker in Chapter 12. He explores the process of writing up research, and in particular reflecting on the process of getting published, particularly in journals. The chapter reflects 'what can be said, by whom, how, and where' – exploring the politics of publishing as well as some thoughts on how this can be navigated. The chapter thus reflects on the state of the publishing field and how it disciplines the writer to create submissions that conform to a certain style and creates barriers to those who step outside of these conventions. However, it is not only journals that shape the craft, but also communities of scholars. Parker reflects on how CMS has by repute developed its own language, which can be seen to be exclusionary and pretentious, and on the geo-intellectual divide between North American and other (typically European) outlets for writing. He also considers how the institutions of publishing shape our writing, by requiring it to be marketable, and by encouraging practices that lead to impact. By bringing these reflections to our attention, Parker prompts us to become more reflexive in our writing and mindful of the politics of publishing (and to what is given voice and what is not), as well as encouraging us to resist it.

In the final chapter, Emma Jeanes and Tony Huzzard offer some concluding thoughts by drawing together the key themes emerging from the book and then draw out the role of the researcher in the preceding discussions. Underpinning much of what is explored above are the role and identity of the individual researcher and how they inform and are informed by the researcher's choice of research paradigm, personal style 'in the field', approach to working with colleagues or career ambitions, to name but a few. Critical research claims to lay much emphasis on the importance on reflexivity, and also lays claim to an underlying ethics, so in the concluding chapter we focus on the ethics of critical research, the role of reflexivity and the identity of the researcher in shaping research. We draw examples of ethics and reflexivity from throughout the text and reflect on the implications for the critical management researcher.

References

Ackroyd, S. (2009) 'Research designs for realist research', in D.A. Buchanan and A. Bryman (eds), *The Sage Handbook of Organizational Research Methods*. London: Sage, pp. 532–548.

Adler, P.S., Forbes, L.C. and Willmott, H. (2007) 'Critical management studies', *Academy of Management Annals*, 1(3): 119–179.

Alvesson, M. (2009) 'At-home ethnography: Struggling with closeness and closure', in S. Ybema, D. Yanow, H. Wels, and F. Kamsteeg (eds), *Organizational Ethnography: Studying the Complexities of Everyday Life*. London: Sage.

Alvesson, M., Bridgman, T. and Willmott, H. (2009) 'Introduction', in M. Alvesson, T. Bridgman, and H. Willmott (eds), *The Oxford Handbook of Critical Management Studies*. Oxford: Oxford University Press.

Alvesson, M. and Deetz, S.A. (2000) *Doing Critical Management Research*. London: Sage.

Alvesson, M., Hardy. C. and Harley. B. (2008) 'Reflecting on reflexivity: Reflexive textual practices in organization and management theory', *Journal of Management Studies*, 45(3): 480–501.

Alvesson, M. and Sköldberg, K. (2009) *Reflexive Methodology: New Vistas for Qualitative Research* (2nd edn). London: Sage.

Alvesson, M. and Willmott, H. (1992) *Critical Management Studies*. London: Sage.

Alvesson, M. and Willmott, H. (1996) *Making Sense of Management*. London: Sage.

Bendix, R. (1956) *Work and Authority in Industry: Ideologies of Management in the Course of Industrialization*. New York: John Wiley.

Benson, J.K. (1977) 'Organizations: A dialectical view', *Administrative Science Quarterly*, 22(1): 1–21.

Braverman, H. (1974) *Labor and Monopoly Capital: The Degradation of Work in the Twentieth Century*. New York: Monthly Review Press.

Brewis, J. and Wray-Bliss, E. (2008) 'Re-searching ethics: Towards a more reflexive critical management studies', *Organization Studies*, 29(12): 1521–1540.

Bryman, A. (2012) *Social Research Methods* (4th edn). Oxford: Oxford University Press.

Burnham, J. (1945) *The Managerial Revolution*. London: Penguin.

Burrell, G. and Morgan, G. (1979) *Sociological Paradigms and Organizational Analysis*. Aldershot: Gower.

Clegg, H. and Dunkerley, D. (1980) *Organization, Class and Control*. London: Routledge & Kegan Paul.

Cunliffe, A. (2003) 'Reflexive inquiry in organizational research: Questions and possibilities', *Human Relations*, 56(8): 983–1003.

Deal, T.E. and Kennedy, A.A. (1982) *Corporate Cultures: The Rites and Rituals of Corporate Life*. Harmondsworth: Penguin.

Denzin, N.K. and Lincoln, Y.S. (2011) *The Sage Handbook of Qualitative Research* (3rd edn). London: Sage.

Donaldson, L. (1996) *For Positivist Organization Theory*. London: Sage.

Duberley, J. and Johnson, P. (2009) 'Critical management methodology', in M. Alvesson, T. Bridgman, and H. Willmott (eds), *The Oxford Handbook of Critical Management Studies*. Oxford: Oxford University Press.

Ellis, C. (2004) *The Ethnographic I: A Methodological Novel about Autoethnography*. Walnut Creek, CA: AltaMira Press.

Enteman, W. (1993) *Managerialism: The Emergence of a New Ideology*. Madison: University of Wisconsin Press.

Fournier, V. and Grey, C. (2000) 'At the critical moment: Conditions and prospects for critical management studies', *Human Relations*, 53(1): 7–32.

Geertz, C. (1973) *The Interpretation of Cultures*. New York: Basic Books.

Gibbons, M., Limoges, C., Nowotny, H., Schwartzman, S., Scott, P. and Trow, M. (2000) *The New Production of Knowledge. The Dynamics of Science and Research in Contemporary Societies* (2nd edn). London: Sage.

Habermas, J (1984/1987) *The Theory of Communicative Action* (Vols I–II). London: Polity Press.

Horkheimer, H and Adorno, T.W. (1947/1972) *Dialectic of Enlightenment*. New York: Herder and Herder.

Jackson, N. and Carter, P. (1991) 'In defence of paradigm incommensurability', *Organization Studies*, 12(1): 109–127.

Jones, C. (2009) 'Poststructuralism in CMS', in M. Alvesson, T. Bridgman and H. Willmott (eds), *The Oxford Handbook of Critical Management Studies*. Oxford: Oxford University Press.

Keleman, M. and Rumens, N. (2008) *An Introduction to Critical Management Research*. London: Sage.

Knights, D. and Willmott, H. (1989) 'Power and subjectivity at work: From degradation to subjugation in social relations', *Sociology*, 23(4): 535–558.

Lazonick, W. and O'Sullivan, M. (2000) 'Maximizing shareholder value: A new ideology for corporate governance', *Economy and Society*, 29(1): 13–35.

Lukacs, G. (1923/1971) *History and Class Consciousness*. Cambridge, MA: MIT Press.

Mills, C.W. (1956) *The Power Elite*. New York: Oxford University Press.

Nichols, T. and Beynon, H. (1977) *Living with Capitalism*. London: Routledge & Kegan Paul.

Parker, M. (1995) 'Critique in the name of what? Postmodernism and critical approaches to organization', *Organization Studies*, 16(4): 553–564.

Parker, M. (2002) *Against Management: Organization in the Age of Managerialism*. Cambridge: Polity Press.

Rasche, A. and Scherer, A.G. (2014) 'Jürgen Habermas and organizations studies: Contributions and future prospects', in P. Adler, P. Du Gay, G. Morgan and M. Reed (eds), *The Oxford Handbook of Sociology, Social Theory and Organization Studies: Contemporary Currents*. Oxford: Oxford University Press.

Reed, M. (2009) 'Critical realism in critical management studies', in M. Alvesson, T. Bridgman and H. Willmott (eds), *The Oxford Handbook of Critical Management Studies*. Oxford: Oxford University Press.

Reynolds, M. (1998) 'Reflection and critical reflection in management learning', *Management Learning*, 29(2): 183–200.

Scherer, A. (2009) 'Critical theory and its contribution to CMS', in M. Alvesson, T. Bridgman and H. Willmott (eds), *The Oxford Handbook of Critical Management Studies*. Oxford: Oxford University Press.

Silverman, D. (2011) *Qualitative Research* (3rd edn). London: Sage.

Spicer, A., Alvesson, M. and Kärreman, D. (2009) 'Critical performativity: The unfinished business of critical management studies', *Human Relations*, 62(4): 537–560.

Thompson, P. (2004) 'Brands, boundaries and bandwagons: A critical reflection on critical management studies', in S. Fleetwood and S. Ackroyd (eds), *Critical Realist Applications in Organisation and Management Studies*. London: Routledge, pp. 51–66.

Thompson, P. and Ackroyd, S. (1995) 'All quiet on the workplace front? A critique of recent trends in British industrial sociology', *Sociology*, 29(4): 615–633.

Thompson, P. and McHugh, D. (2009) *Work Organizations: A Critical Approach* (4th edn). Basingstoke: Palgrave Macmillan.

Van Maanen, J. (1988/2011) *Tales of the Field: On Writing Ethnography*. Chicago: University of Chicago Press.

Voronov, M. (2008) 'Toward engaged critical management studies', *Organization*, 15(6): 939–945.

Voronov, M., Wolfram Cox, J., LeTrent-Jones, T.G. and Weir, D. (2009) 'Introduction: Intersections of critical management research and practice: A multi-domain perspective', in J. Wolfram Cox, T.G. LeTrent-Jones, M. Voronov and D. Weir (2009) *Critical Management Studies at Work. Negotiating Tensions between Theory and Practice*. Cheltenham: Edward Elgar, pp. 1–16.

Wolfram Cox, J., LeTrent-Jones, T.G., Voronov, M. and Weir, D. (2009) *Critical Management Studies at Work. Negotiating Tensions between Theory and Practice*. Cheltenham: Edward Elgar.

Willmott, H. (1993) 'Breaking the paradigm mentality', *Organization Studies*, 14(5): 681–720.

Wray-Bliss, E. (2003) 'Research subjects/research subjections: Exploring the ethics and politics of critical research', *Organization*, 10(2): 307–325.

PART I

APPROACHING THE FIELD

TWO

Problematization meets mystery creation: Generating new ideas and findings through assumption-challenging research

Mats Alvesson and Jörgen Sandberg

Introduction

A key objective of research is to develop new ideas and theoretical contributions. This is somewhat different from what is normally emphasized in methodology, namely, procedures that enable precision in description and analysis. In the latter, the issues of interest include validity, reliability, 'data collection' (depth and richness in the production of empirical material) and 'data processing' (how data are codified, categorized, analysed, interpreted and written). Such methodological procedures can be 'tight' or 'soft'. For example, a tight procedure may stress a fixed interview schedule and codification, while a soft procedure may emphasize the importance of having 'been there', in-depth interviewing, and interpretations that are fair to the experience of subjects.

Our purpose in this chapter is not to develop methodological procedures for generating more accurate and 'objective' representations of reality or of the authentic experiences and meanings of people; rather, our purpose is to discuss ways of generating interesting and potentially influential new ideas and theoretical contributions. This is of particular interest for critical studies in which the key aim is not so much the 'mirroring' or 'mapping' of reality, but instead the encouragement of novel ideas and path-breaking thinking. Breaking away from dominant constructions and institutions calls for some latitude from an overly strict focus on empirical details and slavishly following methodological procedures. But as good ideas and contributions require a grounding in empirical examinations – or, in a strong sense, how reality looks and can be understood – critical and theory-developing research are not in contradiction to, or disconnected from, empirical ambitions. Nevertheless, doing research – both theoretical and/or empirical – with the intention of developing new ideas often requires 'data' to stimulate imagination and creativity, rather than a narrow focus on ensuring that data mirrors reality: whether in the form of representing a phenomenon 'out there' (facts) or in the form of the experiences, beliefs, feelings or cognitions of subjects under study (meanings).

More specifically, for a theory to become interesting and influential it needs to attract attention from other researchers and practitioners, to lead to enthusiasm, to generate 'aha' and 'wow' moments, to trigger responses such as 'I have not thought about this before' or 'perhaps I should rethink this theme', and possibly to act as an effective tool for animating dialogue and reflexivity among practitioners. During the last four decades, originating with Davis's (1971) seminal sociological study, a large number of researchers have shown that rigorously executed research is typically not enough for a theory to be regarded as interesting and influential: it must also challenge an audience's[1] taken-for-granted assumptions in some significant way (e.g. Astley, 1985; Bartunek et al., 2006; Weick, 2001). In other words, if a theory does not challenge some of an audience's assumptions, it is unlikely to receive attention and become influential even if it has been rigorously developed and received substantial empirical support. Of course, not all forms of assumption challenging are in line with a critical management studies (CMS) agenda – CMS assumptions of the rotten nature of capitalist society, patriarchy, managerialism and other typical subjects can (and should) themselves also be scrutinized – but the research ideal of assumption challenging is broadly congruent with, and supportive of, the CMS project of unsettling dominant worldviews and constructions of reality. Emancipation means that a fixed set of beliefs are opened up for critical examination with the intention of increasing ethical awareness and autonomy (Alvesson and Willmott, 2012).

However, although this growing body of literature has clearly shown the importance of assumption challenging for developing novel research ideas, it has been considerably less clear about *how* we can productively go about challenging assumptions as a means for developing more interesting and influential theories. In previous studies, we have suggested two major ways of producing new ideas through assumption-challenging research, namely through *problematization* (e.g. Alvesson and Sandberg, 2013) and through *mystery creation* (e.g. Alvesson and Kärreman, 2011). The problematization methodology is used for critically scrutinizing and challenging dominant assumptions in a field, while the mystery methodology uses empirical material as a

---

[1]Here we mainly have in mind the academic audience targeted. However, 'audience' is a complex issue as it typically is not a unitary group but consists of several subgroups within a theoretical field. For further detail, see Alvesson and Sandberg (2013: Chapter 5).

source for constructing breakdowns and mysteries in social life. The former emphasizes critical examination of existing theory and studies within a field with the aim of questioning established truths and lines of thinking. The latter means that one tries to mobilize empirical material as a dialogue partner to talk back to established knowledge and through that encourage rethinking.

In this chapter we elaborate how these two assumption-challenging methodologies can be *combined*, as a way to come up with something new and unexpected, not just to represent reality or to apply, conform to, or modify a framework. Of course, new ideas come partly through serendipity and creative ingenuity, and partly by using existing theories/ideas in a novel way, but using 'creative' methodologies can also be beneficial in this process. We start by describing what we call the problematization methodology, followed by the methodology for mystery creation. Then we show how they can be productively set in interaction to generate new ideas and contributions.

Constructing research questions through problematization

It is important to consider what strategies researchers use for constructing and formulating research questions from existing literatures. Although a range of issues influences the purpose of a study, such as the researcher's knowledge and interest or what kind of research is likely to attract funding, the most crucial influencing factors are probably existing theory and empirical studies. The framing impact of earlier research is typically very strong. No researcher starts to study mergers, strategies, leadership or teamwork without 'knowing' something about previous thinking and studies in the area. The most prevalent strategy for constructing research questions in the context of established work is gap-spotting (Sandberg and Alvesson, 2011). It is by looking for different knowledge 'gaps' in existing literature that research questions are constructed. One common strategy is trying to spot *confusions* in the literature that need to be rectified. The most prevalent strategy is *neglect-spotting* in which the researcher tries to identify areas that are overlooked, under-researched, or lack empirical support and, in response to this neglect, construct a research question. A third route is *application-spotting*. Here, the researcher searches for an absence or shortage of a particular theory or perspective in a specific area of research, and then seeks to apply the theory in this new area. For example, CMS advocates commonly use a specific framework, such as gender, Foucault or Marxism. The specific framework is applied, perhaps even imposed on the object of study, which means that the object of study is typically being constructed in line with the favoured approach. Gender students find discrimination and Foucauldians find power exercising disciplinary effects. A common motive for such application-spotting studies is that nobody has applied the specific framework to a specific (sub-)area of research before.

By applying it for the first time, the study generates knowledge that fills an identified gap in the literature.

While gap-spotting research is a central ingredient in most theory development, it is unlikely to produce interesting and influential knowledge contributions. As pointed out above, for research to be seen as interesting and influential, it is not enough to improve existing theory; it also needs to challenge its audience's taken-for-granted assumptions in some significant way. Gap-spotting studies and their emphasis on filling gaps in existing theory tend to *reinforce* rather than *challenge* existing theories in any significant way and are, therefore, incapable of producing something new and interesting. A gap-spotting researcher applies, reproduces and varies or adds to existing knowledge, but does not substantively challenge it. This is because in gap-spotting research, the assumptions underlying the existing litera-ture are more or less taken as given and, thus, reproduced. When the assumptions underlying a specific theory are reproduced, the theory is reinforced rather than challenged in any substantive way. This assumption-reproducing way of working, such as applying a framework, a vocabulary and a set of 'truths', therefore, coun-teracts what is typically seen as interesting – ideas and knowledge that challenge an audience's assumptions and show that what they thought was true or self-evident is actually not so (Alvesson and Sandberg, 2013; Davis, 1971).

In order to support efforts to more deliberately and systematically identify and challenge the assumptions underlying existing literatures, we suggest the use of *problematization* as a methodology for generating research questions. By this we do *not* mean a minor critical scrutiny of a concept or a truth claim, but a more open-minded critical inquiry, where the basic assumptions underlying existing literatures are examined and unpacked.

Advocating a genuine problematization approach does not mean that a prob-lematizer is 'a blank slate' or position-free. A developed pre-understanding is a key feature of any researcher (as an academic and social being), and is brought into play in any intellectual enterprise. Any problematization necessarily takes its point of departure within a specific metatheoretical position (i.e., epistemological and ontological stance: Tsoukas and Knudsen, 2004: Chapter 1) as well as within the cultural framework into which the researcher has been socialized through upbring-ing, education and work. The ambition is therefore normally not – nor is it typically possible – to totally undo one's own position; rather, it is to unpack it sufficiently so that some of one's ordinarily given assumptions are scrutinized and reconsidered in the process of constructing novel research questions. Here *reflexivity* is key: the care-ful thinking through of one's position and how it easily locks the researcher into taken-for-granted assumptions and a view of the world as a set of 'truths' (including 'truths' offered by CMS perspectives).

The focal point in problematization as a methodology for generating research questions is to illuminate and challenge those assumptions underlying existing theo-ries (including one's own favourite theories) about a specific subject matter. This is rarely done, at least very seldom seriously demonstrated in research publications.

Critique of others or phenomena 'out there' is not the same as problematizing one's own received wisdom. Also critical approaches being reproduced and applied score low on problematization.

The aim of the problematization methodology proposed here is to come up with novel research questions through a *dialectical interrogation* of one's own familiar (or home) position, other theoretical stances, and the domain of literature targeted for assumption challenging. There are of course differences in terms of what a targeted theory domain looks like. Sometimes it is fairly weak, open, or pluralistic regarding specific theoretical ideas. Sometimes it is more distinct, and may deviate more or less from other ingredients in the interrogation. In some cases it may be difficult to separate the domain from the home position, as the boundaries may not be so clear. (Of course one's home position can be the target, but here we assume that the researcher is not exclusively focusing on the home position, but is partly or mainly focusing on another theoretical stance.) In other cases, such as when the home theoretical position and a new domain literature are clearly different, it is easier to separate one's home position from the domain targeted.

The idea of dialectical interrogation calls for the availability of different positions and lines of thinking. This should optimally include some clear variation or difference between the theoretical positions represented by the home position, other stances and targeted domains. Such variation in positions provides better options for opening up not only the domain literature about the subject matter, but also one's favoured home position. Hence, dialectical interrogation calls for going against one's preferred understandings of the world and programmed problematizations, and as this is difficult, intellectual resources need to be used. A set-up for dialectical interrogation, with position and counter-position initiating dialogue, will offer support. Reading other theories will give an indication of what is being missed by one's preferred position. It will stimulate rethinking of one's established ideas and facilitate imagination and creative reframing of the subject matter and/or novel ways of using a theoretical framework.

A key task in generating research questions through problematization, then, is to enter a dialectical interrogation between one's own and other metatheoretical stances so as to identify, articulate, and challenge central assumptions underlying the existing literature (including those assumptions underlying the existing literature in the CMS field), and to do so in a way that opens up new areas of inquiry. Rather than working with a fixed set of assumptions, one tries to develop awareness of alternatives.

Although not working with a fixed set of categories or levels of assumptions, we regard the following types of assumptions as particularly important to consider: in-house, root metaphor, paradigm, ideology, and field assumptions. *In-house* assumptions exist within a particular school of thought in the sense that they are shared and accepted as unproblematic by their advocates. *Root metaphor* assumptions represent the broader images used to conceptualize a specific subject matter, such as seeing organization as 'culture', 'machine', 'network' or 'pyramid'. *Paradigm* assumptions refer to the ontological, epistemological and methodological assumptions that underlie a specific body of literature. *Ideology* assumptions include various political, moral, and gender-related assumptions that underlie a specific literature field. Finally, *field* assumptions point to a broader set of assumptions that are shared by several schools of thoughts within a discipline. Taken together, this typology of assumptions can potentially be used for identifying and articulating assumptions in existing literature.

To enable identification and problematization of assumptions via dialectical interrogation between one's own and other metatheoretical stances, we have proposed the following methodological principles as being central: (1) identifying a domain of literature by summarizing its existing knowledge and choosing a specific audience (parts of the research community and/or parts of the educated public), (2) identifying and articulating assumptions underlying this domain, (3) evaluating them critically and then focusing on problematic assumptions and, based on that, (4) identifying and developing an alternative set of assumptions, (5) considering the alternative

Table 2.1 The problematization methodology and its key elements (Alvesson and Sandberg, 2013)

Aim of the problematization methodology					
Generating novel research questions through a *dialectical interrogation* of one's own familiar position, other stances, and the literature domain targeted for assumption challenging					

A typology of assumptions open for problematization					
In-house Assumptions that exist within a specific school of thought	*Root metaphor* Broader images of a particular subject matter underlying existing literature	*Paradigm* Ontological, epistemological, and methodological assumptions underlying existing literature	*Ideology* Political-, moral-, and gender-related assumptions underlying existing literature	*Field* Assumptions about a specific subject matter that are shared across different theoretical schools	

Principles for identifying and challenging assumptions					
1. *Identify a domain of literature:* What main bodies of literature and key texts make up the domain?	2. *Identify and articulate assumptions:* What major assumptions underlie the literature within the identified domain?	3. *Evaluate articulated assumptions:* Are the identified assumptions worthy to be challenged?	4. *Develop alternative assumptions:* What alternative assumptions can be developed?	5. *Relate assumptions to audience:* What major audiences hold the challenged assumptions?	6. *Evaluate alternative assumptions:* Are the alternative assumptions likely to generate a theory that will be regarded as interesting by the audiences targeted?

assumptions in relation to its audience, and (6) evaluating the alternative set of assumptions and crafting a research idea to be presented to the audience, who should, if one is successful, react by responding 'this is interesting!' – and mean it (Alvesson and Sandberg, 2013). This methodology is presented in Table 2.1.

This methodology aims to say something new and thought-provoking to an audience of researchers and other interested people (professionals, managers, educated public). For this reason, challenging assumptions is of interest not only to the researcher doing the work but also to the audience he or she seeks to communicate with. In particular, assumption challenging is seen as a *means* (not a goal as it is sometimes viewed in more critical theory and, in particular, poststructuralist research; see for example, Knights, 1992, who emphasizes negative knowledge) for coming up with new and creative ideas and research contributions. Typically, the researcher him- or herself belongs, at least partly, to the target audience, but of course there may be differences. It is vital not to be purely self-focused or academically introverted, but work on and against the assumptions, while bearing in mind others interested in the subject matter in question.

We refer the reader to Alvesson and Sandberg (2013: Chapter 5) for a full exploration of the methodology, but here we address only its most important principle – which also represents a crucial stage in the problematization process – principle no. 2: Identify and articulate assumptions. A key issue here is to transform what are commonly seen as truths or facts into assumptions. In doing so the implicit or hidden is made explicit and open for scrutiny. This is demanding, and most people are not so interested or successful in doing it. It often calls for a hermeneutic process of noting, interpreting, moving between, and reinterpreting different cues, thereby indicating assumptions not directly expressed, or perhaps not being consciously grasped or considered by authors. Hermeneutic ideas such as the circle (constant and recurrent moves) between pre-understanding and understanding are helpful here (e.g. Alvesson and Sköldberg, 2009).

We see a range of methodological tactics available for identifying assumptions in existing literatures. Some assumptions, held by specific groups/schools, can be identified by scrutinizing internal debates and the interfaces between a specific group of authors who frequently refer to each other and neighbouring areas, moderately relating one's work to the focused group's work, and using a similar narrative style and vocabulary. For example, various authors have challenged the idea that organizations typically form unitary and unique cultures (e.g., Van Maanen and Barley, 1984), or even clear and stable subcultures (Martin and Meyerson, 1988), by seeing culture as a process – a form of traffic – rather than as something stable (Alvesson, 2013).

A particularly important ingredient in creatively identifying assumptions is to engage in perspective shifting. This means that a variety of theoretical ideas are invoked in order to facilitate sensitivity towards various assumptions. As researchers with problematization ambitions – like other mortals – we do not only function intellectually and rationally. It is also central to realize our emotional preferences and how our own identity can give rise to blindness, one-sightedness, or a generally reduced ability to seriously consider aspects other than those we normally tend to see. It is therefore important to try to work with one's own identity and associated emotional commitments and blinders, through distancing and identity shifting. For example, distancing and identity shifting[2] can be achieved by accessing alternative theories, talking to people with views different from one's own, and voluntarily step-ping into the shoes of advocates of other perspectives (i.e. associated with various paradigms, knowledge interests, theories, or social identities). A critical researcher may try to identify him- or herself with a person in charge of an organization or another elite representative. A symbolic interactionist may attempt to take the out-look of a macro-researcher seriously. A poststructuralist may think about a problem that calls for a solution – rather than a deconstructionist ironic reading – and then imagine him- or herself as a functionalist trying to deliver a robust and clear result. All of these moves aim to increase reflexivity and imagination and thereby facilitate the often rather difficult project of identifying assumptions.

Since not all assumptions are likely to be strong candidates for problematization and the development of new assumptions and research questions, it is often fruitful to identify a surplus of assumptions that can be challenged and to formulate these in various ways, thereby offering different possibilities for further work. In the later stages of the process, some initially interesting assumptions may be reassessed as being less interesting to challenge than initially thought. One could also use the tac-tic of identifying a few assumptions that appear promising for challenging. How to evaluate them and what to do with them in the subsequent work is very much a mat-ter of what the variety of assumptions looks like in the context of empirical work.

An example: Values

Let us give an example – values. This is a key element in a range of different areas, not just focused 'value studies', but also in the context of organizational cultures, conflicts, leadership, careers, motivation, gender, sustainability, power, resistance and so forth.

A conventional assumption is that people have values. This is often taken for granted and not reflected upon. Many authors, for example, define organizational culture in terms of shared values. Many would see this as a self-evident fact, beyond doubt and consideration. This leads to research questions such as 'What kind of val-ues are prevalent in an organization and how do they influence outcomes?', 'What kind of leadership style is expressed as a result of specific values held?', 'How do

---

[2]We don't have in mind that the researcher should and can permanently change all his or her basic assumptions about the subject matter in question. Rather, we suggest that researchers temporarily try to distance and shift identity as a tactic to better see the assumptions underlying their own favourite position.

masculine (Western, upper-class, consumerist, etc.) values and so forth dominate a specific setting? Measurement or, if values are seen as 'deep', in-depth interviews, are then viewed as possible and appropriate ways of studying values.

A counter-assumption could be people take value positions – i.e. there are various values in circulation, and people use these values in various ways so as to promote their interests or get along. Values would not then be seen as fixed traits, something people (or organizational groups) 'hold', but instead as something that people connect to or disconnect from. An alternative assumption would then be that values and value talk are a tactical resource for corporate actors. Values become then process, and it is not possible to nail them down through measurement or the interpretation of 'fixed meanings'. For example, sustainability, profit, growth, quality, gender equality, competitiveness, and so forth would signal alternative values for actors in particular contexts. Actors could then move between these alternative values, depending on their specific situation.

These two statements can be seen as varied – a conventional assumption and an alternative one – but they nevertheless have something in common. Specifically, both assumptions assert that the individual is somehow the central agent, holding or flexibly using values. The individual is at the centre of matters and is a container or a manager of values.

One can challenge and de-centre this notion and draw attention to how other forces are at play. A counter-assumption could be that the individual is not the agent, but is produced by discourses or social forces controlling or governing the value positioning of the individual. The idea would then be that value-laden discourses tend to frame, guide and constrain subjects in an integrated and coherent way, leading to the individual being fixed and appearing to 'hold values'.

Yet another assumption could be that various forces and mechanisms are regulating individuals in a more varied and shifting manner. The latter idea would be to emphasize how multiple forces are in operation, leading to flexible and fragmented modes of value-positioning prescribed by various instances or mechanisms operating on the individual. Pressures to sometimes be an isolated individual (to be assessed and developed as such), or to sometimes be a 'chain gang' like a team member (expected to be loyal and compliant), call for flexibility in terms of values and valuing. Sometimes autonomy and individualistic values may be expressed; sometimes loyalty, teamwork and community may define how the subject is supposed to approach and value the world.

We can thus work with four assumptions:

The individual holds values.

The individual is a strategic and tactical user of values.

Social and discursive forces operate on the individual and lead to a fixed association and subordination with (organizationally expressed) values (being present until a new regime produces another value-positioning).

Social and discursive forces operate on the individual in a myriad of varied ways, creating fragmentation and hopping between different values.

These four assumptions can inform the construction of research questions and the execution of studies. One may either fixate on one type of assumption and work with this (whilst trying to consider the alternatives), or take seriously all possibilities and bear these in mind during empirical inquiry.

Problematization in empirical work

Developing an array of possible alternative assumptions in relation to those guiding the literature one is working with is essential for generating new ideas and contributions. Another major way of generating new ideas is to problematize the empirical work itself. The methodology literature often separates these two methods, but a good interplay between the two is typically required to produce new ideas and contributions. The ideal is a productive interaction between problematization of the literature and doing empirical work that strongly problematizes the empirical material. One conventional and established way to challenge dominant theoretical ideas is the use of empirical material as the final arbitrator of ideas and hypotheses. Here the fit between theory and data is viewed as central. Misfit or falsification can thus be seen as a source of problematization – similar to what Kuhn (1970) referred to as anomalies possibly creating problems for an established paradigm and triggering development towards (paradigm) revolution. Theory not supported by data should then be reconsidered and new theory developed.

Constructing and solving mysteries in empirical work

Unlike many others with a strong faith in the robustness of data (such as quantitative or grounded theory methodologists, who celebrate discipline and diligence rather than imagination), we claim that data, or – our preferred term – empirical material, are simply not capable of unambiguously showing the right route to theory or unproblematically screening out good ideas from bad. As we see it, the interplay between theory and empirical material is more about seeing the latter as a source of inspiration and a partner for critical dialogue than as a guide and ultimate arbitrator. Acknowledging the constructed nature of empirical material, which is broadly accepted in the philosophy of science (Alvesson and Sköldberg, 2009; Kuhn, 1970; Gergen, 1978; Denzin and Lincoln, 2000), has major consequences for how we consider the relationship between theory and empirical material, and calls for giving up the old idea of data and theory being separate.[3]

---

[3]We are talking here primarily in an ontological and epistemological sense. It can still, for analytical purposes, be fruitful to deal with 'data' and 'theory' separately.

One central aspect here is that assumptions tend to guide all understandings of data (empirical material), in that theories and vocabularies produce specific worldviews that tend to order reality in predictable ways, and confirm one's preconceptions. If a manager gives a talk and this is viewed as 'leadership', a theory about the latter produces the talk as leadership action (different from any other forms of talk not being 'leadership'). Any empirical material is sensitive to the assumptions guiding the research process that produces the material. It then becomes very difficult for empirical material to kick back at assumptions, unless these are clarified, opened up and problematized. Problematizing established assumptions makes it possible for researchers to approach field studies and other forms of empirical work in a much more open-minded manner and to consider more fully the variety of ways in which we can see empirical material. This is very different from aiming to 'fix' data through measurements or codification that freezes a specific meaning and direction of a representation of some phenomenon of interest. (For detailed exposure of how this is typically problematic, see Alvesson, 2011; Alvesson and Sköldberg, 2009; Potter and Wetherell, 1987). Such measurement or codification tends to reproduce and reinforce assumptions, although there is always some scope for the empirical material to be at odds with some parts of the framework and assumptions guiding the entire enterprise.

It is crucial that researchers seek to challenge the value of an established theory or a framework, to explore its weaknesses and problems in relation to the phenomena it is supposed to explicate, and to do this not just in situations in which the empirical material is obviously at odds with it. Problematizing means generally opening up, and pointing out the need and possible directions for rethinking and developing established theory. In order to develop new and interesting insights that challenge dominant assumptions, it is important to mobilize empirical material in such a way that it can encourage rethinking. The idea here is not to approach the area of study as 'a site where academics can demonstrate their stance towards the world, rather than a place where the world stands as a potential empirical critique of our assumptions about it' (Miller, 2001: 226).

Consequently we suggest a methodology for theory development through encounters between theoretical assumptions and empirical impressions that involves an active search for opportunities to let empirical material inspire the rethinking of conventional ideas and categories (developed in Alvesson and Kärreman, 2011). It is the unanticipated and the unexpected – the things that puzzle the researcher due to the deviation from what is expected – that are of particular interest in the encounter. Accordingly, theory development is stimulated and facilitated through the selective interest of what does *not* work in an existing theory, in the sense of encouraging interpretations that allow a productive and counterintuitive understanding of ambiguous social reality and that differ from established frameworks and routine findings. The ideal research process then includes two key elements: creating a mystery and solving it (Asplund, 1970). A mystery is empirical findings that deviate from what is expected and lead the researcher into a (temporary) state of bewilderment and loss: a mystery appears when we cannot understand something, and it calls for a new set of ideas that diverge from established assumptions and wisdoms, in order to resolve the mystery.

An illustration from our own research is in the area of 'leadership'. Here, the managers studied claimed to do leadership and provided accounts of their work fully in line with contemporary leadership ideals (helping people develop, working with visions and values, rejecting 'micro-management', and so forth). However, when asked about their specific practices, they mainly referred to administrative, technical, and operative issues. This was out of tune with the 'leadership' they professed to believe in and practise. Here we found excellent inspiration to reinterpret what 'leadership' is about. Specifically, it is more a discourse used by managers to boost their identity and legitimize their work than a guiding force behind their managerial practices (Alvesson and Sveningsson, 2003).

The empirical material, carefully constructed, thus provides strong impetus to rethink conventional wisdom and to find new ways of understanding a given phenomenon, making it less self-evident and more surprising, and thus generative of novel insights. However, the ideal is *not*, as in neo-positivist work such as grounded theory (Glaser and Strauss, 1967; Strauss and Corbin, 1994), to aim for an 'intimate interaction with actual evidence' that 'produces theory which closely mirrors reality' (Eisenhardt, 1989: 547). This is an effective hindrance of imagination, as reality-mirroring easily means marginal theorization and trivial results. Chiefly, our goal is to explore how empirical material can be used to develop theory that is interesting, rather than obvious, irrelevant, or absurd (Davis, 1971). However, this calls for a more active construction of empirical material in ways that are imaginative, and not just passively waiting for data to show us the route to something interesting, as is the typical, perhaps unrealistic, hope in more conventional research. For example, careful work with data as advocated by grounded theory is hardly sufficient to trigger imagination that leads to really novel and challenging ideas (Alvesson and Sköldberg, 2009). Of course, the approach that we suggest calls for some relaxation of the pressure for conventional rigour. Instead, the ambiguity of empirical material and the uncertainty of our interpretations are acknowledged. In particular, the researcher needs to carefully consider how any empirical material can be understood in more than one way, and that unconventional understandings may lead to new insights and the creation of a mystery in a study. For an extensive description and exemplification of the mystery methodology, see Alvesson and Kärreman (2011).

Combining problematization and mystery construction

This 'mystery methodology' for how to work with empirical material can interplay with the 'problematization methodology' suggested above. The latter opens up and adds insights via alternative assumptions that can guide research; the former can be more sensitive and imaginative as a consequence of a decreased tendency to press empirical impressions into pre-established categories and theories. The mystery methodology can also more directly encourage and fine-tune assumption challenging during empirical work. In many cases, one can imagine that there are problematization elements in both the review of the literature and the construction of empirical material, and that both 'parts' of the research process interact and support each other.

Research consistent with the spirit of this methodology is typically characterized by iterations and intersections between assumption challenging in relation to the literature and to the empirical material. Ideally, a preliminary problematization of the literature leads to a specific curiosity in fieldwork, which feeds back into how the literature is read (and reread), which again informs how to address and use empirical material, and so on. Importantly, empirical impressions must be considered as a vital input into the refinement of assumption-challenging outcomes. New assumptions may be convincing based on a critical scrutiny of the literature, but may later appear less promising in the face of empirical impressions. While there is hardly a one-to-one relation between assumptions and data, sometimes the latter may offer fuel for rethinking assumptions, and thus productively feed into an ongoing problematization process. This process is, as we have emphasized, not just restricted to the early stages of research, leading to fixed research questions derived from a literature review, but typically ongoing, emergent and/or shifting, right up to the point where the final research report or article is submitted for publication.

Let us underscore that the problematization methodology and its fieldwork (mystery) cousin imply a somewhat different *researcher identity* than the common one. Both methodologies call for drawing upon a broader set of theories and vocabularies as resources for challenging dominant assumptions and constructions of empirical material, greater emphasis on (self-)critical and hermeneutic interpretations of the frameworks and ideas in operation, as well as some boldness in counteracting consensus. A fair degree of scepticism is important. This typically means less detailed knowledge of all that has been done within a narrowly defined field, and a reluctance to divide up theory and data as separate categories and address these as distinct parts and sections in a report. It may also mean facing some antagonism from defenders of an established position. In short, our approach calls for a shift of emphasis in researcher identity: from cultivating an incremental gap-spotting research identity, to a reflexive and path-(up)setting scholar, with some preference for irony and promiscuity over a fixed, programmatic position. It also calls for some shift in professional norms, celebrating ideals other than 'find and fill the gap' and consistently working within and applying a specific framework.

Returning to values

The interplay between challenging the assumptions underlying theoretical ideas and trying to bring out surprises in fieldwork can be illustrated in various ways empirically. Statements by interviewees (or people observed expressing sentiments in specific episodes) can be interpreted based on assumptions about value-holding as well as value-jumping. In most cases it is not always clear-cut how to address empirical phenomena: is there some variation but also some underlying coherence, or is there some tendency to express not only a particular orientation but also fragmentation and variation? Different surprises and mysteries that allow for the challenging of established theoretical ideas can be produced in different ways. Proceeding from the conventional view of people and groups having values, one can point at empirical indications suggesting variation, fragmentation and shifting between values. A 'mystery' would then be the disinclination or inability to produce coherence and direction. How does it come to be that values are not integrated and directed in a clear way? How can we understand this and develop new ideas, for example on the individual as a value-jumper?

But one may also take seriously and proceed from other assumptions expressed in the literature, such as the notions of contemporary individuals as being 'other-directed', customer-oriented, lacking character and conviction, formed by contemporary capitalism and organizational life to be oriented to cope with a variety of demands, expectations, people and situations, and as being quite flexible and malleable. Given these assumptions, the indications of an individual or a group wholly or at least partially sticking to certain values and commitments, could be viewed as an interesting mystery. How can we understand instances of people holding on to a sense of integrity/rigidity/coherence, in a social world calling for adaption to social contingencies? How is someone capable of 'having' and being fairly consistent in 'holding' these values?

This is not to say that any data can be used for any purpose. Empirical material often kicks back against some ideas and interpretations; sometimes the material offers limited support for a specific interpretation. But different theoretical ideas often lead to different constructions of empirical material, and the latter is seldom so short of ambiguities that it only allows one clear kind of codification and interpretation. In order to develop new ideas, then, the dialectical interplay between theoretical assumptions and empirical material calls for bringing on board both the assumptions and possible counter-assumptions that the researcher can mobilize and work with to open up empirical material for alternative readings. To repeat, the purpose is not to maximize the fixity of empirical material through denying ambiguity and codification, but to use these in order to develop interesting ideas.

Conclusion

Given the centrality of scrutinizing and challenging assumptions for producing interesting and influential research, we think it is necessary to question an exclusive focus on building upon published empirical studies and applying existing theory within social studies. Consensus-challenging work is important, and key here is problematization of taken-for-granted assumptions within a specific research area. A supplement to this is a willingness to look for surprising field experiences and letting these kick back against one's theoretical framework.

We thus formulate two key principles and how they can be combined for developing interesting and novel research insights:

1. Critically scrutinize dominating assumptions and, when motivated, suggest alternative ones.
2. Find and solve a mystery in empirical studies.

We certainly do not claim that this is suitable for all researchers and research projects, and we are not saying that problematization of conventional theory and questioning of established ways of ordering data should generally replace mainstream views of research (e.g. treating theory and data as separate and emphasizing the collection and analysis of data as a 'theory-free' enterprise). It is important to maintain diversity in ways of doing research. However, given the dominance of the conventional view (as expressed in most method books and journal articles) and frequent complaints (e.g. Clark and Wright, 2009; Daft and Lewin, 2008; Grey, 2010; Starbuck, 2006)[4] about research often lacking new, surprising ideas and insights, we encourage researchers to be less inclined to one-sidedly employ assumption-reproducing research questions and lines of analysis. Instead, less reproductive and more *disruptive* modes should also be promoted and used, as they are likely to lead to the development of more interesting and significant research results. Of course, views of what is interesting differ between people, but demonstrating that earlier held assumptions are problematic, and that alternative ones make sense, will lead to an experience of 'this is interesting' (Davis, 1971).

Such disruption should focus on the assumptions in the literature of a field, as well as conventional ways of dealing with empirical material. An interplay between challenging assumptions of dominant theories within a field, and looking for unexpected and challenging interpretations in fieldwork is important. The former facilitates the latter, while fieldwork can encourage the kicking back and revision of ideas on both dominant and alternative assumptions. In the space between alternative assumptions and alternative meanings of empirical material, and the dialogue therein, creativity and imagination can be cultivated. This is not to deny the significance of discipline – our approach is not a licence to do whatever one wants with literature or fieldwork material. Having said that, typically it is possible to carve out more than one meaning from an aspect of the literature as well as from empirical material. These possibilities for alternative options do not appear to be used by most researchers. Our methodology can perhaps change this.

---

[4]For an extensive review and discussion of these complaints, see Alvesson and Sandberg (2013: Chapter 7).

More generally, the proposed combination of the problematization and the mystery methodology also contributes to – and relies upon – more reflexive and path- (up) setting scholarship, in the sense that it counteracts or supplements the domination of cautious, strongly specialized, and incremental research ideals. A major problem is that much research tends to be quite predictable, and does not significantly advance the management field. In fact, most research applies and reinforces, rather than challenges, existing theories in the field. CMS researchers regularly target the usual suspects, reproduce and apply Foucauldian, feminist etc. perspectives in a predictable way, and thereby lose some of their critical edge and capacity to foster new insights. Researchers can develop a more critical, reflexive, and path-(up)setting scholarly identity by continuously scrutinizing, interpreting, critically investigating, and occasionally reconsidering their own and their research field's assumptions. We see a strong need for this kind of scholarly identity in the contemporary academic climate of specialization, journal publication focus and an emphasis on careers rather than having anything valuable to say. CMS is not altogether an exception. More creative and unexpected work is needed to make research more interesting and influential.

References

Alvesson, M. (2011) *Interpreting Interviews*. London: Sage.

Alvesson, M. (2013) *Understanding Organizational Culture* (2nd edn). London: Sage.

Alvesson, M. and Kärreman, D. (2011) *Qualitative Research and Theory Development*. London: Sage.

Alvesson, M. and Sandberg, J. (2013) *Constructing Research Questions. Developing Interesting Research through Problematization*. London: Sage.

Alvesson, M. and Sköldberg, K. (2009) *Reflexive Methodology* (2nd edn). London: Sage.

Alvesson, M. and Sveningsson, S. (2003) 'The good visions, the bad micro-management and the ugly ambiguity: Contradictions of (non-)leadership in a knowledge-intensive company', *Organization Studies*, 24(6): 961–988.

Alvesson, M. and Willmott, H. (2012) *Making Sense of Management* (2nd edn). London: Sage.

Asplund, J. (1970) *Om Undran infor Samhallet*. Lund: Argos.

Astley, W.G. (1985) 'Administrative science as socially constructed truth', *Administrative Science Quarterly*, 30(4): 245–273.

Bartunek, J.M., Rynes, S.L. and Ireland, D.R. (2006) 'What makes management research interesting, and why does it matter?' *Academy of Management Journal*, 49(1): 9–15.

Clark, T. and Wright, M. (2009) 'So farewell then … Reflections on editing the *Journal of Management Studies*', *Journal of Management Studies*, 46(1): 1–9.

Daft, R.L. and Lewin, A.Y. (2008) 'Rigor and relevance in organization studies: Idea migration and academic journal evolution', *Organization Science*, 19(1): 177–183.

Davis, M.S. (1971) 'That's interesting! Towards a phenomenology of sociology and a sociology of phenomenology', *Philosophy of Social Sciences*, 1(4): 309–344.

Denzin, N.K. and Lincoln, Y.S. (eds) (2000) *Handbook of Qualitative Research*. Thousand Oaks, CA: Sage.

Eisenhardt, K. (1989) 'Building theories from case study research', *Academy of Management Review*, 14(4): 532–550.

Gergen, K. (1978) 'Toward generative theory', *Journal of Personality and Social Psychology*, 36(11): 1344–1360.

Glaser, B.G. and Strauss, A.L. (1967) *The Discovery of Grounded Theory*. New York: Aldine.

Grey, C. (2010) 'Organizing studies: Publications, politics and polemic', *Organization Studies*, 31(6): 677–694.

Knights, D. (1992) 'Changing spaces: The disruptive impact of a new epistemological location for the study of management', *Academy of Management Review*, 17(3): 514–536.

Kuhn, T.S. (1970) *The Structure of Scientific Revolutions*. Chicago: University of Chicago Press.

Martin, J. and Meyerson, D. (1988) 'Organizational culture and the denial, channeling and acknowledgment of ambiguity', in L.R. Pondy (ed.), *Managing Ambiguity and Change*. Chichester: John Wiley.

Miller, D. (2001) 'The poverty of morality', *Journal of Consumer Culture*, 1(2): 225–243.

Potter, J. and Wetherell, M. (1987) *Discourse and Social Psychology: Beyond Attitudes and Behaviour*. London: Sage.

Sandberg, J. and Alvesson, M. (2011) 'Ways of constructing research questions: Gap-spotting or problematization?' *Organization*, 18(1): 23–44.

Starbuck, W.H. (2006) *The Production of Knowledge: The Challenge of Social Science Research*. Oxford: Oxford University Press.

Strauss, A. and Corbin, J. (1994) 'Grounded theory methodology: An overview', in N.K. Denzin and Y.S. Lincoln (eds), *Handbook of Qualitative Research*. Thousand Oaks, CA: Sage, pp. 273–285.

Tsoukas, H. and Knudsen, C. (eds) (2004) *The Oxford Handbook of Organization Theory*. Oxford: Oxford University Press.

Van Maanen, J. and Barley, S.R. (1984) 'Occupational communities: Culture and control in organizations', in B.M. Staw and L.L. Cummings (eds), *Research in Organizational Behavior*, Vol. 7. Greenwich: JAI Press, pp. 287–365.

Weick, K.E. (2001) 'Gapping the relevance gap: Fashions meet fundamentalist in management research', *British Journal of Management*, 12(S1): S71–75.

THREE

Researcher collaboration: Learning from experience

Emma Jeanes, Bernadette Loacker and
Martyna Śliwa

Introduction

The notion of 'researcher collaboration' typically refers to the relationship between researchers and their participants, case site, or funding organization (Engstrom, 1984; Katz and Martin, 1997). Less commonly discussed, though no less important for the process and outcome of research, is the relationship between researchers. Given the recent 'reflexive turn' in research methodology – and critical management (CM) research in particular (Alvesson et al., 2008; Linstead, 1994) – it is perhaps surprising that more attention has not been paid to the role of inter-researcher relations in framing, shaping and producing research (Wray-Bliss, 2003). This is also curious since so much of our research is focused on the working relationships of others, and on power relations. In failing to evaluate our own, often hierarchical relationships (Rogers-Dillon, 2005) we fail to be critical or reflexive about, and in, our research.

The topic of researcher collaboration has remained largely in the realm of gossip and informal conversation. Indeed, the genesis of this chapter, which initiated the book project, arose out of such a conversation: a meeting that was ostensibly about sharing research ideas and coordinating individual projects turned into a conversation about the meaning of collaboration and the expectation and regulation of collaboration in that particular research group. These concerns, we contend, are not uncommon. Conversations with colleagues lead us to believe that a surprising number of us have experienced unequal or challenging working relationships, as well as fulfilling ones. Formally, however, these issues are rarely discussed and often play little or no role in texts that address the process of research. The issue of researcher collaboration is becoming a question of increasing relevance as institutional pressures require, or at the very least ask, researchers to collaborate more frequently, and often in situations that we might not otherwise choose. As a result there is a tendency for individual research projects to give way to collaborative research endeavours. Given the potential for these relationships to shape the research, and the researcher, we argue that more explicit discussion of them is warranted.

This project evolved iteratively – as collaborations often do – such that the final writing team for this chapter differed from the one at the outset. However, what brought the authorial team together was a shared concern for the precarious and often unspoken nature (in the formal or written sense) of these issues, a desire to explore some of these issues, and in doing so reflect on how relationships could be made more rewarding, democratic, non-exploitative and free(r) from conflicts. The authors are CM researchers, collaborating with and inquiring of – in the main – fellow CM researchers, who might reasonably be anticipated to draw upon their inclusive politics of equality (evident in their writing) in the research process itself. Clearly the issue of researcher relationships is not an exclusively 'critical' concern, but the quest for ethical relations is crucial for CM scholars if they wish to succeed (at least partially) in their emancipatory agenda in terms of both process and outcome.

Rather than rely on our own experiences, we sought to draw upon a broader range of experiences and reflections from the field of CM research from which others can learn. To this end the chapter aims to give voice to researchers, highlighting the precarious and, at times, unequal nature of collaboration. It then seeks to explore the nature of these relations and reflect on why such relationships may arise and what might be done to improve relations. In line with the book's purpose to encourage reflections on research practices within the field of CM, we hope that the empirical material and discussion presented in this chapter will inspire scholars to reflect on their own researcher collaborations, and to see considerations regarding the processes and outcomes of these collaborations as an inherent aspect of the methodological approach to, and ethics of, research projects (an aspect that also has important broader consequences for shaping relations within the scholarly community) as well as the outcome of the research endeavour.

The chapter begins with a brief summary of existing framings and conceptions of researcher collaboration. It then gives an account of our research methods, and subsequently explores issues related to researcher collaboration that have emerged from our empirical research on the collaborative practices of critical scholars. The analysis mainly reflects on the understandings of collaboration, with whom people collaborate, the intentions and reasons for collaboration, and experiences of and challenges in collaboration. It also offers additional reflections on the nature, value and process of collaboration. The discussion concludes by outlining the main insights from these accounts, which we hope will inform collaborative practice, particularly addressing the issue of (in)equality within collaborative relationships and the need for more reflexivity in CM field-specific collaboration practices.

Reasons for, types and effects of researcher collaboration

The phenomenon of research collaboration has greatly increased over the past few decades. The contemporary research environment has been described as characterized by a 'partnership or perish' (Berman, 2008: 167) climate, whereas entering into collaborative relationships has been considered an essential route for individuals to acquire the skills, knowledge and social relations necessary to participate in science (Bozeman and Corley, 2004). This can be explained by a number of both macro-level and institutional trends that affect the way research is conducted (Katz and Martin, 1997; Morrison et al., 2003). Of particular importance here has been the emergence of incentives and demands by policy-makers and research funding bodies, seeking to encourage collaborative research (Smith, 2001). Current performance measurement regimes, such as the Research Excellence Framework (REF) in the UK, also stipulate performance indicators in terms of the quantity and quality of publications, with both sets of criteria more likely to be met by researchers working collaboratively rather than individually.[1] A growing specialization of science, coupled with a greater complexity of investigated problems and cross-disciplinary work, further promotes collaborative work (Leahey and Reikowsky, 2008).

Together with the rise in collaboration, the subject of research collaboration has attracted a certain amount of scholarly attention, albeit mostly beyond the field of CM. In particular, scholars have sought to establish what can be defined as collaboration, what are the motivations behind and benefits of collaboration, and what strategies and patterns of collaboration tend to be adopted by researchers. While research collaboration has been – seemingly straightforwardly – defined as 'the working together of researchers to achieve the common goal of producing new scientific knowledge' (Katz and Martin, 1997: 7) or 'a research endeavour that pools the resources of any variety of researchers, agencies, scientists, clinicians and representatives from different disciplines' (Engstrom, 1984: 78), the concept of collaboration has occasionally also been regarded as far from obvious and unproblematic (Katz and Martin, 1997). As a way of operationalizing collaboration, Katz and Martin (1997: 7) suggest applying a number of criteria allowing for distinguishing between collaborators and other researchers. In their view, collaborators typically are:

(a)   those who work together on a research project throughout its duration or for a large part of it, or who make frequent or substantial contribution;

---

[1] See http://www.ref.ac.uk.

(b)   those whose names or posts appear in the original research proposal;

(c)   those responsible for one or more of the main elements of the research (e.g. the experimental design, construction of research equipment, execution of the experiment, analysis and interpretation of the data[,] writing up the results in a paper).

The identification of activities that are considered collaborative is important for this chapter, since one of the questions of concern is the way in which scholars negotiate the distinctions between collaborators and non-collaborators, and the implications of such distinctions in personal, emotional and political terms.

We were also interested in what motivates researchers to enter into collaborative relationships. Here extant literature offers a useful starting point, as it suggests a number of reasons and motives behind researchers' engagement in collaboration. Chief among them are the opportunities to share with others: workload and experience (Hauptman, 2005), knowledge (Katz and Martin, 1997; Beaver, 2001), skills and expertise (Bammer, 2008), equipment and resources (Stillman et al., 2005), intellectual interests and ideas (Hauptman, 2005; Smith, 2001), and the general risks associated with the research process (Morrison et al., 2003; Ritchie and Rigano, 2007).

Typically, authors who have studied collaboration in different disciplines highlight its 'instrumental' and 'measurable' influences, such as a positive effect on research productivity (Ponomariov and Boardman, 2010), impact factors (Bouyssou and Marchant, 2011), the number of citations attracted by a given publication (Sooryamoorthy, 2009) and, thus, the greater visibility and prestige seemingly connected to collaborative efforts (Katz and Martin, 1997). In this manner, collaboration tends to be perceived as improving researchers' prospects of securing important contacts, funding or future employment (Beaver, 2001). While less frequently mentioned, the – difficult to capture through measurement – personal and emotional impacts of collaboration are also raised in the literature. For example, several authors associate collaboration with: greater creativity, a solution to the loneliness frequently accompanying the research process (Smith, 2001), as well as chances to provide researchers with a sense of pleasure and positive emotional energy (Katz and Martin, 1997; Melin, 2000; Ritchie and Rigano, 2007). Generally, most of the literature places an emphasis on the advantages of researcher collaboration. However, a few authors, Katz and Martin (1997) among them, also refer to certain costs of collaboration, mainly in terms of financial resources, time, and increased administrative burdens.

Our interest in the practices of collaboration has, moreover, drawn our attention to extant typologies addressing the levels, patterns and strategies of collaboration. In relation to collaboration *levels*, Katz and Martin (1997) distinguish between inter-individual, inter-institutional and international levels of collaboration, whereas Smith (2001) makes a distinction between interpersonal, team and corporate levels. John-Steiner (2000) furthermore discusses four types of research collaboration *patterns*, referring to the extents of formality and hierarchy (see also Morrison et al., 2003), namely: distributed, complementary, family, and integrative types. Yet another criterion – collaboration *strategies* – is adopted by Bozeman and Corley (2004) who distinguish between six, in their view, independent types of collaborating researchers: the Taskmaster, the Nationalist, the Mentor, the Follower, the Buddy, and the Tactician. These typologies provide us with certain insights into the motivation behind, nature of, and concerns regarding collaboration.

However, the recent increase in research interest in collaboration has been particularly visible in the medical and natural sciences (John-Steiner, 2000). Here a bibliometric methodology is usually employed in order to quantify collaboration, identify appropriate measures of collaboration, and correlate measures of collaboration with other variables such as research output (Liao and Yen, 2012), propensity to collaborate (Birnholtz, 2007), and factors that may influence this, such as tenure or international networks (Van Rijnsoever et al., 2008). While bibliometric studies tend to operationalize collaboration in terms of the co-authorship of scholarly publications, authors within this area do not focus on or critically appraise the relations and (in)equalities among collaborating researchers, or explore other forms of collaboration. Questions of power and hierarchies within collaborative relationships and practices, however, become problematized when viewed from the perspective of social sciences and, more specifically, CM studies, where scholars raise questions of reflexive methodology (Alvesson and Sköldberg, 2000), and espouse ethical and political commitments to equality and to scrutinizing the power relations imbuing their own research practices (Hardy et al., 2001). Cheek (2008) stresses that it is essential to reflect on one's role as a researcher throughout the research process (see also Ritchie and Rigano, 2007), and more broadly on collaboration, especially as it has generally come to be understood as a benign, positive aspect of a research endeavour. Cheek (2008) encourages researchers to consider the assumptions underlying collaboration, and to question its taken-for-granted desirability, and how collaboration and discussions about it are connected to the political research context within which they occur. The latter is seen as crucial in order to effectively navigate through the different demands of academic or corporate research funding bodies (see also Smith, 2001: 137).

Ritchie and Rigano (2007) highlight the need for exploring the relations, which are little discussed in the literature, such as expectations and the emotional aspects of collaborating with others. An inherent part of collaborative relationships are 'errors', instances of 'confusion' and 'regrettable decisions' – all of which emotionally affect the involved parties and have an impact on their relationships, well-being, careers and so on. Recognizing and learning from such experiences require a commitment to honesty and reflexivity (Goldstein, 2000). By taking a critical look at collaborative processes and relationships, especially the power relations and practices within them, and the ensuing risks, challenges and emotional responses of those involved, we seek to contribute to understandings and evaluations of research collaboration among CM researchers. In turn, we reflect on the implications for CM scholars.

Reflexively exploring researcher collaborations

When working on the chapter, we aspired to develop our own collaboration as a democratic, trust-based and joyful process, considering it a worthwhile endeavour in personal and intellectual respects (Ritchie and Rigano, 2007; see also Goldstein, 2000). We aimed to share the responsibilities equally between the three of us, and to jointly shape the direction of the chapter's development, ensuring that the 'voices' of each of us were present in the text.

Our empirical study consists of seven interviews we conducted with critical scholars who were selected on the basis of their seniority (3 professors, 2 mid-career and 2 early-career researchers), gender (3 females, 4 males), and experience (including experience of collaboration). The interviews drew on an internationally diverse cohort, with five of the seven participants having worked as academics in at least two countries. The interviews were conducted with colleagues whom we knew, but did not necessarily have a close (or collaborative) working relationship with, in order to balance the familiarity required for achieving an open, trusting conversation with the avoidance of any potential conflict of interest. For the purposes of anonymity, all names that appear in the empirical section are pseudonyms.[2]

The semi-structured interviews were developed on the basis of the literature and our own knowledge of the subject matter. Each interview lasted between 1 and 1.5 hours. The interviews were not designed to be representative but allowed for in-depth exploration of the issues. Despite the small number of participants, theoretical saturation (Glaser and Strauss, 1967) was suggested when their accounts, supplemented by the researchers' own knowledge of the field – in terms of their own experience and the accounts of the experiences of others, and their prior research in this field – resulted in consistent themes being drawn from the data.

All interviews were recorded and transcribed. Themes were drawn from the data and agreed upon based on a series of conversations between us. Aiming to engage in reflexivity and to learn from each other at all stages of the research and writing process, we strove to mutually question and problematize our theoretical and methodological pre-understandings as well as our paradigmatic and field-specific assumptions (such as that collaborations are rewarding *or* exploitative; CM researchers are less instrumental and/or more reflexive than mainstream management scholars) (Alvesson and Sandberg, 2011: 253–255; see also Chapter 2, this volume). Questioning and refining the modes through which we collectively constructed and developed knowledge and insights was also central to the process of analysing and interpreting our empirical material (Alvesson and Sköldberg, 2000: 8). In writing up

---

[2]In addition to the pseudonyms, we indicate the seniority level of our interviewees: ECR = early-career researcher, MCR = mid-career researcher, SCR = senior career researcher.

the chapter, we took turns to ensure that we all worked on each of the sections, as we wished for the final text to reflect, throughout, the merging and interweaving of our voices.

The fact of collaborating on a piece about researcher collaboration was not without impact on our own reflexive processes regarding our relationship as co-authors. Within the course of writing we started to consciously scrutinize our own practices and attitudes underlying collaboration. In doing so, we were aware of challenges and uncertainties accompanying the attempts to address and negotiate personal and scholarly views, perceptions and attitudes to reach an 'equality of voices' and contributions. We therefore made a deliberate effort to 'look after' the emotional aspect of writing together and encounter each other, in scholarly terms, as 'critical friends'.

Reflections on researcher collaboration

In the following we discuss the collaborative practices and relations of the CM scholars interviewed. More specifically, we reflect upon the various meanings, intentions, experiences, challenges as well as the evaluations associated with researcher collaborations that inform and shape both the research and the researcher, and the nature of future collaborations.

Meanings of research collaboration

Our participants' understandings of what constitutes research collaboration, include, for some, such diverse forms of collegial engagement as establishing and participating in reading groups, commenting on each other's work, co-organizing conferences and symposia, and carrying out editorial responsibilities. For most, a distinction was made between collaboration – meaning 'labouring together' – and 'exchange', though precisely what was meant by 'exchange' in this context was not always clear (the exchanging of ideas could often be the basis of collaboration, whereas 'swapping names' on papers was evaluated more negatively). Collaboration was also understood as a particular relationship or project, a way of working or a 'mutual process of learning', and in relation to a particular community or working environment. However, there was also an implicit hierarchy of collaboration. For example, one participant noted that they 'romanticize' the 'ideal collaboration' as a community of scholars discussing and exchanging ideas but describing such collaboration as 'not formal'. Generally, collaboration was seen as existing between people, not institutions (Smith, 2001).

The two areas of activity that were universally recognized and particularly relevant for the scholars we interviewed were those associated with being a member of a research team, in particular applying for research funding and jointly fulfilling project obligations, and those activities involved in the publication of academic texts, especially co-writing and co-authoring.[3] While meanings of collaboration also appeared to shift during researchers' careers (Ritchie and Rigano, 2007), the accounts given illustrate that co-writing forms the most prevalent meaning accompanying researcher collaboration and that meanings and experiences of collaboration were significant in forming and shaping careers.

Who academics collaborate with

Collaboration partners are not chosen at random. For most of our participants it is important to work with someone whom they know and with whom they have a personal relationship (Melin, 2000). In some cases, these relationships are friendships that can be traced back to the early stages of their academic career (Smith, 2001).

Choosing to collaborate with friends (see also Katz and Martin, 1997), is often explained by reference to an ideal of a research collaboration in which there is a 'meeting of minds', referred to by one participant as 'pure pleasure', and by another one as a 'dream' about a 'wordless understanding' that leads to a collective generation and expression of ideas in an atmosphere of trust. For some, the friendship and the 'cementing' of the relationship were a primary driver for collaboration (Ritchie and Rigano, 2007):

> I don't think I would even consider meeting someone at a conference: 'well, let's write something together'... I do think it works better within friendships, because it does require quite a bit of good intentions from both sides. It's not easy if somebody deletes your stuff or changes things ... In order to know that you have similar ideas about something, I think that already requires quite a bit of conversations and time spent together. (Jacob, MCR)

Most interviewees stated that they look for long-term, or 'buddy' (Bozeman and Corley, 2004) collaborative relationships, and well-known 'duets' were cited in positive terms. Such relationships were seen as better suited for addressing the emotional and intellectual complexity of collaborative processes and in some cases for improving the quality and efficiency of the work. One participant reflected on the synergistic effects of the 'duet' by noting how their close collaborators 'help me in getting [my voice] across more clearly and I help them in getting their voice across more clearly'.

Despite the emphasis on friendships and long-term relationships, often with peers or (former) supervisors, several interviewees also indicated they worked with a broader community of scholars. For example, some of the more established scholars

---

[3]The distinction is important and reflects the different styles of writing articulated, for example: some academics literally 'work together' (to the extent of sitting in front of a computer together to write) while, at the other extreme, scholars 'divide tasks'. It also reflects the distinction between writing and contributing to the work in another fashion (such as providing the ideas) or even just being named as an author.

referred to mentoring relationships and, thus, to collaborations with junior colleagues (Ritchie and Rigano, 2007: 142; Morrison et al., 2003). Other participants stated that they had worked with people they had met only a few times at conferences, and that they used conferences and international networks to cultivate collaborative partnerships. Thus, not all collaborations were based on close personal relationships. One participant even indicated that they had never met some of their collaborators.

There was also evidence of potential collaborator scrutiny, with evaluations of their 'skills', 'reading and attainment', 'general intelligence', 'track record', 'spark', 'chemistry' and 'self-irony'. There was a concern to ensure there were 'shared passions', 'common ideas and language', 'openness and respect'. The notion that a collaborator could 'add something' was also crucial, or as one participant expressed it: 'am I going to get enough from her?'

Intentions and reasons for collaboration

The motivations for collaborations reflect both scholarly and instrumental underpinnings, often simultaneously (see also Katz and Martin, 1997). Several accounts were given referring to collaboration as a 'default' way of working and as a means to avoid being 'lonely' in one's work (Smith, 2001). Yet for others it was part of a more deliberate strategy to develop an international profile or become more 'efficient' and produce 'outputs' that would count in terms of helping one secure employment or career progression (Van Rijnsoever et al., 2008). Collaboration was also viewed as 'necessary', such as for achieving research funding, or 'required' in the context of institutional or academic pressures in general.

Some academics spoke about the instrumental aspect of their own approach to working with others. As 'tacticians' (Bozeman and Corley, 2004), they opted for collaborations to complement their own skills or make up for deficits (Morrison et al., 2003; Leahey and Reikowsky, 2008):

> It often doesn't really pay off to learn a methodology from the start because you know in the long run you won't need it so much. So it's just the other people's knowledge, competencies ... that have to pool together. (Sabine, MCR)

Time pressure seemed to serve as another common motivation for collaboration:

> It allows getting things done quicker. If I do everything myself, I just can't write as much ... So the fact that I work with someone else does save me time and makes it easier for me to get [ideas] out. (Claudia, ECR)

The importance of outputs was reflected in the speed of turnaround and the joys of being able to 'share the burden' and 'hand it on' as well as the 'discipline' of co-working (Morrison et al., 2003). It was also presented as part of a strategy for achieving high-ranking publications:

> In the recent paper I've been doing … it's been going on for about two and a half, three years, we've had one rejection from a 4 star and now it's at a 3 star … Latterly, [co-author's name] wanted to bring on board an American professor that I'd never met … It's just somebody that has written in this area and was likely actually a previous reviewer when we got rejected … We brought them on board like a Trojan horse and they were happy to do that. They had a real effect. (Bob, SCR)

Comparisons of inputs (time and effort) to outputs as a means of evaluating the projects were also prevalent in many accounts (see also Melin, 2000; Smith, 2001). However, the adoption of an instrumental approach to managing one's collaborative relationships does not tend to sit comfortably with the simultaneously upheld ideal of the non-careerist purposes[4] and outcomes of collaborations:

> The goal is not to get published, I mean of course you want to get published, but that's not the goal of the enterprise. It is about getting an idea that you have on paper. (Jacob, MCR)

In contrast, another academic described the ideal collaborator in output-orientated terms:

> [S/he] would have time, be very interested in producing output because at my stage in career, I unfortunately have to be interested in really getting published. So a person who is under the same pressure, I think that would lead to a more productive relationship if both of us would push or be pushed. (Sabine, MCR)

For many, struggles between instrumental and non-instrumental purposes were not easy to resolve in an unambiguous manner and illustrate a variety of possible inconsistencies. One academic, for example, spoke about how, while not being 'strategic', he had become, nevertheless, 'opportunistic' in his approach to research collaboration. Another declared his lack of interest in publication rankings, and at the same time admitted to directing his efforts at submitting manuscripts to highly ranked journals. Another, young, scholar only approaches very senior and experienced academics for collaborative projects, and yet claimed not to collaborate with them because of their 'big names' (see also Bozeman and Corley, 2004). A senior academic highlighted the responsibilities he took on to assist his doctoral students' publishing while simultaneously admitting not being able to fulfil his tasks and duties within collaborative projects. Where reasons behind the differences between their ideal and actual approach to collaboration were considered, the current institutional environment with which our participants consider themselves obliged to come to terms was often invoked as an explanation.

However, despite the strategic, pragmatic and 'semi-opportunistic' approaches to collaboration, the desire for intellectual discussions and inspiration, and the aim to

---

[4]It is noticeable that it is always *others* who are 'intellectually instrumental and corrupt' in their collaborations.

produce 'something of value' was evident in all the accounts (Smith, 2001; Ritchie and Rigano, 2007). Also present were personal anxieties about one's own capabilities, and not 'trusting oneself' to work as effectively alone. Whilst the interviewees described how they used people 'to their advantage' and to 'help fulfil personal goals', there was much to suggest this is partly driven by a need to compare favourably with colleagues.

Experiences of collaboration

The awareness of power asymmetries and institutional pressures was manifest in accounts of their own position within collaborative relationships. For example, some of our participants mentioned how, over time, their position had shifted from being the one who approached others and asked them to collaborate, to finding themselves on the receiving end of such requests. Other senior academics made a distinction between their early experiences of research collaboration and those since they had become professors or heads of large research projects. The perceived 'obligation' to support junior colleagues was often cited as a source of anxiety in terms of potential exploitation, sometimes predicated on their own experiences. However, their concerns could often be contrasted with their current approach. One participant noted that:

> The first time I collaborated with someone who would be more senior to me, was a professor at work who I wrote a handbook chapter with. And he wrote something, and sent it to me and this is like ... shit basically. Then I kind of rewrote the whole thing ... and then it was like okay. Yeah fine, he didn't really read it ... and then it got published ... that partially confirms some of my assumptions about what it means to work with a more senior person, essentially they just exploit you. (Thomas, SCR)

But later went on to advise junior scholars to:

> Work with the best people you can ... learn a lot from that. Realize that you are probably going to have to do a lot more of the work ... But also be clear about ... what the boundaries are ... The other person should really bring something substantive to the table ... [Be] cognizant if you're being exploited, but also questioning your own ideas about what it means to be exploited ... because I think sometimes ... [it's] learning.

Another senior colleague similarly noted that there is 'always a slight imbalance', whereas junior and mid-career researchers more frequently indicated their 'anger' at this inequality. Our participants also distinguished between collaborations they entered of their own free will and ones that might have been imposed upon them, for example by their superiors who require them to contribute to particular research projects (Smith, 2001). In some extreme cases, such 'forced' research collaboration confirmed inequalities within the project team; though, examples of 'hierarchy ... slipping in' were also evident in mutually engaged collaborations. Despite the evidence of 'power under the surface', participants generally agreed that 'equality' including 'alphabetical order' in publications was, or should be, an assumption (John-Steiner, 2000).[5]

The interviewees also provided insights into the relevance of collaboration for their professional and scholarly self-positioning, whereby academics reflected on the interplay between working with others and working on their own, and on the ways in which different experiences of research collaboration constitute exposure and, in doing so, tap into their personal insecurities and uncertainties, and affect their sense of self-worth (Ritchie and Rigano, 2007). One of the participants, for example, commented on how a particular collaborative relationship, which ended in a conflict between him and his co-author, has enabled him to show his worth as high-quality scholar:

> The motivation to doing that on my own was ... in this antagonism with my co-author [co-author's name]. I thought, 'I'm going to show you, you fucker, again, that I can write some a, really good paper'... And it's been very important to me actually. I've learned that ... I can produce work of the highest quality now, journal articles, without other people if I so choose ... it's been extremely empowering. (Bob, SCR)

Such accounts illustrate that collaborations present power relations that are often intellectually, personally and thus emotionally intense (Ritchie and Rigano, 2007). There is frequent evidence of 'anger' at others, as well as personal anxiety and guilt about one's own contribution (to the extent that one participant indicated he became 'afraid to open ... emails').

The participants noted the need to get used to 'different styles' and 'rates of work' and 'responses'. The terms of engagement and approaches to collaboration vary from those who prefer to work together in blocks of time, or engage over a longer period of time and 'turn taking', and whether they like to share roles or take on different tasks (ideas, writing, editing and so on). Most indicated they preferred working face-to-face and to deadlines. Relationships were supported by 'backslapping emails', using emoticons and attaching pictures and introducing social elements. The importance of (ideally physical) proximity was often highlighted as a significant factor in managing the collaborative relationship, not least 'to heal rifts' when they occur.

Overall the interviewees have experienced a mixture of good and bad collaborations. Most of them seem to be positive about the need to collaborate because of the sense of intellectual stimulation, fulfilment and enjoyment they potentially get out of the process, and the satisfaction they are able to feel with its outcomes. According to the accounts given, collaboration offers various opportunities to learn and develop, to correct and discipline each other in a productive way and, more broadly, to share the joys and sorrows accompanying the research process. However, asymmetries within collaborative relationships as well as institutional pressures

---

[5]One participant noted that they worked to the '70:30 rule' whereby authorship was alphabetical unless the second (alphabetical) author had done 70% of the work. However, this is both hard to determine and possibly not as universal an understanding as implied.

academics face, give rise to a number of risks and challenges associated with collaborative work. It is to these that we now turn.

Challenges of collaborations

The accounts reflected the risks and tensions of the collaborative relationship that is dominated by too much closeness and proximity. The most frequently mentioned area of difficulty referred to the extent to which different collaborators contributed to co-writing texts or met the requirements of funded projects. Typically cited were cases of collaborators not meeting deadlines or 'backing out' after making the commitment (sometimes many years before). It was generally assumed that colleagues had 'good intentions', saying 'yes, of course' before not delivering and letting the project 'drop off the radar'. This usually meant others picking up the rest, and sometimes 'the lion's share' of the work. The frustration with free-riding and broken promises was articulated as a 'lack of responsibility'. In some ways even more problematic were collaborators' 'shifts in involvement' where the extent of commitment is at stake:

> I've worked with some people who I've found frustrating... [You] put in a lot of time, go back, thinking about things and then you send it to the other side: 'Okay, I've got one day in my diary, I've spent the day on it you know, basically I checked all the things off on my part so it is fine' ... It's not simply just work because they deliver ... but then there's also depth of work and commitment. (Thomas, SCR)

Similarly, the quality of work raised challenges:

> [I]t's been sometimes difficult then to kind of say, 'Well this isn't good enough. Go back and do it again' kind of thing... [I] end up in that position doing it myself. (Thomas, SCR)

Unequal distributions of workload[6] often resulted in a feeling of exploitation and could lead to the termination of a collaboration (Morrison et al., 2003). However, inequality of contribution was identified as an aspect of collaboration that could not easily be resolved. It was generally agreed that these were difficult issues to approach and, as a consequence, they were often accepted. One participant noted:

> It's also hard for me to really approach somebody and say, 'I have the feeling you have not done enough for the paper'... Actually, I've done it twice with the same person and I was really explicit and mentioned it before I gave this person another chance and said, 'Okay, maybe I can see from your excuses and everything that you were really under pressure during that time. But now I have another project and it would be nice if now you could do 80% and I've already done the 20%'... [but] it turned out the same again. (Sabine, MCR)

---

[6]One participant observed that in Italy some publications indicate the proportion of contribution, which she felt was a good idea.

Challenges were also faced in negotiating the different styles of working and balancing the need to be 'open to learn' and coping with having 'work edited out' whilst at the same time 'retaining control'. Indeed, a 'bad collaborator' was described by one participant as someone with an 'intransigent intellectual view'. This was often made more difficult when there was a hierarchy:

> And working with more senior people ... The thing which I found really difficult here is the kind of struggles and battles which go on between you trying to assert yourself and saying, 'No, we should do it this way' and them saying, 'No, we should do it that way', particularly when they don't listen. (Thomas, SCR)

Another interviewee raised the notion of collaboration serving to homogenize thinking and conceptual development, particularly where there was a compulsion to collaborate and/or a dominant 'voice' in the process.

Most participants also indicated that they preferred working in one-to-one (or at least small-scale) collaborations. Where this was often not possible was in the case of large, externally funded research projects. One academic described some of the difficulties experienced in collaborative projects:

> Once this multi-person research team grew bigger, it became really difficult because each of those members of the research team had very different agendas and different kinds of understandings of what is right and wrong. (Thomas, SCR)

Additional problems arose over the ownership and use of data, in some cases without the permission of the data collector. Another commonly emerging frustration, which most of our participants commented on, was the decision regarding the order of authors' names to appear in the publication. Here, the interweaving of the personal and professional dimensions of the relationships with the co-author(s) added a layer of difficulty to resolving the problem of unequal contribution and the perception of an unfair sequencing of the authors' names.[7] In the extract below, one academic explained the personal consequences of a situation in which, despite feeling that he had made the most significant contribution to a publication, his two remaining co-authors had placed his name as third in the order of authors:

> That definitely had an influence on the friendship ... So that was hard. But it's interesting that the sensitive issues are not ... about having completely different ideas and that you don't manage to create an argument together. Now it was about something extremely benign, right, it's about order of authors. I felt tricked or I felt that he was using me and it was a bit of a shock because I never thought that [co-author's name] would do something like this. (Jacob, MCR)

As already alluded to, the tendency to avoid confrontation was commonplace; to be open is thus perceived as a challenge. Often participants 'let things go ... because of the

---

[7]This was of particular issue for those who, by dint of their surname, often found themselves last on publications regardless of effort.

friendship' but at the same time acknowledged that this 'leads you not to be truthful' about the collaborative process (see also Ritchie and Rigano, 2007). It was often hoped, in the context of longer-term relationships, that things would 'even out in the end'. Interestingly, this did not always put an end to the collaborative relationship, or what one participant described as 'the battered wife syndrome'. These tensions were equally evident in collaborative relations between peers and within a hierarchical relationship.

Such, often unspoken, challenges exemplify that collaborative relationships are complex power relations with more or less asymmetry. The examples given illustrate that collaborative relations constitute different personal and project-related dependencies and micro-power struggles, on all levels of hierarchy. Against this background, we highlight and summarize below how our participants reflect on their collaborative experiences.

Evaluations of collaborations and reflections

On balance, all our participants expressed their preference for collaborations that are participative and democratic in their orientation and, in doing so, stressed that their ideal collaborations are ones where their voice is not lost or dominated by that or those of the co-author(s) (Morrison et al., 2003). The ability to navigate this precarious terrain, and thus to negotiate collaborative practices and standards, can develop with experience:

> Writing is also a form of negotiation. What do we regard as good? What do we regard as bad? Very often, I say, 'Yes, you are right'. But sometimes I think 'Actually, it is wrong'. Now I started to maybe build up a little more confidence to ... make my voice stronger and also change things. (Claudia, ECR)

The insights exemplify that there is both a wish and pressure to collaborate, as well as a desire to work on one's own scholarly reputation and 'brand' (Ritchie and Rigano, 2007). However, participants also noted how the 'social control' or 'sense of responsibility for others' meant they tended to prioritize collaborative projects at the expense of 'crowding' or 'squeezing out' their own projects, and often their 'core' professional identity. This sometimes led to a series of 'vaguely connected projects' on their CV and to a sense of frustration.

However, despite different collaboration experiences, altogether our interviewees shared quite similar ideas on what makes up a 'good' collaboration or collaborator. One participant observed:

> Collaboration is a relationship, as the name indicates, so only collaborations can be good and not persons ... it's like a marriage. (Katrine, SCR)

In the context of discussing good collaborations, some of the interviewees also problematized their own collaborative behaviour, for example in self-critically admitting that they sometimes fail to 'deliver' or to 'deliver good quality' as they are involved in too many collaborative projects. There were also a few who reflected on how their collaborators felt about shared projects and the collaborative process itself. Some participants made, above all, the 'rules of the academic field' responsible for 'bad' and unproductive collaboration practices. In contrast, other scholars gave more reflexive accounts of the rules of the publication and collaboration 'game' – even if they complied with them:

> It sounds tough but ... it's your own fault in some ways, right? We have our masters and now we are slaves when it comes to publication. (Claudia, ECR)

The interviewees generally stressed the importance of finding the right collaborators. However, what made collaborative relationships successful, such as a close personal connection or 'understanding', also raised some of the more precarious challenges and dependencies, and resulted in unfairness that was difficult to address.

In summary, we can state that researcher collaboration presents a multifaceted, often intense and dynamic process (Ritchie and Rigano, 2007). This implies that there are a variety of aspects that might lead to the 'success' and/or 'failure' of the collaboration. However, our interviewees', and also our own, reflections on previous collaboration experiences highlight that collaborative processes and outcomes are often differently perceived, for example in regard to issues such as the value of time and ideas as contributions. Thus success (or failure) might be differently evaluated by parties involved in collaborative research projects.

Final thoughts

This chapter is interested in the investigation of and reflection on the meanings, experiences, and personal and scholarly challenges accompanying the process of researcher collaboration, particularly in light of the limited discussion of these issues in the literature (but see Cheek, 2008; Ritchie and Rigano, 2007). We hope the reflections of CM scholars contribute to an understanding of the unfolding nature of collaborative processes, related challenges and reflections on how collaboration shapes personal and professional relations as well as the research process itself in order to give voice to these experiences and consider the implications and possible responses.

The accounts highlight that the experiences of and attitudes towards researcher collaboration are diverse and varied, and frequently multiple and somewhat conflicting views are held at the same time. However, our participants share broadly similar ideas of what 'good' collaboration means and requires, even if there are no definitive 'norms' for collaboration. Reliability, commitment to the project, a 'common language' and understanding, openness and trust are mentioned as crucial elements for a good collaboration process. Several accounts of our interviewees also emphasize that the concrete practices and experiences often differ from this idea(l). Both personal reasons and institutional conditions are introduced as explanatory factors.

Even if the critical scholars interviewed present themselves, on balance, as appreciators of collaborative projects there are also many challenges faced in collaboration. The blurring of personal and professional boundaries seems to be one of the major challenges, and is widespread given the prevalence of the 'buddy' collaborator (Bozeman and Corley, 2004). The proximity and intensity that often characterize research within the social sciences, and CM research more specifically, can serve as a joyful and creative dynamic, but also as a source of power, deprivation and exploitation (Ritchie and Rigano, 2007) that can be challenging to negotiate. There was evidence of hierarchy, too, demonstrated by shifts in how more senior scholars collaborate now when compared to their past practices, and also the experiences of junior scholars when working with senior faculty. The accounts offer words of caution regarding the risks and consequences of unequal collaborations, even when they are founded in friendship or hitherto equal and respectful relations.

Our study concludes, like Katz and Martin (1997), that the concept of researcher collaboration and collaborators can by no means be taken for granted. The accounts given illustrate that the categories, standards and norms defining collaboration are variegated – often shaped by previous collaboration experiences and organizations or communities of which researchers are a member. Yet, the assumptions and aspirations in regard to collaboration seem to be rarely explicitly discussed or pronounced (John-Steiner, 2000). Many accounts exemplify that, in the course of collaborative projects, the lack or avoidance of discussion and thus the silence around expectations, perceptions and understandings of collaboration, often cause or strengthen unease, feelings of injustice and inequality among those collaborating (Ritchie and Rigano, 2007). Recognizing the widespread nature of these experiences may help give voice to these concerns.

These findings may be surprising in light of those interviewed who – as social scientists, and often critical scholars – would be sensitive to notions of power and also of reflexivity. The accounts reflect statements of what reasonable and fair collaboration comprises juxtaposed with practices that would call their own good practice into question, suggesting that whilst many were reflective of their collaborations they did not always demonstrate reflexivity in their intra-scholarly collaboration. Questionable practice was sometimes guiltily acknowledged, but other times it was not – perhaps remaining unseen, or seen 'differently' (in this particular case). This is worth noting, given that many of those affected by potential inequality were the more junior members of the profession, with more senior colleagues on occasion appearing not to recognize the role they can play in ensuring their unhappy experiences are not repeated with the next generation.

In practical terms, therefore, more needs to be done to openly reflect on, problematize and frame collaboration such that it can emerge as joyful, productive and fair for all parties. This is unlikely to be a formally managed process (as this was clearly articulated as a barrier to effective collaboration) but a community-level concern and negotiated accordingly. The discussion of collaborative relationships is an important concern since these relationships influence and (in)form the type of research undertaken (projects taken or avoided), the inclusion or exclusion of scholars in collaborative efforts, the negotiation of the types of questions asked and what is written, as well as the personal impact on scholars and interests of justice. Attention should also be paid to what 'good' collaboration means and what constitutes it. 'Good' collaboration typically involves 'like-minded' people and thus can become not only exclusionary but also self-referential, less creative or reflexive in its process and outcome.

In accordance with the book's purpose to explore and inform the research process of critical scholars, we have sought to make a critical-reflective comment on the field-specific research practices that collaborative endeavours involve. Yet we acknowledge that this aim can only be achieved to a limited extent. In particular, the small scale of the study undertaken will inevitably surface a limited range of the issues at stake.[8] Different cultural, institutional, disciplinary or group contexts will undoubtedly highlight different concerns and varying evaluations and responses to them. It is beyond the scope of this chapter, which seeks primarily to surface the issues, to provide extensive concrete 'solutions'. However, raising self-awareness, stimulating discussion and putting researcher relationships at the heart of reflexivity – theoretically and in practice – is an important first step. With its focus on the emotional and intellectual complexities and on the potential tensions, asymmetries and frictions of collaborations, it is hoped that the accounts presented encourage and enable considered and open discussions on the nature and ethics of researcher collaborations aspired to, especially among early-career researchers who are in the process of becoming critical scholars.

References

Alvesson, M., Hardy, C. and Harley, B. (2008) 'Reflecting on reflexivity: Reflexive textual practices in organization and management theory', *Journal of Management Studies*, 45(3): 480–501.

Alvesson, M. and Sandberg, J. (2011) 'Generating research questions through problematization', *Academy of Management Review*, 36(2): 247–271.

Alvesson, M. and Sköldberg, K. (2000) *Reflexive Methodology. New Vistas for Qualitative Research*. London: Sage.

Bammer, G. (2008) 'Enhancing research collaborations: Three key management challenges', *Research Policy*, 37(5): 875–887.

Beaver, D. (2001) 'Reflections on scientific collaboration (and its study): Past, present and future', *Scientometrics*, 52(3): 365–377.

---

[8] One of the editors noted problems arising from data pooling in which data are shared between researchers, raising issues about the use of data, such as potential ethical risks to the participants, issues of equality and access for contributing researchers, and the quality of the research produced.

Berman, J. (2008) 'Connecting with industry: Bridging the divide', *Journal of Higher Education Policy and Management*, 30(2): 165–174.

Birnholtz, J.P. (2007) 'When do researchers collaborate? Toward a model of collaboration propensity', *Journal of the American Society for Information Science and Technology*, 58(14): 2226–2239.

Bouyssou, D. and Marchant. T. (2011) 'Bibliometric rankings of journals based on impact factors: An axiomatic approach', *Journal of Infometrics*, 5(1) 75–86.

Bozeman, B. and Corley, E. (2004) 'Scientists' collaboration strategies: Implications for scientific and technical human capital', *Research Policy*, 33(4): 599–616.

Cheek, J. (2008) 'Researching collaboratively: Implications for qualitative research and researchers', *Qualitative Health Research*, 18(11): 1599–1603.

Engstrom, J.L. (1984) 'University, agency and collaborative models for nursing research: An overview', *Image: The Journal of Nursing Scholarship*, 16(3): 76–80.

Glaser, B.G. and Strauss A.L. (1967) *The Discovery of Grounded Theory: Strategies for Qualitative Research*. Chicago: Aldine.

Goldstein, L.S. (2000) 'Ethical dilemmas in designing collaborative research: Lessons learned the hard way', *International Journal of Qualitative Studies in Education*, 13(5): 517–530.

Hardy, C., Phillips, N. and Clegg, S. (2001) 'Reflexivity in organization and management theory: A study of the production of the research "subject"', *Human Relations*, 54(5): 531–560.

Hauptman, R. (2005) 'How to be a successful scholar: Publish efficiently', *Journal of Scholarly Publishing*, 36(2): 115–119.

John-Steiner, V. (2000) *Creative Collaboration*. New York: Oxford University Press.

Katz, J.S. and Martin, B.R. (1997) 'What is research collaboration?' *Research Policy*, 26(1):1–18.

Leahey, E. and Reikowsky, R.C. (2008) 'Research specialization and collaboration patterns in sociology', *Social Studies of Science*, 38(3): 425–440.

Liao, C.H. and Yen, H.R. (2012) 'Quantifying the degree of research collaboration: A comparative study of collaborative measures', *Journal of Infometrics*, 6(1): 27–33.

Linstead, S. (1994) 'Objectivity, reflexivity, and fiction: Humanity, inhumanity, and the science of the social', *Human Relations*, 47(11): 1321–1345.

Melin, G. (2000) 'Pragmatism and self-organization: Research collaboration on the individual level', *Research Policy*, 29(1): 31–40.

Morrison, P.S., Dobbie, G. and McDonal, F.J. (2003) 'Research collaboration among university scientists', *Higher Education Research & Development*, 22(3): 275–296.

Ponomariov, B.L. and Boardman, P.C. (2010) 'Influencing scientists' collaboration and productivity patterns through new institutions: University research centers and scientific and technical human capital', *Research Policy*, 39(5): 613–624.

Ritchie, S.M. and Rigano, D.L. (2007) 'Solidarity through collaborative research', *International Journal of Qualitative Studies in Education*, 20(2): 129–150.

Rogers-Dillon, R. (2005) 'Hierarchical qualitative research teams: Refining the methodology', *Qualitative Research*, 5(4): 437–445.

Smith, D. (2001) 'Collaborative research: Policy and the management of knowledge creation in UK universities', *Higher Education Quarterly*, 55(2): 131–157.

Sooryamoorthy, R. (2009) 'Do types of collaboration change citation? Collaboration and citation patterns of South African science publications', *Scientometrics*, 81(1): 177–193.

Stillman, F.A., Wipfli, H.L., Lando, H.A., Leischow, S. and Samet, J.M. (2005) 'Building capacity for international tobacco control research: The global tobacco research network', *American Journal of Public Health*, 95(6): 965–968.

Van Rijnsoever, F.J., Hessels, L.K. and Vandeberg, R.L.J. (2008) 'A resource-based view on the interactions of university researchers', *Research Policy*, 37: 1255–1266.

Wray-Bliss, E. (2003) 'Research subjects/research subjections: Exploring the ethics and politics of critical research', *Organization*, 10(2): 307–325.

PART II
IN THE FIELD

FOUR

Critical ethnographic research: Negotiations, influences, and interests

Daniel Nyberg and Helen Delaney

Introduction

Doing ethnographic work can be both a triumphant and tumultuous experience. The ethnographer often moves between feeling inspired, bored, awkward, humble, respectful, frustrated, and even hurt. In short, 'the ethnographer who becomes immersed in other people's realities is never quite the same afterward' (Reeves Sanday, 1979: 527). In this chapter, we are interested in not only how and why ethnographies can change the researcher, but also how critically orientated ethnographic research can alter and influence the research participants, the setting, and ultimately the research community. We argue that most ethnographies have, consciously or not, political impacts and that critical management researchers are equipped with important theoretical lenses to reflect upon this impact. Through acknowledging and exploring the political role, influence, and interests of ethnographic fieldwork, we hope that critical management researchers will be better prepared and reflective about the complicated nature and progressive potential of doing ethnographic work.

Like most academic concepts, what we mean when we talk about ethnography seems to be a moving target. In general, ethnographies are normally characterized as the holistic and descriptive study of people's actions in their natural everyday physical context in order to understand the meaning of the social world (Hammersley and Atkinson, 2007; Silverman, 1985; Watson, 2012; Zickar and Carter, 2010). Studies have also convincingly argued for researching virtual communities (Hine, 2000; Markham, 1998), documented lives (Sullivan, 2012), their own self or community (Alvesson, 2009;

Reed-Danahay, 1997), and even fictional lives (Parker, 2012). Ethnography aspires to contribute qualitative interpretations to describe or reveal something about society, communities, organizations, or individuals. This normally requires longitudinal field-work with access to the community's or organization's natural occurring production of texts through, for example, observations of everyday situations and events, often combined with interviews to understand the meaning attached to behaviours and practices (Alvesson and Deetz, 2000). A wealth of valuable scholarship regarding organizational ethnography is available for the interested reader, which provides introductions and reviews of the field, candid discussions of the trials and tribulations of doing organizational fieldwork, and elaborations on the power relations involved in research and writing the text (to name but a few – see Kunda, 2006; Mahadevan, 2012; Rosen, 2000; Schwartzman, 1993; Van Maanen, 2006; Ybema et al., 2009). In this chapter, we are interested in a type of ethnography that is especially relevant for critical management research, critical ethnography. Given that critical ethnography is a subset, so to speak, of conventional ethnography, there are naturally several significant overlaps in definition and practice between the two. Therefore, in our discussions of critical ethnography invariably this chapter will cover many issues and tensions that are also relevant for traditional ethnography. However, we will also demarcate some questions and issues that pertain specifically to critically orientated ethnographic research.

One of the questions that often arises is: how is critical ethnography different from traditional ethnography? Such a question implies there is an agreed-upon definition of critical ethnography, which of course is impossible given the variety of different disciplines that contribute diverse philosophical assumptions about the purpose and practice of critical ethnography (Foley, 2002; Springwood and King, 2001). Nevertheless, some writers have identified key features of critical ethnography, which we will now outline. Critical ethnographies aim to produce an in-depth understanding of the lived experiences of people in order to reveal the complexities underlying dominations, tensions, ambiguities, conflicts, constraints, or injustices in distribution or access to social goods (Jordan and Yeomans, 1995). In other words, critical ethnographic work places centre-stage the relations and effects of power, ideology, and hegemony in more pronounced ways than traditional ethnographies (Forester, 2003). Some writers argue that critical ethnographies should go beyond the level of describing the experience and existence of the individual or group, and consider the political economy of capitalism that constitutes the social relations, and the construction of meanings and identities in the research setting (Jordan and Yeomans, 1995: 396). For some, critical ethnographers see their work as a form of social or cultural criticism (Kincheloe and McLaren, 2002) that should have a social consciousness or political impact or purpose. As Thomas (1993: 4) succinctly argues, 'conventional ethnography describes what is, critical ethnography asks what could be'. Our emphasis is on empirically grounded critique, where the research participants, rather than the researcher, open up the space for criticism between 'what is' and 'what could be'. It is this space that the researcher can analyse and channel in arguing for social change. This is often problematic, however, and one of our intentions is to discuss some of the difficulties in trying to produce social change via critical ethnography. We will further argue that the theories underlying most critical ethnographies are useful in reflecting upon the role of ethnographers in navigating the precarious and unpredictable tension of being part of what they are studying.

This chapter is structured as follows. Firstly, using examples from our previous fieldwork, we explore how the role of the ethnographer is continually co-constructed between the researcher and the researched in ways that can feel both energizing and constraining for both parties. Secondly, the chapter discusses the political influence of the critical ethnographer on the research setting. Using examples from our fieldwork experiences, we show how critical research requires negotiation and reflection on how to navigate sensitive issues in and out of the field such as disclosure of information, building rapport, and being reflexive. Thirdly, we expand the concept of interest to develop the notion of critique in critical ethnographies. We problematize and reflect upon the consequence of holding a critical perspective in organizational research and the importance of reflecting upon assigning interests to actors or groups that are part of the study. We conclude the chapter by suggesting a continuous dialogue with the (partially) produced ethnography to understand how it came to be.

Being a critical ethnographer: Negotiations, constructions, and constraints

Social research is never neutral and the text is always supporting or questioning existing institutions, ideologies, and interests (Alvesson, 2008). Critical research acknowledges this and does not pretend neutrality (Alvesson and Deetz, 2000). However, this stands in contrast to one of the most basic premises of research: researchers 'can and should be passive, objective and dispassionate in carrying out their research' (Ferdinand et al., 2007: 521). In this section, we draw attention to how critically orientated ethnography negotiates the various pressures, expectations, and constraints regarding who you are in the field.

While traditional ethnography scholarship is very useful at explicating the various roles the researcher can occupy – see Raymond Gold's (1958) typology of participation – we argue that these typologies generally conceal the powered, unstable, shifting, and constructed nature of being in the field. While some critical ethnography literature invites the researcher to reflect on their relationship with their participants (Duberley and Johnson, 2009; Jordan and Yeomans, 1995), on the whole, detailed accounts of how the critical ethnographer navigates the competing pressures that influence who they can be or how they can act in the field are rarely described at length (see Ferdinand et al., 2007, and Mahadevan, 2012, for interesting exceptions). Therefore, in this section we explore how the researcher never solely constructs their role. Rather, it is continually negotiated, overtly or subtly, with the various stakeholders of the research – especially if the research participants are aware that the researcher holds a critical orientation to the field. While critical ethnographies are often interested in the regimes of control that their research participants are subject to, it is also equally important to explore how the researcher and the research process can be the target of control attempts. In order to better illustrate this, we begin with the following 'tale from the field'.

Story 1: Regulating the researcher's role

As part of her doctoral thesis, Helen undertook an ethnographic study of an 18-month leadership development programme that comprised a group of 30 emergent leaders and six facilitators. This programme involved observing five residential workshops of between 2 and 5 days, and an accompanying virtual learning environment (see Nicholson and Carroll, 2013, for more information). Helen was interested in concepts such as identity work/regulation, power, resistance, discourse, and self-transformation on this programme. Her role within this setting shifted a number of times throughout the 18 months, and was deeply influenced by requests from the programme facilitators.

> At the first residential, Helen participated frequently in events – joining in on group activities, participating in some discussions, asking participants questions about their experience, and at other times solely observing – and therefore could be seen as a participant-as-observer in Gold's (1958) typology. Some of the participants were quite curious about who Helen was and her research interests, although Helen was never entirely explicit about her critical interests with the emerging leaders. On one occasion, one of the facilitators, Carrie, asked her to describe some of the things she was noticing with regard to identity work, to which Helen briefly explained the different identity positions the facilitators seemed to exhibit on the course. As part of her response, Helen noted how it was difficult to determine the identity position of one facilitator, in comparison with the quite obvious and strong positions of the others.

> After this first residential, Helen was asked to meet with three of the facilitators in order to 'share our experience of bringing Helen as [a] researcher into a residential/ programme space' (as described by a facilitator). This meeting was primarily led by the facilitator Cassandra who requested that Helen 'just observe' from now on rather than participate. The rationale for this was that they did not want the participants becoming confused with Helen's role (i.e. they might see her as a fellow participant or a facilitator), to the detriment of their learning and development. Helen was asked not to disclose her thesis topic to the participants, instigate research-related conversations, or to talk in one-on-one scenarios with participants or facilitators. Cassandra expressed concern that the presence of a critical researcher may jeopardize the development process for some of the participants, and therefore Helen's impact on the environment needed to be mitigated. Cassandra was particularly concerned about the interaction Helen had with Carrie about the identity positionings of the facilitators, because it had a) touched on a sensitive issue within their organization (a facilitator trying to establish their identity position), and b) could've distracted Carrie from her focus on the participants. She was also concerned that Helen had talked to some of the participants and

the facilitators did not know what was said. The tenor of this conversation was that the participants and facilitators needed to be protected from the researcher's presence. The facilitators were also uncomfortable that they were being observed and suggested that they were not to be a focus of the research.

This meeting was later described by Carrie as '[Helen] being inducted into how we do things … [which] can mean throwing out lots of unsettling, disquieting stuff into visibility'. This can be read as Helen being initiated into their community and how the facilitators interact, as well as an instance of attempting to regulate the researcher and their research. This meeting was quite anxiety inducing for Helen as a novice researcher, and she began to doubt her ability as a fieldworker, which had an impact on her role in the next residential.

The second residential was at an outdoor pursuits/education centre, and based on the requests from the facilitators, Helen participated less, which at times felt awkward given the physical nature of the workshop. During the residential, Helen was still drawn into group conversations with the facilitators and participants regarding leadership and their experiences of the programme thus far; however, she felt on edge for a lot of the residential as she had internalized the surveillance of the facilitators' requests about her behavior.

In the third residential, Helen became a complete observer, almost a fly on the wall (although the impossibility of actually being a complete observer will be discussed below). Helen did not instigate research-related conversation with the participants, and except for one activity, she did not participate in the group activities. However, this raised the concern of being too distanced from the group and it became hard to capture the informal conversations surrounding the observed interactions. Therefore, by the fourth and fifth residential, Helen increased the level of interaction and acted as an observer-as-participant, interacting with the participants up to a certain point. The facilitators seemed to be more comfortable with Helen's presence at this stage in the programme as it was nearing the end of the development process and therefore presumably the perceived risk of the researcher's influence was lessened. Nevertheless, Helen still felt quite aware that some of the facilitators may be watching her, and regulated her behavior as a result.

The variation of researcher roles from the ethnography described above can be seen as an illustration of the continuous negotiation of different expectations of the research. Doing critical research can therefore raise self-doubts, anxieties, and insecurities that may unsettle the researcher's identity. Thus, our experience of the research process, illustrated through the shifting roles in the ethnography depicted above, disagrees with some of the literature, which assumes that researchers choose their role (see Angrosino and Mays de Perez, 2000). As evident in Helen's example, there is no unbridled agency to construct the role of the ethnographer. Rather, who you are in the field is shaped by the conflicting expectations from the research participants, the 'gatekeepers' (often managers) who grant access, the nature of the work and workplace, the research institution you are part of, and you as a researcher.

Therefore, the process of researcher role negotiation is important for the ethnographer to record during the fieldwork for a number of reasons. These interactions can be analysed in order to better understand the organization and how it operates.

In the case above, the attempts to regulate the research focus (i.e. the explicit suggestion to not research the facilitators who are a main actor in leadership development),
suggests that there may be some anxiety, vulnerability, or insecurity among the
facilitation team regarding their role, perceptions, purpose, and/or cohesiveness,
and hence their desire to protect themselves from a critical researcher. It also points
to a possible need to control the leadership development space, and raises questions
about how the facilitators position and perceive the emerging leaders (i.e. vulnerable
and in need of protection). These interactions may indicate how the organizational
member interacts with their staff, colleagues, and so on, and the rhetorical moves
they use to try and establish power. The intentions, requests, or messages from
the organization or people in power in these moments may also contradict how
they present themselves to employees, workers, peers, or clients. These moments of
negotiation (which may at times feel more like regulation or disciplining attempts)
may unsettle and/or reinforce one's commitment to maintain a critical perspective
in the research. For example, if the organization seems particularly resistant or controlling towards the research(er), this may signal how important it is to pursue this
type of critical inquiry. Therefore, these moments of negotiation may colour how
the researcher interprets their empirical material and how they write the final text.
It is therefore vital to bring forth these moments as crucial data excerpts worthy of
analysis and reflection.

Alongside the ongoing experimentation and negotiation of the ethnographer's
role in the field, the ethnographer often makes choices (and sometimes, mistakes)
regarding how much they should disclose about their research. A critical ethnographer may not be able to fully disclose their research questions in case certain actors
feel vulnerable. This is because critical research generally aims to 'disrupt ongoing
social reality for the sake of providing impulses to the liberation from or resistance
to what dominates and leads to constraints in human decision making' (Alvesson
and Deetz, 2000: 1). In most contemporary organizations, such a project may aim
to increase the autonomy of the workforce, decrease surveillance, and/or initiate
resistance to the constraints the workers are facing. However, in order to gain access
to a community or an organization, you may need to 'sell' or 'pitch' the research to
actors in some form of position of power who may often favour the status quo or
even increased power. Critical researchers are dependent on the people in positions
of power to gain access. These are often the same people who may feel most 'at risk'
from the findings. In addition, not only do gatekeepers have expectations around
full disclosure of the researcher's ideas and intentions, they may also expect 'useful'
managerialist knowledge in return. Hypothetically, it would be possible to inform
managers about critical perspectives, ideas, and findings – indeed, some critical management studies writing is calling for this kind of engagement (Spicer et al., 2009).
The critical ethnographer therefore may need to gently alter how the 'gatekeeper'
sees academic knowledge as well, trying to move them away from a purely technical or instrumental stance, and translating the potential benefit of more critically
inclined research. But such an effort may be blocked (explicitly or implicitly) by a

functionalist interest in prescriptive solutions and efficiency. The alternative may be to only be critical in the academic debate, withhold information to the involved stakeholders, or compromise on how the research is represented (i.e. writing multiple documents to suit different knowledge interests). This can at times be an uncomfortable process as it raises feelings of being coy, misleading, or deliberately vague which may be problematic for a researcher who is aware of ethics, asymmetry, inequality, and silence. This is particularly pertinent for ethnographers who are close to the people they are studying.

The political influence of the critical ethnographer

In ethnographic research, both the research setting and the academic community shape and are shaped by the research, to various degrees. The Entertainment of the research field and academic community enables the study, but at the same time limits the researcher's own understanding. That is, the possible knowledge about what one can study is limited by being part of the setting studied. The researcher is necessarily involved in the activities and there is no exterior observational point, since we are part of what we try to understand (Barad, 2007). Thus, the ethnographer is never an outsider looking in, nor an insider looking out. The ethnographer, like the research participants, is part of the observed practices and activities. While the researcher and the participant share the situations, they do not necessarily share how they make sense of them, nor may they share the same interest in the situation. For example, in Story 1 above, Helen's interest in the intent, purpose, and effect of leadership development as a critical management researcher may be quite different from that of the aspirational manager who is participating in the programme to progress up the corporate ladder. This suggests that the critical ethnographer's reflexive practice would involve considering how their own interests are influenced by the community they are studying, as well as how their interests and research may influence the fieldwork setting.

In doing critically informed ethnographic research, you may find yourself in situations where you may change the activities and practices under focus. For some, creating a political impact should be the end to which critical ethnography aspires (i.e. Jordan and Yeomans, 1995). Whether a political impact is intended or not, a feature of critical ethnographic work is to consider the positionality of the researcher (Madison, 2012). Positionality, according to Madison (2012: 7) requires us to 'acknowledge our own power, privilege, and biases just as we are denouncing the power structures that surround our subjects'. This requires reflexivity in order to be aware of one's potential impact and influence. In this section, we illustrate the political role of the ethnographer by including extracts from ethnographic studies that we previously conducted (for further details, see Nyberg, 2008, 2009).

Story 2: Changing seats

The first extract is from an eight-month-long ethnography that Daniel conducted in an Australian insurance company with approximately 1,700 employees. The particular focus of this study was three call centre departments located in the same building at the company headquarters. The research was mainly observational and Daniel was a semi-participant: he 'shadowed' individual employees during their time at work and participated in lunch and coffee breaks, but did not have any formal work role in the organization. These semi-participatory observations also included meetings, discussions with supervisors, as well as more informal interactions with peers. The following extract from one of the call centres, *Business Relations*, is taken from field reflections:

> Walking towards the *Business Relations* cubicles I saw the manager and the two team leaders of *Business Relations* sitting at a table separated from the cubicles. They looked at me and I walked towards them while greeting the organizational members I passed. At the table, Eric, the manager, asked me who I wanted to observe. The team leaders, Anne and Karen, turned around and looked at me, waiting for an answer. I knew that the follow-up question to my answer would be 'why?' Thinking about that, I chose Mary. Eric then asked me 'why Mary?' I responded that my earlier observations had been with people who were placed in the centre of the cubical landscape and Mary was on the fringe of the two teams in *Business Relations*. Eric did not agree and told me that 'all of them have equal opportunity to interact'. To which I did not comment. Anne said smilingly that my answer to Eric's question was really good. Not thinking anymore about our conversation, I spent the day observing Mary doing her work.

> A couple of weeks later, when I walked into the *Business Relations* area, I saw that Anne's team had changed seats. All the team members were in different places in the office. I froze, remembering the conversations a couple of weeks before. Did this have anything to do with our earlier conversation? Have they done this before? Why did they do it?

These field reflections illustrate the importance of considering how the researcher may influence what is observed. As a researcher in the field, you are confronted with 'ethically important moments ... the difficult, often subtle, and usually unpredictable situations that arise in the practice of doing research' (Guillemin and Gillam, 2004: 262). The extract above illustrates one of these everyday moments in research practices. Given their enduring presence in the research organization, the ethnographer can often be asked to share their opinion regarding the dynamics of the workplace. These are 'ethically important moments' which can be complicated to navigate, especially given that a critical ethnographer may offer analyses that bring to light issues around power, identity, and inequality that the organizational actors have not considered or do not wish to confront. The interactions between the ethnographer and the employees may alter how the employees perceive their organization, their place in it, and/or the researcher.

The researcher's interest in conducting the ethnography can also become entangled with other actors' interests. As Daniel's extract above suggests, managers in the organization may use the researcher's presence to reflect upon their methods of controlling the workforce. Similarly, workers may use the researcher's presence to avoid taking on extra responsibilities and to both gain and discuss opinions about the managers in the workplace. In Daniel's study, he felt like the customer service operators (CSOs) sometimes used his presence as a researcher to avoid taking on work tasks or to have breaks, with rationales like 'I cannot do that because Daniel is observing me today' or 'I have to go to lunch now with Daniel'. Spending considerable amounts of time in the field means that the ethnographer becomes attuned to the politics of the organization, which requires reflexivity in understanding how their presence is used by different actors. Even when one tries to be a complete observer, some research participants may (inadvertently) mimic a similar researcher gaze (i.e. stepping 'out' of the mire of everyday organizational detail to adopt a more analytical stance), or the 'gatekeepers' may continue to monitor the researcher to ensure they are 'just observing'.

As the accounts above have pointed out, research participants may be or become suspicious about the ethnographer's presence, at times due to their political influence on the research setting (Hammersley and Atkinson, 1995; Punch, 1986). The ethnographer's attempts to build a good rapport with their research subjects is often justified in the sense that it helps build up trust. Some writers have asked whether these 'tricks of the trade' used to put research participants at ease could be seen as a 'mild form of manipulation, if not exploitation' (Ferdinand et al., 2007: 534). It could be that with the gain of trust or familiarity, the political situations mentioned may deteriorate – or put differently, critical ethnographers may find it more difficult to establish rapport with their research subjects precisely because of their critical orientation (Springwood and King, 2001). This can be seen in Helen's example, whereby some of the facilitators seemed uncomfortable that she was connecting with the leaders on the programme. The critical researcher may also find it difficult to create rapport with their research subjects if they are researching a site, practice, group, or individual they wish to challenge, deconstruct or eliminate, such as a misogynist, racist, capitalist and so on (Springwood and King, 2001). In other cases, the researcher may be seen as a confidant and the act of 'confessing' may have performative effects for the organizational member (Foucault, 1990). That is, by inviting the worker/manager into an interaction where they are encouraged to talk about their experience of work (perhaps with an emphasis on power, control, agency, identity, voice, inequality, emotions, etc.) the moment of disclosure can have an effect on how they perceive and interact with their organization. These more intimate moments of self-disclosure may also make it difficult for the researcher to hold their critical gaze, especially if they have previously positioned an occupational group (i.e. managers) as 'oppressors'.

In conducting a critical ethnography it is important to reflect upon ethically important moments, in terms of how they might impact the field, what type of impact is sought after, how you are shaping what you are studying, and, perhaps more importantly, the ethical implications of how the research process is affecting the participants. We recognize that there is always something out of the reach of reflexivity, and that it is impossible to completely do this prior to setting foot in the field, or on your own, therefore we favour an approach to reflexivity that sees it as an in-the-moment, relational process, which we describe in more detail below (see also Foley, 2002, for an overview of different types of reflexivity in critical ethnography).

Guillemin and Gillam (2004) outline three steps that can be useful in order to increase reflexivity during the research process. First, it is important from the outset to acknowledge that the ethnographer's presence will influence the organization or community studied, and that being in field means that one will occasionally be confronted with interactions and negotiations about this dynamic. Second, by being aware of the situations one can develop a sensitivity to ethically important moments and record them in a separate notebook. Daniel's extract above is an example of how this practice helped him to come to terms with how he may have influenced the organization. Third, it is possible to develop micro-strategies to pre-empt and address situations where you are influencing the organization or community studied, as well as processing unanticipated situations. This could involve initially and continually constructing your role as a researcher (for example, on several occasions Helen had to describe what her role did and did not involve with the programme participants, both formally through documentation, and in informal interactions); knowing when to avoid, exit, or redirect conversations gracefully; and when to be honest that you are interacting as an ethnographer, not a colleague, judge, expert, therapist, manager and so on. Exploring reflexivity inevitably leads one to questions such as: who am I as a researcher responsible for and to? What impact or contribution should my research have? These are questions we contend with in the next section.

Plurality of interests

In order to consider the impact or contribution of critical ethnographic research, it is important to understand how organizational actors are generally positioned. In most critical management research those who are supposed to dominate and those who are supposed to resist are already established: managers dominate and workers resist. Their interests are given and assumed to conflict. The worker is somewhat stereotyped as dominated/oppressed and in need of liberation from the academic researcher, while the manager is stereotyped as the oppressor wanting to increase surveillance and control. Critical management research then aims to give voice to the workers in liberating them from management domination. More specifically, critical ethnography is meant to expose political struggles, oppressive practices, and control regimes, possibly with an emancipatory intent (Duberley and Johnson, 2009). However, what if the participants with constraints upon their decision-making do not want to be 'saved'? Or what if the managers are not interested in dominating the workers? Who are we then supposed to 'save'? Arguably, this clear division is murkier and how individual organizational members make sense of their position is contextually dependent. Most middle or lower managers today are also constrained in their actions, like the workers they are supposed to supervise. With increased complexity in the labour market, class divisions do not necessarily neatly follow manager–worker divisions. While we acknowledge societal class divisions, (multinational) corporations are not necessarily mirrors of their societies.

For example, in the ethnography of the call centre described above, some of the workers found the close surveillance liberating. The close surveillance allowed the workers to be protected from customer complaints and the surveillance was associated with prizes for individuals and teams performing well under its measurements. This notion of comfort was observed when CSOs told the customers that 'the system gives you the quote' or 'the system gives you the rating' (Nyberg and Sewell, 2014: 321). Here, the CSOs are effectively absolving themselves of responsibility by blaming the shortcomings in customer service on the computer system, and it was often observed how the supervisors sided with their CSOs against both the restrictive technology and problematic or difficult customers. Importantly, surveillance in the form of recording the CSO–customer interchange could also confirm that the CSO had followed the script and other protocols. If they became the target of a customer complaint, the surveillance protected them from criticism. Thus, the research participants were well aware of the close surveillance but accepted it on the basis of protection and rewards, such as days off, movie tickets, or cash prizes.

This is not to say that all of the workers experienced the surveillance positively. Indeed, one of the call centre workers said:

> There is almost no flexibility, the computer tells us everything. I used to work for another insurance company and there was a lot of wheeling and dealing. Here you are a representative of the computer. You cannot do anything for the customer, which is very disempowering ... I cannot do anything myself! Everything has to go through the manager. She has complete control over what is happening ... To do brainless work full-time is just mind numbing. It's like a part of you that is developed is not used, like they take your arm off. (Nyberg and Sewell, 2014: 320)

Further, not only are the workers caught in monotonous surveillance relations, the managerial activities in performing surveillance also lack complexity and discretion. The managerial role is almost as mundane as that of the workers. In effect, managers and workers – parties who are traditionally seen as being on opposite sides of the 'frontier of control' – arguably define the purpose and consequences of control through localized acts of sense-making beyond any sterile theorization of their supposed position.

The ethnographic study referred to above shows that the common critical claim of false consciousness does not stand up since the workers were aware of the surveillance and its consequences. They often considered it constraining, although at times they saw it as rewarding and liberating. Some participants chose money and protection over autonomy. The critical theorist's intention to portray the insider's agenda (Jermier, 1998) can result in the discovery that the participants do not share similar interests with each other or the critical theorist's political agenda. This can be problematic in giving voice to participants who have contradictory politics, or giving credence to a perspective that the theorist does not support. The portrayed informants may not think that the socioeconomic conditions should change or that the asymmetrical structures of control are problematic. Going against the subjects would then construct a position of privilege and power for the critical ethnographer (Katz, 2004). It is here that the problem of false consciousness arises, since the researcher is not describing or representing the voice of the participants (Katz, 2004). Instead, the elitist claims denigrate the voices. The lack of shared interests between the critical ethnographer and the workforce 'means that no amount of "reflexivity" will solve this problem: no single researcher is likely to be as diverse as the subjects he or she studies' (Katz, 2004: 300). This complicates the call from some critical ethnographers that we 'must aim to learn and impart skills which will allow our subjects to continue investigating the world in which they will go on living' (Jordan and Yeomans, 1995: 401). Or perhaps more emphatically, that we need to make 'the everyday world ... problematic for those we leave behind in the field' (Jordan and Yeomans, 1995: 401–2). Rather than dissolving the distinction between researcher and researched, such an attitude could reinforce the powered position of the researcher as the one who knows and imparts.

The example from Nyberg and Sewell's (2014) study above illustrates the problems of taking interests for granted by showing other interpretations that are slightly more nuanced to most everyday politics in organizations. The study opens up the debate about how to represent the voice of organizational members, the basis of the critique, and the position of the critic. This is important since there is a potential mismatch between the political aim of societal critique and the method of studying local expressions. It is therefore important to consider the basis of the critique to understand both the positions of the ethnographer and the participants.

The basis of critique

The majority of critical management research provides a theoretical basis for the critique of the social injustice that management and organizations may reproduce. What unites critical scholars from diverse backgrounds, such as Marxist labour process theory, critical theory based on the Frankfurt School, and more recently scholars inspired by Habermas, is an a priori established yardstick for the critique. For example, using Habermas's (1984) concept of communicative rationality, critical management research can reveal how social structures, reproduced locally, distort equal and democratic communication. The a priori standard of an 'ideal-speech' situation works as a yardstick to evaluate the power relations inherent in social structures and between actors within organizations. Whether or not the ideal-speech situation can be obtained is of secondary value, since it is still useful to unmask social values, partial interests, and power relations (Adler et al., 2007; Duberley and Johnson, 2009). Forester (2003) illustrates the fruitful application of Habermas's ideas in a critical ethnography of meetings of city planning staff in a small New York municipality. Forester shows how the communicative actions in the meetings shape beliefs, consents, and attention to particular issues, which helps explain how actors are content with unequal situations and domination. The basis of the critique is theoretical, with the participants acting as informers for an emancipatory struggle towards equality, consensus, and freedom from domination beyond the borders of the organization. However, this Habermasian position of critique is based upon a 'leap of faith' in that it presumes that it is in people's interest, beyond the ethnographer, to reach these values or goods (Flyvbjerg, 1998).

The problem facing critical management researchers aligned with more postmodern or poststructuralist thinking has been to convincingly argue for the foundation of their critique. Alvesson and Sköldberg (2000: 131) put this abruptly in arguing that 'we can hardly go around asking people about their psychic prisons or false consciousness or communicative distortions and so on'. People are socialized to accept their situation as a natural order, with criticism requiring critical distance (Duberley and Johnson, 2009). The theoretical position of the ethnographer is then obtained by presumed universal and objective positions; in Walzer's (1983: xiv) words, the critical scholars have 'to walk out of the cave, leave the city, climb the mountain, fashion for oneself (what can never be fashioned for ordinary men and women) an objective and universal standpoint. Then one describes the terrain of everyday life from far away, so that it loses its particular contours and takes on a general shape'. However, we should not confuse the research subject's lack of theoretical understanding with false consciousness, and there is a real danger in claiming to be able to distinguish between people's true and false interests (Adler et al., 2007). Even so, if we cannot trust the natives to be theoretically critical of their own conduct, what are the alternative positions of social critique to Marxist or Habermasian theoretical foundations?

Instead of engaging in distant critique, from the mountain top, Walzer (1983: xiv) argues for standing 'in the cave, in the city, on the ground': we do not need to discover the critical higher ground, it is already there in the society, community, and organization. The basis for empirical and close critique 'of existence begins, or can begin, from principles internal to existence itself' (Walzer, 1987: 21). Instead of universal claims of class interests as the basis for critique, Walzer argues for the plurality of often-recognized social goods to reveal domination. In *Spheres of Justice* (1983) he argues that different domains in society have their own ways of separating good from bad, right from wrong, and that each of these spheres is governed by different principles of justice. For example, the good of medicine should be distributed according to need, higher education according to talent, money according to skill in the market, and so forth. Inequality and domination are built into these spheres, and we can use the ethnographic material to outline distribution and access to goods without a separate 'yardstick' of morality. Critical ethnography is then based on understanding a plurality of goods instead of interests. Critique is based on the insiders' perspective of what equality means and the participant's capacity to access the distribution of public goods in other spheres. The domination of markets over other spheres and the recognition of goods are visible in everyday situations through observing empirical moments of critique.

Boltanski (2011), supporting Walzer's pluralism and empirical basis of critique, suggests turning to situations where people engage in critique – that is, disputes. In everyday disputes or disagreements actors justify their positions and validate their arguments, and their positions can be used to ground critique. In promoting a pragmatist sociology of critique, Boltanski (2011: 30) advocates 'making use of the point of view of the actors – that is to say, base itself on their moral sense and, in particular on their ordinary sense of justice, to expose the discrepancy between the social world as it is and as it should be in order to satisfy people's moral expectations'. In disputes, actors do not merely refer to individual interests or authority; quite the opposite, they refer to public goods (Walzer, 1983) or orders of worth (Boltanksi and Thévenot, 2006) in arguing their case. For example, in situations of discrimination in hiring processes, the candidate in disputing the decision does not refer to her/his individual interest in terms of 'I want the job' or 'I need the job'. In disputing the job, the candidate would refer to principles of equality or justice. The understanding of these types of everyday situations can thus form the basis for critique. Critical ethnography is well suited to understanding, through critique and disputes, the process of how the social world is being made as well as the social injustices of this construction.

Conclusion

We started this chapter by outlining how the critical ethnographer influences the field as well as how the field influences the researcher. We showed how there is a continuous political negotiation between the different actors in carrying out a critical ethnography. The final academic text, the critical ethnography, is an outcome of how you negotiated your role in the organization (what you were allowed to see and hear), your role in the political struggle/negotiation (whom you were seeing and hearing), the theoretical perspective that influenced the study (how you chose to hear and see things), the academic negotiation (how you were allowed to present what you saw and heard), and your critical perspective (for whom or what you are seeing and hearing).

We highlight a number of ethical issues that critical ethnographers may wish to reflect upon, such as:

- How could my assumptions, biases, interests, and presence influence the fieldwork setting?
- How may I need to negotiate the ethical dilemma of what information to reveal and conceal to different parties?
- How may my identity/position as a critical researcher facilitate and inhibit the creation of relationships of trust and rapport with participants?
- To what am I responsible, and to whom?
- How am I positioning myself and the research participants in terms of power, political purposes, and/or interests?
- Do I have an intention to create political or social change through this research, and if so, what may be some of the unintended consequences of such an effort?

We have tried to challenge the assumption that researchers and participants may share single and mutual interests. In advanced capitalist societies with workers trading in shares and placing their money in private pension funds that own large parts of multinational corporations, the division between capitalists, agents of capitalists, and workers is becoming increasingly blurred. There is thus a danger in assuming the same interest between the participants, or the participants and the researcher. We have argued that the position of critique need not be vertical: from a distant and privileged position in an ivory tower looking down at the participants. The theory-laden, emancipatory, or ironic critique is not the only way of reflecting upon the field. The alternative would be horizontal, where the researcher uses one field or sphere to understand another, or the disputes in society to understand the praxis of critique. A position of resistance towards institutions is often assumed to be dependent on creating a distance towards the field or community. Alternatively, as outlined above, one can use closeness to understand the sphere one is studying. The closeness still allows for reflexivity by understanding how other spheres interact with the current field, for example how goods and resources are distributed within fields, and the institutional constraints of certain forms of domination. This allows for connections to be made between the research subject's immediate experiences and their social conditions, which can be used by the ethnographer to position the research.

This chapter has challenged several traditional assumptions regarding the purpose and plausibility of doing a critical ethnography, particularly of going in 'all guns blazing' to change the organization or group researched. While we do support the aim of some critical ethnographic research to change institutions, one should be careful in assuming the possibility to conduct informed and consensual research that shares a political or critical interest with any or all of the participants.

References

Adler, P.S., Forbes, L.C. and Willmott, H. (2007) 'Critical management studies', *Academy of Management Annals*, 1(1): 119–179.

Alvesson, M. (2008) 'The future of critical management studies', in D. Barry and H. Hansen (eds), *The Sage Handbook of New Approaches in Management and Organization*. London: Sage, pp. 13–27.

Alvesson, M. (2009) 'At-home ethnography: Struggling with closeness and closure', in S. Ybema, D. Yanow, H. Wels and F. Kamsteeg (eds), *Organizational Ethnography: Studying the Complexities of Everyday Life*. London: Sage, pp. 156–174.

Alvesson, M. and Deetz, S. (2000) *Doing Critical Management Research*. London: Sage.

Alvesson, M. and Sköldberg, K. (2000) *Reflexive Methodology: New Vistas for Qualitative Research*. London: Sage.

Angrosino, M.V. and Mays de Perez, K.A. (2000) 'Rethinking observation: From method to context', in N.K. Denzin and Y.S. Lincoln (eds), *Handbook of Qualitative Research*. London: Sage, pp. 673–702.

Barad, K. (2007) *Meeting the Universe Halfway: Quantum Physics and the Entanglement of Matter and Meaning*. Durham, NC: Duke University Press.

Boltanski, L. (2011) *On Critique: A Sociology of Emancipation*. Cambridge: Polity Press.

Boltanski, L. and Thévenot, L. (2006) *On Justification: Economies of Worth*. Princeton, NJ: Princeton University Press.

Duberley, J. and Johnson, P. (2009) 'Critical management methodology', in H. Willmott, T. Bridgman and M. Alvesson (eds), *The Oxford Handbook of Critical Management Studies*. Oxford: Oxford University Press.

Ferdinand, J., Pearson, G., Rowe, M. and Worthington, F. (2007) 'A different kind of ethics', *Ethnography*, 8(4): 519–543.

Flyvbjerg, B. (1998) 'Habermas and Foucault: Thinkers for civil society?' *British Journal of Sociology*, 49(2): 210–233.

Foley, D.E. (2002) 'Critical ethnography: The reflexive turn', *Qualitative Studies in Education*, 15(5): 469–490.

Forester, J. (2003) 'On fieldwork in a Habermasian way: Critical ethnography and the extra-ordinary character of ordinary professional work', in M. Alvesson and H. Willmott (eds), *Studying Management Critically*. London: Sage, pp. 46–65.

Foucault, M. (1990) *The History of Sexuality, Volume 1: An Introduction*. New York: Vintage Books.

Guillemin, M. and Gillam, L. (2004) 'Ethics, reflexivity, and "ethically important moments" in research', *Qualitative Inquiry*, 10(2): 261–280.

Gold, R.L. (1958) 'Roles in sociological field observations', *Social Forces*, 36(3): 217–223.

Habermas, J. (1984) *The Theory of Communicative Action, Vol. 1: Reason and the Rationalization of Society*. Boston: Beacon Press.

Hammersley, M. and Atkinson, P. (1995) *Ethnography: Principles in Practice*. London: Routledge.

Hine, C. (2000) *Virtual Ethnography*. London: Sage.

Jermier, J.M. (1998) 'Introduction: Critical perspective on organizational control', *Administrative Science Quarterly*, 43(2): 235–256.

Jordan, S. and Yeomans, D. (1995) 'Critical ethnography: Problems in contemporary theory and practice', *British Journal of Sociology of Education*, 16(3): 389–408.

Katz, J. (2004) 'On the rhetoric and politics of ethnographic methodology', *Annals of the American Academy of Political and Social Science*, 595(1): 280–308.

Kincheloe, J.L. and McLaren, P. (2002) 'Rethinking critical theory and qualitative research', in Y. Zou and E.T. Trueba (eds), *Ethnography and Schools: Qualitative Approaches to the Study of Education*. Lanham, MD: Rowman & Littlefield, pp. 87–138.

Kunda, G. (2006) *Engineering Culture: Control and Commitment in a High-tech Corporation*. Philadelphia: Temple University Press.

Madison, D.S. (2012) *Critical Ethnography: Method, Ethics, and Performance* (2nd edn). London: Sage.

Mahadevan, J. (2012) 'Translating nodes of power through reflexive ethnographic writing', *Journal of Organizational Ethnography*, 1(1): 119–131.

Markham, A.N. (1998) *Life Online: Researching Real Experience in Virtual Space*. Walnut Creek, CA: Altamira Press.

Nicholson, H. and Carroll B. (2013) 'Identity undoing and power relations in leadership development', *Human Relations*, 66(9): 1225–1248.

Nyberg, D. (2008) 'The morality of everyday activities: Not the right, but the good thing to do', *Journal of Business Ethics*, 81(3): 587–598.

Nyberg, D. (2009) 'Computers, customer service operatives and cyborgs: Intra-actions in call centres', *Organization Studies*, 30(11): 1181–99.

Nyberg, D. and Sewell, G. (2014) 'Collaboration, co-operation, or collusion? Contrasting employee responses to managerial control in three call-centres', *British Journal of Industrial Relations*, 52(2): 308–332.

Parker, M. (2012) 'Being there, teleography and The Wire', *Journal of Organizational Ethnography*, 1(1): 23–30.

Punch, M. (1986) *The Politics and Ethics of Fieldwork*. London: Sage.

Reed-Danahay, D. E. (1997) *Auto/Ethnography: Rewriting the Self and the Social*. London: Berg.

Reeves Sanday, P. (1979) 'The ethnographic paradigm(s)', *Administrative Science Quarterly*, 24(4): 527–538.

Rosen, M. (2000) *Turning Words and Spinning Worlds: Chapters in Organizational Ethnography*. Amsterdam: Harwood Academic Publishers.

Schwartzman, H.B. (1993) *Ethnography in Organizations*. Newbury Park, CA: Sage.

Silverman, D. (1985) *Qualitative Methodology and Sociology*. Aldershot: Gower.

Spicer, A., Alvesson, M. and Kärreman, D. (2009) 'Critical performativity: The unfinished business of critical management studies', *Human Relations*, 62(4): 537–560.

Springwood, C.F and King, C.R. (2001) 'Unsettling engagements: On the ends of rapport in critical ethnography', *Qualitative Inquiry*, 7(4): 403–417.

Sullivan, P. (2012) 'The personality of public documents: A case study in normalising Aboriginal risk', *Journal of Organizational Ethnography*, 1(1): 52–61.

Thomas, J. (1993) *Doing Critical Ethnography*. London: Sage.

Van Maanen, J. (2006) 'Ethnography then and now', *Qualitative Research in Organizations and Management: An International Journal*, 1(1): 13–21.

Walzer, M. (1983) *Spheres of Justice: A Defense of Pluralism and Equality*. New York: Basic Books.

Walzer, M. (1987) *Interpretation and Social Criticism*. Cambridge, MA: Harvard University Press.

Watson, T.J. (2012) 'Making organizational ethnography', *Journal of Organizational Ethnography*, 1(1): 15–22.

Ybema, S., Yanow, D., Wels, H. and Kamsteeg, F. (eds) (2009) *Organizational Ethnography: Studying the Complexities of Everyday Life*. London: Sage.

Zickar, M.J. and Carter, N.T. (2010) 'Reconnecting with the spirit of workplace ethnography', *Organizational Research Methods*, 13(2): 304–319.

FIVE

Critical action research

Tony Huzzard and Yvonne Johansson

Introduction

Action research is typically characterized in terms of collaboration or 'researching with' the field with a view both to generating new scientific knowledge and promoting democratic social change (Greenwood and Levin, 2007: 1). In the recent *Sage Handbook on Action Research* (Reason and Bradbury (2008: 1) it is defined by the editors as: 'a participatory democratic process concerned with developing practical knowledge in the pursuit of worthwhile human purposes, grounded in a participatory worldview'. Our point of departure in this chapter is that action research, as defined here, can have ambitions which are closely aligned with a critical approach to studying management. At stake here is the broad goal of micro-emancipation through participation (Alvesson and Willmott, 1992). Moreover, the emphasis on reflexivity in action research, both as practice and as validation (Coghlan and Brannick, 2010: 41ff.; Warwick and Board, 2012), is consistent with the call for reflexivity in, for example, Critical Management Studies (Fournier and Grey, 2000).

On the other hand, the close engagement with the field implied by action research might be at odds with the calls of certain critical scholars for eschewing 'performativity' (Fournier and Grey, 2000). In recent years, however, as discussed in Chapter 1, critical management scholars have argued more strongly for engagement with the field (Spicer et al., 2009; Wolfram Cox et al., 2009). However, we will argue in this chapter that performative engagement through action research is not without its tensions. The difficulty is that action research sees knowledge creation as a joint enterprise between researcher and researched, an approach that normally entails a rather intimate, high-trust collaborative relationship or ethics of care which, intuitively, would seem to compromise the requirement for distance that is generally seen as essential in critical approaches not least those that aim at denaturalization (Fournier and Grey, 2000). What, then, does it mean for a critical scholar of management to conduct action research?

For us, critical action research not only concerns researching with practitioners in an intervention to develop or improve work organizations, but also entails joint knowledge creation with practitioners and reflexivity with the ambition to emancipate individuals from certain structural constraints (Kemmis, 2001). This view sees critical action research in terms of social analyses of organization and power in a local situation with a view to improving things, notably for those who are subjected to oppression or domination (Kemmis and McTaggart, 2000). A critical approach also aims to uncover how particular perspectives, structures and practices produce 'untoward effects, with the aim of finding ways to change things so these consequences can be avoided' (Kemmis, 2008: 125). Our aim in the chapter is to discuss the possibilities and pitfalls of doing action research critically.

The chapter is an attempt to stimulate the reader through particular reflections from research practice rather than provide a critical action research toolkit. As well as pinpointing various approaches in the action research literature, we will present and reflect on a case study which broadly conforms to a critical approach to action research according to criteria proposed by Johansson and Lindhult (2008). This enabled us to explore and explain how the dominant ideology or doxa of evidence-based medicine impacted on attempts to develop new structures of horizontal knowledge creation among practitioners through research and development (R&D) networks in a regional health authority. The approach adopted can be seen as an example whereby a critical perspective was brought to bear in the collaboration between the researcher and participants in the field. This prompted a reflexive approach to conversations on practical knowledge and action. Notably, the approach entailed both instances of closeness to and distance from the field. By the former we mean participation in joint activities in the field and thus frequent interaction with participants, whereas the latter entails the researcher also seeing his or her role as part of an abductive research process drawing on relevant theories as a means for reflecting on specific elements of a project as it unfolds (Johansson and Lindhult, 2008: 101).

We proceed by discussing the literature on action research, its more critical variants, and the dilemmas involved in terms of doing work in the field, and illustrate some of the issues at stake from the case. The question of concern to us here, however, is: to what extent can action research interventions be 'critical'? Can an action research intervention challenge existing structures of domination, or are such structures merely reproduced or reinforced? What role does reflexivity play in such processes? A key dilemma for the critical action researcher is, on the one hand, maintaining a close, high-trust relationship with actors in the field and, on the other hand, having sufficient distance or autonomy from them to be able to write critically about her engagement with the field. We illustrate this dilemma and how its tensions might be played out in practice.

Action research: a short background

What is action research and what is it not? As a broad approach for engaging with the field, its introduction is usually attributed to the comparative research of Kurt Lewin in the 1940s on the conditions and effects of various forms of social action (Lewin, 1946). He described action research as a spiral of steps, each of which is composed of a circle of planning, action, and fact-finding about the result of the action. Clearly the term 'action' here denotes some sort of intervention by the researcher. Also a common theme is that of solving problems through participation. Such problem-solving invariably extends the role of the researcher to that of being a change agent. Moreover, the relationship between researcher and the field is usually also recast: in non-interventionist approaches the relationship is that of 'research on' the field, whereas in interventionist approaches such as action research the relationship becomes one of 'research with' the field. In other words, an intervention entails engaging together with practitioners in a joint learning process from which both theoretical and practical knowledge (mode 1 and mode 2 knowledge, respectively: Gibbons et al., 2000) can emerge together.

Action research may involve traditional data generation techniques such as surveys, interviews and observation. But what distinguishes action research from other forms of engagement with the field is its concomitant interest in the action of the researcher that guides his or her intervention (Greenwood and Levin, 2007; Reason and Bradbury, 2001, 2008). Knowledge on the action and its effects in context are of equivalent interest to theoretical knowledge. The difficulty here from a critical perspective, however, is that action that achieves desired effects usually entails not only consensus between researcher and practitioners but also a shared commitment among practitioners to the change effort. Accordingly, action research, if it is to be effective on its own terms, must acknowledge the contested nature of organizations or at least make discussable dissensus in the context of the asymmetrical power relations that are an inevitable feature of organizational life. Indeed, critics have argued that action research cannot easily prevail against entrenched structures of domination and that recent efforts at developing workplaces 'are best seen as defensive manoeuvring' (Ackroyd, 2009: 545).

A proper discussion of these questions perhaps requires us to look at action research historically as answers are contingent on the historical and cultural factors through which they are framed. The sceptical scholar may well dismiss action research as not being part of the critical agenda as in practice it does not always live up to its emancipatory ambitions. In most organizations, senior managers as agents of financial interests may have an effective veto on any processes of change that are deemed to be in conflict with their interests and the interests that they represent. This view sees action research as assisting the problem-solving of elites, thus bolstering their dominant position within the capitalist enterprise (see Ramsay, 1985). This scepticism perhaps explains why Lewin's early work was located by Burrell and Morgan (1979: 144) as formally within functionalist sociology. Much of the language of action research has been evident within the (managerial) domains of organizational development and change management, yet, as Cooke (1999) shows, this is to detract seriously from the radicalism of Lewin's early work in its historical and cultural context. Although through a contemporary lens Lewin's work seems somewhat conservative, his original ambitions were arguably far more radical in their emancipatory intent in the context of the time than is often made out (Lewin, 1946).

Critical approaches to action research

A radical or critical intent to action research is more clearly detectable, however, in the work of subsequent authors. A notable example of this is the book by Paolo Freire (1970), *Pedagogy of the Oppressed*, in which he laid out his version of what has become known as 'participatory action research'. Working in the educational setting of teaching Brazilian adults to read and write, he adopted a Marxist class analysis to explore what he saw as an oppressive relationship between 'the colonizer' and the 'colonized'. He argued against the then dominant paradigm of education whereby learners were seen as empty vessels to be filled with knowledge. Rather, learners should be considered as co-creators of knowledge. In arguing for the overthrowing of oppression and changing the balance of power between the oppressor and the oppressed he wrote:

> Freedom is acquired by conquest, not by gift. It must be pursued constantly and responsibly. Freedom is not an ideal located outside of man [sic]; nor is it an idea which becomes a myth. It is rather the indispensible condition for the quest for human completion. (1970: 47)

Here we see an ambition to secure what others have called emancipation (Kemmis, 2001).

More recently, authors have developed the notion of participatory action research into what has been termed 'critical action research'. The ambition of this is 'to bring together broad social analyses: the self-reflective collective self-study of practice, the way language is used, organization and power in a local situation, and action to improve things' (Kemmis and McTaggart, 2000: 568).

The issue here, however, is the extent to which it is practical or possible to translate these ideas into interventions in formal organizations. How far can one go in terms of overthrowing capitalist structures of domination? Doubts about this have led authors to scale back somewhat on claims about the possibilities of freedom by focusing instead on more modest ambitions. These might be those, for example, proposed outside the domain of action research, such as micro-emancipation (Alvesson and Willmott, 1992) or small wins (Weick, 1984). But whatever the label, there is always the danger that (critical) action research is used as just another vehicle for actors in the field to be subjected to a dominant ideology from the outside – not, perhaps, that of capitalist exchange but, rather, that espoused by the critical social scientist from the regime of power/knowledge she inhabits.

A critical ambition in action research can also be located elsewhere. In Scandinavian working life research there has been a significant action research tradition for a number of decades. By the 1980s much of this work was inspired by critical theory, notably the work of Jürgen Habermas on ideal-speech situations (Habermas, 1984/1987) to design interventionist methods based around principles of democratic dialogue aimed at reducing, in theory at least, asymmetries in power relations (Gustavsen, 1992; see also Kemmis, 2001). However, this work can be critiqued on the grounds that democratic dialogue, whilst clearly aspiring to form part of the critical agenda in theory, may not live up to its aims in practice (Ekman-Philips and Huzzard, 2007). Moreover, it can also be argued that genuine participation is also an ideal that is impossible to realize, particularly in more recent attempts at interventions of a broad nature across organizations that aim at change at a regional or systems levels in, for example, health care (Huzzard et al., 2010). Finally, it is also argued that democratic dialogue and participation foreground consensual practices. The danger is that such a heavy emphasis on consensus through, for example, collective experimentation might actually reinforce dominant structures rather than undermine them. On the contrary, *conflict* reveals power structures and it is only through conflict that efforts can be made to secure the micro-emancipation at the heart of critical action research ambitions. Accordingly, the Scandinavian action research tradition has been critiqued for upholding the status quo, or at least conceding change on management's terms rather than anything that has a more emancipatory intent (Johansson and Lindhult, 2008).

So how, then, might we summarize the distinctive characteristics of a critical approach to action research? This question has been usefully addressed by Johansson and Lindhult in an article from 2008 in which they contrasted action research approaches with a critical orientation with those that had what they termed a pragmatic orientation. This contrast can be seen in terms of their respective assumptions and practical implications: the latter is deemed more suitable in contexts where concerted and immediate action is needed, and the former where potentially transformative action is needed but has to be preceded by critical thinking and reflection which should reveal dominant ideologies and coercive structures. Broadly speaking, the authors associate the critical orientation with the work of Freire (1970) in its emphasis on the emancipation of underprivileged groups. The pragmatic orientation, on the other hand, is much more to do with generating local knowledge with practitioners with a view to improving workable praxis but broadly leaving social relations untouched. This, in retrospect, would appear to characterize much of the Scandinavian action research tradition, despite its clear origins in critical theory (Gustavsen, 1992; Kemmis, 2001). The distinction between the pragmatic approach and the critical approach is set out in Table 5.1.

Table 5.1 Comparing a pragmatic and a critical orientation to action research (Johansson and Lindhult, 2008: 102)

Issue	Pragmatic orientation	Critical orientation
Purpose	Improvement in workability of human praxis	Emancipation
Action focus	Experimental, cooperation	Resistance, liberation
Orientation to power	Power as ability to do, collaborative relation, practical agreement is striven for	Dominant interests, coercive, conflict is acknowledged
Role of researcher	Closeness, practical knowledge	Distance, episteme, reflective knowledge
Research focus	Action, dialogue	Reflection
Development focus	Experiential learning, learning by doing	Consciousness raising, reflexivity
Type of dialogue	Cooperative, experience-based, action-oriented	Promote openness to the other
Situation	Fragmentation, compartmentalization	Asymmetrical power relations, invisible, restricting structures

The dilemmas of doing action research

As stated, doing action research critically entails a real dilemma. On the one hand the researcher needs to maintain a close, high-trust relationship with actors in the field in order to research *with* them rather than *on* them – perhaps over a long period of engagement of 2–3 years or even longer. On the other hand, a critical stance also necessitates some degree of distancing from the dominant assumptions of both practitioners and the researcher herself. This is because a critical stance puts greater emphasis on reflection and consciousness-raising, whereas pragmatic approaches are more about action (Johansson and Lindhult, 2008). Accordingly, action research entails an implicit (and perhaps even explicit) contract between the researcher and the field that pulls in two opposite directions. This contract is fundamentally ethical in nature as it confers on the parties a mutual expectation of trust and respectful conduct (see Lundin and Wirdenius, 1990). In the early 2000s, researchers from Sweden's National Institute for Working Life became increasingly concerned that the action research tradition in Scandinavia had too often been pulled in the direction of close collaboration with actors in the field. This, it has been argued, led to there being too much action and too little research,[1] or at least research outputs lacking a critical edge (Svensson et al., 2007). The response to this

---

[1]And perhaps, on occasions, vice versa.

was to propose an alternative – interactive research[2] – that downplayed the emphasis on change agency in action research and saw 'researching with', instead, in terms of a joint learning process. This was seen as an end in itself, without there being any explicit action intervention.

We will now focus our remaining discussion on the dilemma the critical action researcher faces in terms of maintaining high-trust, collaborative relations with the actors in the field and at the same time ensuring sufficient distance such that the generation of theoretical knowledge is not compromised by the implicit ethical contract with the practitioners. We present and discuss an action research project that had the initial aim of supporting the development of a number of R&D networks in various domains of health care. The idea here was to establish new arenas for participation and dialogue among health care professionals that straddled existing organizational and occupational boundaries such that the practitioners concerned could develop new forms of knowledge to inform and support their work practices. The ambition of this initiative was not that of increasing productivity or cost-cutting. However, whilst the project was certainly instrumental in its aims, it nevertheless entailed new forms of social relations inasmuch as the knowledge networks were seen as a potential means for developing new practices and forms of work and participation beyond the existing structures of the health care bureaucracy. Whilst the participants could hardly be seen as oppressed in the sense understood by Freire, the project's aims were nevertheless potentially emancipatory and bore considerable resemblance to participatory action research (see previous discussion).

However, it transpired that the initial aims of the project did not wholly come to fruition as intended in that the participants generally eschewed the opportunity to explore new knowledge through horizontal relationships in practice and fell back on exploiting the knowledge derived from evidence-based medicine. For this reason the critical nature of the research task changed tack to that of a more reflexive conversation around knowledge production more generally. This entailed a joint exploration of the question of why the discourse or doxa of evidence-based medicine had such a dominant effect on practice. As we shall see, this change in focus also entailed a switch in forms of researcher identity and reflexive practice (Alvesson et al., 2008). In turn, this also prompted a re-evaluation by the researcher of her own epistemological points of departure.

In sum, we argue that critical action research necessarily requires the researcher to bring to the dialogue theoretical ideas that may question the assumptions and theories-in-use of the participants, including the researcher. This inevitably implies that we move between the two positions of closeness and distance to the actors in

---

[2]Following Coghlan and Brannick (2010) we see action research as a broad, generic term for a number of different interventionist approaches entailing 'research with', among them cooperative inquiry, participatory action research, and appreciative inquiry. Interactive research is one such approach.

the field during the unfolding of a typical project. The latter allows us to be able to conduct reflexive practice through questioning the assumptions that informed the initial intervention and thereby tease out more hidden forms of power and domination in both the domain of practice and the domain of research (Kemmis and MacTaggart, 2008). Accordingly, as we, together with practitioners, navigate action research learning cycles (Coghlan and Brannick, 2010), perhaps two or three times throughout the duration of a single project, a critical approach will require us to oscillate between closeness and distance as a means of facilitating our own reflexive practice. We now turn to an empirical illustration of this through a case study of a recent action research project undertaken by one of us[3] in the setting of a number R&D networks aimed at developing integrated care in the north-eastern region of Skåne, in southern Sweden.

Critical action research – an empirical illustration

Case background

In 2002, nine R&D networks were set up within the field of health care in the north-east district under the county council of Skåne in Sweden. The networks had ramifications in hospital care, primary care and care provided by municipalities, and created links across professions, workplaces and organizational sectors. The overall aims of these networks were to increase collaboration across sectors and the transfer of knowledge to support knowledge development in practice. The networks were named after the subject areas they focused on: Palliative Care, Documentation, Drugs and the Elderly, Ulcer, Nutrition and Eating, Psychiatric Rehabilitation, Pain, Hygiene, and Discharge Planning (see Figure 5.1).

Each network consisted of 11–50 network participants, amounting to approximately 200 actors in total. Most participants were practitioners, the majority of whom were registered nurses. Their workplaces were the two hospitals in the area, within primary care, psychiatry, care of the elderly and care of physically disabled patients. Furthermore, each network was led by a subject specialist who acted as the coordinator with overall responsibility for network development. The coordinators of the networks were linked together in their own meta-network, led by a facilitator who was also the initiator of the networks and the driving force in their continuing development work. In addition, the networks were connected through a steering group. The role of the steering group was to encourage and oversee the development of the networks. The networks had network meetings between two and six times a year, lasting 2–6 hours on each occasion.

---

[3]This was a PhD project, the full details of which are available in Johansson (2013).

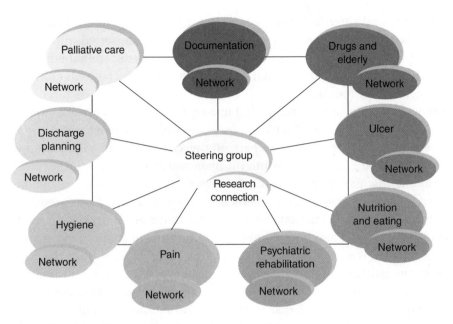

Figure 5.1 The nine R&D networks in north-eastern Skåne

Phase 1: Joint action and learning

The research project was conducted within a research group at Kristianstad University that pursued action research as a common approach for undertaking projects. Collaborative processes of inquiry are considered particularly fruitful in the domain of health and social care service development (Koch and Kralik, 2006). In this particular case, the facilitator of the meta-network contacted the research group as she and the coordinators of the networks were interested in being engaged in a research project focusing on the development process of the networks. With the intention of obtaining a clear project focus with relevance to all the coordinators, an agreement was made that the researcher would start by undertaking interviews with the coordinators to ascertain their views of the role of the networks and their ideas on how to achieve their networks' developmental visions. It also intended to elucidate their reflections on the networks' achievements, on their role as coordinators and what they considered as strengths and limitations of the networks. The overall aim of the collaborative process of inquiry was to support network development and raise awareness on the issue of knowledge creation and thereby potentially initiate a process of change. The intervention intended by means of a dialogical process to encourage the coordinators of the networks in reflection on a subject that emerged from their own interests. Accordingly, the design of the project was broadly in line with Johansson and Lindhult's conceptualization of a critical approach.

From interviews and observations undertaken among the coordinators, it became apparent that the transfer of knowledge into practice was regarded by the coordinators and their facilitator as an urgent challenge. The general consensus was that scientifically generated knowledge could be transferred into practice by means of various activities, such as lectures and other educational efforts, which would thereby lead to change which would improve care for patients and empower health care professionals.

However, the knowledge transfer and implementation did not work out as envisaged. According to the coordinators, knowledge largely remained undiffused within the networks. This prompted, as part of the critical action research approach, feedback and dialogue sessions within the meta-network to enable further problematization and discussion on the issue of knowledge transfer, a process supported by selected quotations from the interviews. Furthermore, a model was presented that had emerged from the initial data analysis which illustrated the coordinators' theory of knowledge transfer and how changes might be brought about in practice. This in essence entailed scientifically based knowledge being diffused from the networks, through the participating organizations and their practitioners, and finally on to patients and clients. The reason for highlighting this model was to contrast it with the alternative approach referred to in the network and communities of practice literature whereby sharing of knowledge takes place horizontally (Bate and Robert, 2002; Goodwin et al., 2004).

The intention behind the introduction of the model was to encourage dialogue and reflection on the topic of knowledge transfer, built upon the idea that engagement in a dialogical process could support further network development (Greenwood and Levin, 2007; Gustavsen, 1992). The model presented served as a trigger of a dialogical process. The coordinators stated that the model corresponded to their understanding and practice of knowledge transfer, but nevertheless it was agreed to challenge this view collectively because of the difficulties they had experienced. By challenging existing routines and the beliefs that underpinned them it was hoped that reflection and developmental learning would be supported (Ellström, 1996). As a result of the first feedback and dialogue sessions undertaken, the coordinators' original theory of knowledge transfer was problematized and discussed more broadly. Concretely this meant that the coordinators highlighted the perspective of the practitioners more explicitly. For example, suggestions emerged to support network participants in the use of case descriptions among practitioners. Such descriptions acted as tools for animating dialogue and thereby participation among the practitioners involved.

After a period of time, a review of the whole collaborative process undertaken was summarized and fed back to the coordinators and their facilitator, followed by a new process of dialogue and reflection. One part of the subsequent dialogical process involved the participants discussing their ideas and noting suggestions on the continuation and direction of the networks, focusing on knowledge transfer. However, the result of this exercise was contradictory. On the one hand, the generation of ideas implied a bottom-up approach, which included suggestions for increased involvement of practitioners in the networks' future efforts. On the other hand, the statements from the written notes suggested ideas that implied a top-down approach. For example, one of the coordinators suggested that large-scale lectures should be given by experts on a regular basis, directed towards different professional categories. Accordingly, suggestions for both bottom-up and top-down approaches were given by the participants.

The dialogue continued during an additional meta-network meeting in which the steering group also participated. During this session, the duality regarding the different approaches to knowledge transfer that emerged during the previous meeting came to the surface once more. One of the participants of the steering group initiated a discussion in which the importance of dissemination of evidence-based knowledge provided by research and measurable results was emphasized. This account was accepted by several of those present. In conclusion, the focus in the dialogue moved from an overall concern about the complex area of knowledge transfer and attempts to get routines into perspective, to a focus on more measurable objectives. This final dialogue session was considered a critical phase as it could possibly initiate a process of change, but no new initiatives or suggestions emerged. Instead, to end the collaborative process, the coordinators were asked to write reflexive notes on what they had learnt from the process during their participation.

The sharing of knowledge took place within the networks at their respective meetings, which to a great extent were arenas for dialogue, the exchange of experiences and the establishing of new contacts. For the purpose of developing their own personal knowledge, the actors' intention was that the knowledge they obtained should be transformed and transferred into practice. This happened to varying degrees. But both network coordinators and network participants felt frustrated about the sluggish rate of development. The key intervention of the action researcher was thus to facilitate a joint focus on the topic of knowledge transfer, and challenge the prevailing approach of the actors towards this. The researcher role during subsequent feedback and dialogue sessions was to combine their frameworks and perspectives on knowledge transfer within a learning community and to facilitate these sessions.

On the other hand, the meta-network did not share or transfer knowledge to any great extent. Rather, the participants shared experiences from their respective networks and discussed future network development. The meta-network meetings took place three to five times a year (decreasing in frequency over time) and lasted in most cases for half a day. The facilitator of the meta-network usually started off the meetings by letting the coordinators of the networks in turn present the respective network achievements accomplished since their last meeting. The facilitator typically also highlighted the new national guiding principles or tendencies and local directives she had come across, for example from her participation in managerial meetings. The remaining time was normally spent on the sharing of experiences and discussions on future network development and measures to be taken.

Phase 2: Critical reflection

Action research projects invariably involve a balancing act between closeness and distance. In this particular case, this meant that the researcher's relationship with the actors varied over time. For example, the interviews and feedback and dialogue sessions were characterized by closeness by means of mutual openness, for example regarding ideas and critical viewpoints. The researcher also sought to achieve familiarity and trust as these aspects influenced the direction of the ongoing process. The analysis undertaken prior to the feedback and dialogue sessions was, on the other hand, characterized by distance, implying a more critical stance regarding the different roles of participants and the researcher, the activities undertaken, the ongoing process and its results. Notably, an activity in practice can be frozen and turned into an object and thereby an observable phenomenon, that is, the activity can be subjected to reflexive practice. As a consequence, a phenomenon observed can be explained and described, and thereby transformed into a theory of practice (Johansson, 2013). But this is a balancing act because closeness suggests maintaining an ethics of care vis-à-vis the actors in the field (Spicer et al., 2009), whereas distance suggests an ambition to make more critical assessments that can easily compromise the ethical contract, implicit or explicit, on which the research engagement is based. Methodologically, the dilemma of handling closeness and critical distance in the project was managed by conducting the research in two partly overlapping phases: first the collaborative phase and then an epistemological break that entailed a critical interrogation of the process with a view to reflecting on and explaining what had happened in the initial intervention.

In addition, a critical dimension was adopted; indeed, a critical interrogation of dominant assumptions was a central element in the ethical contract. The critical gaze in this project was supported by the theoretical lens used in the analysis. The data obtained in the study was interpreted and analysed in a way that drew inspiration from Bourdieu's understanding of social practices, which also constituted a framework for breaking with 'common sense' and explaining the empirical storyline (Bourdieu et al., 1991). At the same time, this lens provided the researcher with theoretical resources to write her thesis critically. The phase whereby the intervention was re-theorized was undertaken in parallel with the final stage of the collaborative process and, directly afterwards, existing structures of domination and tensions involved in the field were teased out. Moreover, the theoretical lens was a supportive tool in the researcher's reflections on her own role in the process and her concerns about how to combine the collaborative and critical aspects of the research practically (Johansson, 2013; cf. Svensson, 2008).

The research project raised the dilemma that no new initiatives or suggestions on network continuation had emerged that could be directly related to the dialogue and reflection sessions undertaken during the final stage of the collaborative process. It was this situation that forced the researcher into adopting a more critical and reflexive gaze. For example, the role of the researcher and the facilitation of the collaborative process were questioned: should she have taken a leading role in the networks' development process? In this case, the decision was taken to let the coordinators and the facilitator take responsibility for any possible developmental actions to be taken (Stringer, 1999). This decision was in line with the standpoint of interactive researchers such as Svensson (2008), who argue that those conducting interactive research should 'tone down' their responsibility for development work and emphasize instead the joint learning process of the engagement as an end itself. In essence this entailed a change in researcher identity – to what Sandberg and Wallo (2013) term being a 'virtual participant'.

Another aspect of reflexivity was the question whether the slowdown that became clear during the final stage of the collaborative process was due to the researcher and participants in the study having different frames of reference, or whether it was the steering group who influenced the direction of the dialogue into what partly seemed to be a consolidation of the coordinators' initial theory of practice (namely, a linear top-down model of implementation of evidence-based practice). The researcher in this project had a lens that rendered visible structures, power relationships and conflicting interests, while the coordinators of the network and the participants in the steering group had a clinical view, which implied a greater focus on standard operating procedures and measurable outcomes (Ford and ogilvie, 1996). In addition, the steering group inevitably had a certain authority, which we would normally expect to influence the content and direction of the dialogue. These differences and power aspects were not clearly articulated, perhaps because they were not properly understood, yet could nevertheless have restrained the process.

In her PhD thesis, the action researcher (Yvonne) noted the dilemma that the participants in the collaborative inquiry process had in terms of their specific theory of change and that she, as a researcher and facilitator of the collaborative process, did not fully share their mindset. However, if she had started out from the paradigm of the participants, it might well have been impossible to challenge their basic approach to knowledge transfer, which is what they had actually sought in the intervention in the first place. Instead, the intervention would have been restricted to dialogue and reflection within existing frames. Looking back, both she and the participants could have established their different roles at the outset with greater clarity and been more explicit as to their expectations. The role of the critical action researcher here is to make this visible as part of the reflexive learning process of the participants.

Collaborative processes in action research are built on trust, in particular a shared understanding that each party will maintain their respective commitments to the ethical contract. Adopting a critical perspective necessarily entails a balancing act that risks undermining this trust by making knowledge claims from outside the collaboration. In the case, critical questions were posed and routine-like ideas and ways of working were challenged during the dialogue and reflection sessions, with the intention that reflection and developmental learning should be supported (Ellström, 1996). From Berglund and Danilda's (2008) perspective, the role of research is not only to listen to the practitioners' voices, but also to be critical and provide contrasting images, reveal new perspectives and problematize established conventions. An aim here was to allow practitioners to examine their own knowledge bases and to situate this knowledge within a broader framework by challenging taken-for-granted perspectives (cf. Ledwith and Springett, 2010).

If action research is about micro-emancipation, then it is important to question whether the critical gaze adopted in the project served the networks' development process. Shortly after the end of the collaboration, results from the process along with the theoretical reconstruction phase were fed back during a local conference directed towards practitioners, to which the participants of the meta-network were invited. The facilitator and some of the coordinators attended the conference and took an active part in the subsequent opportunity for questions and dialogue. No measurable changes in organizational structures could be presented. However, it should be noted that small but important changes are often not explicitly articulated and therefore difficult to make visible (Gunnarsson et al., 2007). The collaborative process undertaken in the project could therefore be seen as a start of a cumulative process of reflexivity which, when seen from a long-term perspective, led to increased consciousness and new ways of thinking and acting. However, the evidence of changes to awareness and how this was reflected in new practices was somewhat mixed. This is illustrated in some of the reflexive notes made by the coordinators at their final dialogue session on what they had learned from the project:

> Learning through reflection on one's own experiences must be encouraged.

> Knowledge is difficult to disseminate through words, instead, knowledge must be perceived and understood.

> All development work is based on learning, dialogue and active practitioners.

> I have learnt that learning processes take time and require much support.

> You have provided me with an eye-opener, to see the structure of the network and how exchange and communication take place.

> You have helped the network to reflect on the networks' existence and mission.

Discussion

The case presented here illustrates how the critical action researcher can combine both closeness to the field in the form of joint action and learning with distance from the field that emphasizes raising awareness through a reflexive approach to knowledge creation. The two approaches combined had the aim of developing health care such that there would be new possibilities for knowledge transfer (the R&D networks) and advertising the networks in different ways (the meta-network). This included newsletters, an active presence at national conferences and so on.

Even though the networks pre-existed the intervention, the ambition of the action research here ex ante can be seen as intervening to support network development which could possibly initiate a process of change. The ambition was to support a dialogical process to encourage the coordinators of the networks to engage in reflection on a subject that emerged from their own interests. We argue that this approximated to the notion of micro-emancipation in that greater voice and discretion were being sought for health care practitioners in both the means and ends of the intervention. The participants were being given new opportunities and spaces to learn and work unencumbered by the constraints of the health care bureaucracy. A strength of the networks, underlined both by coordinators and network participants, was that the network meetings functioned as arenas for discussions, exchange of experiences and establishing of contacts. This is illustrated by the following statements from the reflexive notes from the participants in the Psychiatric Rehab Network:

> I have created new contacts both within the county council and other municipalities.

> It has been invigorating for my professional practice to meet 'like-minded' people and get feedback on my own ways of thinking and acting.

> I bring the discussions we have back to some of my colleagues [at work].

Moreover, the permanent establishment of the networks clearly entailed the potential for new forms of working and organizing (i.e. new social relations) in the form of a new collaborative community for collaboration and clinical practice across organizational boundaries (Freire, 1970; Alvesson and Willmott, 1992; Adler and Heckscher, 2006).

The fact that the ambition of knowledge transfer in the meta-network never really materialized prompted a switch in the research question (actually formulated before the action researcher became involved) from how such a meta-network should be set up to why the knowledge transfer did not always take place. Due to the difficulties experienced in the process of knowledge sharing, the researcher and the participants also made an agreement to challenge the latter's view of knowledge transfer collectively. The purpose was to broaden their perspective in this complex area and possibly initiate a process of change. At this stage the researcher was able to critically address the new research question by drawing on the work of Pierre Bourdieu to ask why, in the meta-network, the actors were resorting to the discourse or doxa of evidence-based medicine rather than drawing on their own experiential knowledge generated from within the networks.

In effect, the critical examination undertaken in the critical reflection phase was a feature more reminiscent of interactive research (Svensson et al., 2007; Sandberg and Wallo, 2013) in that the researcher was able to engage in critical reflection in a way that had become disconnected from any explicit change objective. This enabled her to problematize certain rather optimistic notions about the viability of knowledge sharing in such circumstances. Moreover, the re-theorization highlighted the role of dominant discourses or in terms suggested by Bourdieu – doxa – that constrained the learning processes associated with the intervention and thereby the possibilities for micro-emancipation. On the other hand, this necessarily entailed the researcher taking on the role of 'being the expert'. Although this, in this case, was not a violation of the ethical contract per se, it nevertheless sits uneasily with the notion of the researcher being on an equal footing with the participants.

We have already discussed in this case the balancing act between closeness and distance. In addition, we can highlight further dilemmas that surfaced:

- the preference of the technical knowledge ideal within the health care sector that stresses solutions instead of reflection on experiential learning (see also Willmott, Chapter 11, this volume);
- time constraints among participants in terms of balancing their time spent on work in the networks with their normal professional duties;
- the question of ownership of the change process – this clearly entails an oscillation between two researcher identities, that is, as a change agent when working closely with actors in the field and alternatively working as a more distanced critic.

As we see it, the two stances of closeness and distance oblige the critical researcher to adopt two quite distinct forms of reflexive practice. The participatory nature of the first of these phases clearly entails the ambition to facilitate what Alvesson et al. (2008: 483ff.) call multivoicing. Here the researcher and the participants engaged in collectively negotiating the meanings and challenging of taken-for-granted assumptions through writing their own notes and discussing case descriptions. In this way the researcher was one voice among many and not privileged as an authorial source. At issue here was whether the researcher could speak authentically about the experiences of the participants in the project as well as the nature of the relationship between the researcher and the field.

The nature of reflexive practice changed, however, during the critical reflection phase. Here the researcher engaged in what Alvesson et al. (2008) term 'positioning practices' whereby what is in focus is not the researcher in relation to the participants but, rather, the researcher (and research) in relation to the broader domain or field within which the knowledge claims were being (socially) constructed and how such claims were being secured in the habitus of practice. It was precisely this that informed the choice to draw on the conceptual work of Bourdieu as a means for providing analytical tools to interpret, explain and prompt dialogue on what was felt and experienced by the participants as inertia within the project (Bourdieu and Wacquant, 1992).

Alvesson et al. (2008) also contend that different reflexive practices prompt different researcher roles or identities. That argument is well illustrated by the case discussed in this chapter: in the joint learning phase the researcher assumed the identity of being a co-participant in a process of joint knowledge creation that sought to develop new perspectives among the participants through new arenas for dialogue and learning. In contrast, in the critical reflection phase the researcher identity more closely resembled that of the traditional (critical) researcher by taking a more distanced and dispassionate relationship from the field as a 'virtual participant' in the quest for providing analytical tools for feeding back to the participants such that they were able to reflect on their activities in the networks from outside of their pre-existing assumptions and frames of reference.

Conclusions

This chapter has sought to develop the argument that action research can be fruitfully used by critical scholars of management. We suggest that doing action research critically can entail either an intervention, with the researcher as a change agent, that aims at some form of micro-emancipation (McTaggart and Kemmis, 2000), or a more distanced, reflexive approach that sees the researcher as a facilitator of joint learning processes that can invite participants in the field to engage in reflexive practice and develop greater levels of awareness. But we argue that the two contrasting elements of closeness and distance suggesting contrasting researcher identities can be fruitfully combined. Put differently, this enables the researcher to oscillate between performative (Spicer et al., 2009) and non-performative stances (Fournier and Grey, 2000). Spicer et al., rather than eschewing any notion of performativity, have sought to identify ways in which critical scholars might purposely engage with practice. Clearly rejected in their account, however, is any notion of means–ends calculation for converting inputs into outputs, particularly when the interests of employers or capital are privileged. We have explored various ways in which this sense of critical yet purposeful engagement (see also Voronov, 2008) might be realized in the field. In our case this enabled a more reflective analysis of the structural factors or doxa (Bourdieu et al., 1991) that constrained the possibilities for achieving the initial emancipatory ambitions of the project.

It seems to us that Spicer et al.'s principles or tactics of critical performativity overlap considerably with certain approaches to action research. Indeed, it could be argued that certain versions of critical action research go further than this in their ambition and practices. For example, the emphasis on pragmatism in critical performativity, perhaps acknowledging a debt to earlier pragmatic philosophers such as William James and John Dewey, would seem to be odds with the conceptualization of critical action research proposed by Johansson and Lindhult (2008) (see for example Keleman and Rumens, 2008: 39ff., on the legacy of American pragmatism in critical management studies as well as the advocacy of pragmatism in critical research in the domain of human resource management by Watson, 2010). Either way, we have argued in this chapter that various action research repertoires can be a serious option for the critical scholar in certain contexts, notably where interventions or joint learning processes are aimed at either improving practice or joint learning. However, this is not to say that action research is always necessarily critical, or indeed that all critical scholars see performative engagement as part of the critical management project.

References

Ackroyd, S. (2009) 'Research designs for realist research', in D.A. Buchanan and A. Bryman (eds), *The Sage Handbook of Organizational Research Methods*. London: Sage.

Adler, P.S. and Heckscher, C. (2006) 'Towards collaborative community', in C. Heckscher and P.S. Adler (eds), *The Firm as a Collaborative Community: Reconstructing Trust in the Knowledge Economy*. New York: Oxford University Press.

Alvesson, M., Hardy, C. and Harley, B. (2008) 'Reflecting on reflexivity: Reflexive textual practices in organization and management theory', *Journal of Management Studies*, 45(3): 480–501.

Alvesson, M. and Willmott, H. (1992) 'On the idea of emancipation in management and organization studies', *Academy of Management Review*, 17(3): 432–464.

Bate, S.P. and Robert, G. (2002) 'Knowledge management and communities of practice in the private sector: Lessons for modernising the National Health Service in England and Wales', *Public Administration*, 80(4): 643–663.

Berglund, K. and Danilda, I. (2008) 'Interaktiv kritisk forskning – om att kunskapa genom att initiera evenemang', in B. Johannisson, E. Gunnarsson and T. Stjernberg (eds), *Gemensamt kunskapande – den interaktiva forskningens praktik*. Växjö: Växjö University Press.

Bourdieu, P., Chamboredon, J.C. and Passeron, J.C. (1991) *The Craft of Sociology. Epistemological Preliminaries*. New York: Walter de Gruyter.

Bourdieu, P. and Wacquant, L. (1992) *An Invitation to Reflexive Sociology*. Cambridge: Polity Press.

Burrell, G. and Morgan, G. (1979) *Sociological Paradigms and Organizational Analysis*. Aldershot: Gower.

Coghlan, D. and Brannick, T. (2010) *Doing Action Research in Your Own Organization* (3rd edn). London: Sage.

Cooke, B. (1999) 'Writing the left out of management theory: The historiography of the management of change', *Organization*, 6(1): 81–104.

Ekman-Philips, M. and Huzzard, T. (2007) 'Developmental magic? Two takes on a dialogue conference', *Journal of Organizational Change Management*, 20(1): 8–25.

Ellström, P.-E. (1996) *Arbete och lärande. Förutsättningar och hinder för lärande i dagligt arbete*. Stockholm: Arbetslivsinstitutet.

Ford, C.M. and ogilvie, dt. (1996) 'The role of creative action in organizational learning and change', *Journal of Organizational Change Management*, 9(1): 54–62.

Fournier, V. and Grey, C. (2000) 'At the critical moment: Conditions and prospects for critical management studies', *Human Relations*, 53(1): 7–32.

Freire, P. (1970) *The Pedagogy of the Oppressed*. New York: Herder and Herder.

Gibbons, M., Limoges, C., Nowotny, H., Schwartzman, S., Scott, P. and Trow, M. (2000) *The New Production of Knowledge. The Dynamics of Science and Research in Contemporary Societies* (2nd edn). London: Sage.

Goodwin, N., Peck, E., Freeman, T. and Posaner, R. (2004) Managing across diverse networks: Lessons from other sectors, Findings from a review of the literature. *Summary report for the Service Development and Organisation programme within the NHS Research and Development Programme*. Working Paper: University of Birmingham.

Greenwood, D. and Levin, M. (2007) *Introduction to Action Research: Social Research for Social Change* (2nd edn.). Thousand Oaks, CA: Sage.

Gunnarsson, E., Westberg, H., Andersson, S. and Balkmar, D. (2007) *Learning by fighting: jämställdhet och genusvetenskap i VINNOVAs organisation och verksamhetsområde*. Växjö: Växjö Universitet.

Gustavsen, B. (1992) *Dialogue and Development. Social Science for Social Action: Towards Organisational Renewal. Volume 1*. Maastricht: Van Gorcum.

Habermas, J. (1984/1987) *The Theory of Communicative Action* (Vols I–II). London: Polity Press.

Huzzard, T., Ahlberg, B.M. and Ekman, M. (2010) 'Constructing interorganisational collaboration: The action researcher as boundary subject', *Action Research*, 8(3): 293–314.

Johansson, A.W. and Lindhult, E. (2008) 'Emancipation or workability? Critical versus pragmatic scientific orientation in action research', *Action Research*, 6(1): 95–115.

Johansson, Y. (2013) *Tensions in the Field of Health Care. Knowledge Networks and Evidence-Based Practice. An Action Research Approach*. Lund: Arbetsliv i omvandling/ Work Life in Transition 2013:1.

Keleman, M. and Rumens, N. (2008) *An Introduction to Critical Management Research*. London: Sage.

Kemmis, S. (2001) 'Exploring the relevance of critical theory for action research: Emancipatory action research in the footsteps of Jürgen Habermas', in P. Reason and H. Bradbury (eds), *A Handbook of Action Research*. London: Sage.

Kemmis, S. (2008) 'Critical theory and participatory action research', in P. Reason and H. Bradbury (eds), *The Sage Handbook of Action Research: Participative Inquiry and Practice*. London: Sage.

Kemmis, S. and McTaggart, R. (2000) 'Participatory action research', in N.K. Denzin and Y.S. Lincoln (eds), *A Handbook of Qualitative Research* (2nd edn). Thousand Oaks, CA: Sage.

Koch, T. and Kralik, D. (2006) *Participatory Action Research in Health Care*. Oxford: Blackwell.

Ledwith, M. and Springett, J. (2010) *Participatory Practice. Community-Based Action for Transformative Change*. Bristol: Policy Press.

Lewin, K. (1946) 'Action research and minority problems', *Journal of Social Issues*, 2(4): 34–46.

Lundin, R. and Wirdenius, H. (1990) 'Interactive research', *Scandinavian Journal of Management*, 6(2): 125–142.

Ramsay, H. (1985) 'What is participation for? A critical evaluation of "labour process" analyses of job reform', in D. Knights, H. Willmott and D. Collinson (eds), *Job Redesign: Critical Perspectives on the Labour Process*. Aldershot: Gower.

Reason, P. and Bradbury, H. (2001) 'Introduction: Inquiry and participation in search of a world worthy of human aspiration', in P. Reason, and H. Bradbury (eds), *A Handbook of Action Research*. London: Sage.

Reason, P. and Bradbury, H. (eds) (2008) *The Sage Handbook of Action Research: Participative Inquiry and Practice*. London: Sage.

Sandberg, F. and Wallo, A. (2013) 'The interactive researcher as a virtual participant: A Habermasian interpretation', *Action Research*, 11(2): 194–212.

Spicer, A., Alvesson, M. and Kärreman, D. (2009) 'Critical performativity: The unfinished business of critical management studies', *Human Relations*, 62(4): 537–560.

Stringer, E. (1999) *Action Research* (2nd edn). Thousand Oaks, CA: Sage.

Svensson, L. (2008) 'Efterord', in B. Johannisson, E. Gunnarsson and T. Stjernberg (eds), *Gemensamt kunskapande – den interaktiva forskningens praktik*. Växjö: Växjö University Press.

Svensson, L., Ellström, P.-E. and Brulin, G. (2007) 'Introduction – on interactive research', *International Journal of Action Research*, 3(3): 233–249.

Voronov, M. (2008) 'Toward engaged critical management studies', *Organization*, 15(6): 939–945.

Warwick, R. and Board, D. (2012) 'Reflexivity as methodology: An approach to the necessarily political work of senior groups', *Educational Action Research*, 20(1): 147–159.

Watson, T.J. (2010) 'Critical social science, pragmatism and the realities of HRM', *International Journal of Human Resource Management*, 21(6): 915–931.

Weick, K.E. (1984) 'Small wins: Redefining the scale of social problems', *American Psychologist*, 39(1): 40–49.

Wolfram Cox, J., LeTrent-Jones, T.G., Voronov, M. and Weir, D. (eds) (2009) *Critical Management Studies at Work. Negotiating Tensions between Theory and Practice*. Cheltenham: Edward Elgar.

SIX

Doing research in your own organization: Being native, going stranger

Mathias Skrutkowski

Introduction

This chapter deals primarily with moral and existential aspects related to doing research in your own organization, a research methodology often referred to as covert ethnography (Dalton, 1959; Roy, 1958) or at-home ethnography (Alvesson, 2009), and how they can affect the research practice. The discussion of these aspects draws on the author's personal experiences from an empirical research project. Organizational ethnography is an established and well-regarded empirical method in the academic repertoire of business research, although sometimes avoided for practical reasons, such as difficulties in negotiating access, or the time commitment involved. Another problem, which is often highlighted, is how the reliability of observations made is affected by the presence of the researcher. Covert ethnography is sometimes held out as an alternative, when negotiation of access is likely to be difficult; an alternative which also appears to be less problematic with respect to reliability of observations.

My own experience is that covert research introduces a whole suite of different, more existential problems, which might be seen as an inversion of a broader problematic within ethnographic research: the merit of adopting an insider's perspective versus the risk of going native, and the difficulties in shaking off a certain colonial sediment attached to the ethnographic research tradition. While there is a growing debate on moral issues linked to covert ethnography (cf. the discussion in Hammersley and Atkinson, 2007), confessional tales (Van Maanen, 1988), which stress the personal difficulties involved in covert research, are less common in the literature, at least in the context of critical management studies (CMS). This chapter thus aims to fill that gap, and is specifically addressed to prospective critical ethnographers, particularly less experienced researchers considering whether to embark on a covert research project, with the aim of highlighting possible and potentially unforeseen contingencies of such fieldwork.

My own decision to return to academia and pursue a PhD programme followed a period working for over 5 years as a management consultant. I had reached a stage where I desired a change in my professional life, which had begun to impact my personal life and circumstances in ways I found detrimental. Through personal acquaintances, I had come to learn of the growing academic contributions going under the label of 'critical management studies'. Much of this work struck a note of affinity with my own observations of work in the knowledge economy. At the same time, the theoretical and humanist grounding of the (sub)discipline appealed to me, as I come from a family background with similar traditions. My father was an anthropologist and my mother a classicist. My sister had pursued an undergraduate degree in continental philosophy, and through her I had become acquainted with critical theory and the Frankfurt School, as well as poststructuralism and Foucault.

The application of these perspectives to management studies struck me as interesting, intellectually appealing, and profoundly relevant, in the sense of a much-needed debate about the ethics of a variety of practices associated with contemporary forms of work. I found the combination of a discursive perspective on management theory (Fournier and Grey, 2000; Grey and Willmott, 2002) with insights from social/discursive identity theory (Tajfel, 1974, 1982; Knights and Willmott, 1999; Alvesson and Willmott, 2002) particularly fruitful. My own decision to become a management consultant (a career option imbued with significant status among business school students) was not entirely devoid of motives to do with social prestige, and I could easily see how this served to smooth over moral apprehensions about the (often dubious) work one performed, as well as the salaries earned (in the context of an economy with growing income disparities). The many firm-based rituals of collective self-aggrandizement all served to reinforce this narcissistic identification with an in-group of elite knowledge workers, worthy and ultimately meriting the financial rewards of success.

The idea of pursuing a PhD degree at an institution with a CMS orientation thus started to grow, both as an opportunity to leave consulting behind (as well as the feelings of personal bitterness I had come to harbour about this career choice), and as a concrete instance of what I had hitherto fantasized about, in the sense of a more authentic existence, one more attuned to the intellectual and moral sensibilities of my inner self.

The administrative process of my application to the PhD programme at Lund University extended far beyond what I had expected, and meanwhile my prospective supervisor suggested that I might carry out covert observations of anything interesting that might be going on in the organization I was working for at the time.

Coincidentally enough, a project was indeed initiated, which had a remarkable over-lap with the research interests of the academic grouping I was aspiring to join, in terms of the themes brought out by the project, and as a manifestation of the influ-ence of a particular set of management theories that the academic grouping had an interest in problematizing. I thus started to make records of my own observations in relation to the project, what was said by the management team who ran it, and what were the reactions of my fellow colleagues and the employees of the firm.

As I pursued these clandestine observations, I began to feel increasingly ambiva-lent about what I was doing, and discovered, to my surprise, how those reservations were related to a long chronicle of problems in the qualitative research traditions associated with methods relying on participant observation. The remainder of this chapter will deal with these problems, relating them to both the broader problem-atic of the ethnographic methodological tradition (as discussed in the following sections), and my own, more narrow, experiences in relation to the research project I was carrying out.

The structure of this chapter is as follows. This introduction is followed by an account of the specific method of covert ethnography – how it has come about as a solution to problems of access and reliability – and then a section on existential issues related to covert participant observation and how these are related to the older problematic of the virtues of adopting an insider's perspective versus the risk of going native, and finally a section on moral issues related to covert ethnography, which might be seen simply as an intensification of broader ethical issues, in the sense of an attitude associated with colonial sediments, within the ethnological tradition.

Covert ethnography

The idea of covert ethnography might be seen to have emerged out of problems iden-tified with ethnographic or participant observation methods, problems related to access and reliability. Ethnography and participant observation are long-established methods for qualitative business research. Participant observation was the primary methodological vehicle for the industrial sociologists associated with the Chicago School (Roy, 1958), as well as a group of UK scholars inspired by this school, who also became pioneers in conducting covert research (Lupton, 1963; Benyon, 1975). The distinction between covert and overt research is sometimes blurred, but overt research typically involves a prior stage of negotiating access to study an organiza-tion, where the outcome is an agreement with some organizational representative authorized to grant such access. Covert research, conversely, connotes research pro-jects where this prior stage of negotiating access is omitted, and where access is achieved through other, sometime deceptive or illicit, means.

Perhaps due to the popularity of cultural studies at the time, and inspired par-ticularly by the cultural anthropology of Clifford Geertz (1973), which had turned 'culture' into a highly fashionable concept, ethnographic methods have enjoyed something of a revival since the 1980s. The concept of 'organizational culture', popularized during the 1980s, also lent further legitimacy to the notion of studying and understanding work organizations as cultural entities, much like anthropologists have studied primitive cultures. A common definition of the methodology, according to an established methodological textbook in business research, is as an approach which requires 'intense researcher involvement in the day-to-day running of an organization, so that the researcher can understand it from an insider's point of view' (Bryman and Bell, 2007: 425). The ethnographic method is thus broadly speaking based on the researcher participating 'in people's daily lives for an extended period of time, watching what happens, listening to what is said and/or asking questions through informal and formal interview, collecting documents and artefacts' (Hammersley and Atkinson, 2007: 3). The objective is to study, inter alia, the construction of cultural norms, expressions of organizational values and patterns of workplace behaviour.

Critical ethnography has become a research vehicle of choice within the CMS tradition, since it lends itself naturally to investigating hegemonic regimes of truth, and how they influence the subjectivity and behaviour of employees in contemporary organizations (Johnson and Duberley, 2009). Critical ethnography differs from conventional ethnography in that the research ambition goes beyond merely portraying the cultural worldview of the people studied; it seeks to challenge this worldview and reveal the structural assumptions on which it is founded, in order to understand how it produces asymmetrical structures of power and control (Jermier, 1998). The ultimate purpose of such research is emancipation, whether, as in action research, directly – through engaging with members of the organization under study to engender change – or indirectly – through the analytical critique of management theory and practice provided.

A common obstacle for research projects aiming to rely on ethnographic methods is that of negotiating access to the organization one wishes to study. Top management is often understandably wary of allowing outside people access to study intimate aspects of how their organizations are run. This may be the case even when there is nothing particularly unpalatable they wish to hide from public scrutiny: there is always the risk that an outside observer might misinterpret or even wilfully misconstrue observed organizational practices in a manner which might damage the organization's image. This problem tends to be particularly pronounced for research projects with a (known) critical agenda.

Another related problem, highlighted both by organizational scholars and traditional anthropologists, is the extent to which the presence of the researcher interferes with the natural behaviour of the people he or she has chosen to study. In primitive tribes, the presence of an odd-looking stranger taking notes about one's every step presumably contributes to a heightened feeling of self-awareness, which might stifle the natural occurrence of those expressions of cultural beliefs and norms that the researcher desires to study. Similarly, in organizational settings, people subjected to observation by an organizational ethnographer might become exceedingly conscious of the impressions they create, of themselves and more broadly the organization under study. More broadly, people tend to behave differently in different contexts within the same setting, as highlighted by Goffman (1959) and his notion of front-stage versus back-stage behaviour. The risk of impression management, aiming to come across in a favourable light, on the part of those individuals being studied – or more broadly that they adapt their behaviour to the presence of the ethnographer (aligning their behaviour with, for example, socially sanctioned norms, or with their own perceived role as research objects in a study) – thus becomes a core dilemma in studies relying on participant observation. This is of particular concern if the ambition of the research project is to study the organization from an insider's perspective, since it is a risk that threatens to undermine the reliability of the research findings (Alvesson and Sköldberg, 2009).

Covert ethnography holds out the promise of overcoming the above problems of access and reliability. By concealing one's own identity as a researcher, there is no need to negotiate access. Furthermore, since none of the people being studied are aware of one's ulterior role as researcher, there is little risk of stifling the natural occurrence of those cultural expressions one wishes to study. On the other hand, covert ethnography introduces a whole suite of very different problems. Quite apart from substantial practical issues related to, for example, the limited possibility of taking notes for fear of betraying your covert agenda, or the problem of not being able to complement your empirical observations with other research methods (such as interviews), I will focus primarily on issues to do with moral and existential issues, as I experienced these myself. This is not to say that the practical issues, as well as other potential issues related to fear of discovery, might not be important for other researchers considering adopting the method of covert ethnography. But my own experiences make me better placed to discuss those issues which I have chosen to focus the chapter around. These will be covered in the following sections.

Another advantage of covert research relates to the fact that as a covert researcher one is typically employed by the organization one intends to study. As such, one is by default likely to know something about what goes on there, since one would otherwise probably not have been employed by them. This is an important advantage; many organizational researchers have a very limited understanding of the business practices, manufacturing and production routines, marketing strategies, customer and supplier relationships etc. that constitute the daily grind of the organizations they intend to study – much of the work being done, as well as the jargon spoken, in contemporary organizations is of a highly complex nature. To understand what people are talking about in such organizations often requires a good deal of knowledge about the complexities of the work they do, and what the jargon signifies. The level of understanding will naturally vary with one's prior job experience in the area, and one's length of employment. The more familiar one is with the organization, the more one is really doing research in an environment which is one's own, as opposed to temporarily gaining access to study some exotic firm or culture. This kind of covert ethnography thus slides over into what Alvesson has called at-home ethnography, the idea of which is 'to utilize the position one is in also for other, secondary purposes, that is, doing research on the setting of which one is also a part' (Alvesson, 2009: 160). As for myself, I had worked more than 5 years in my particular field of practice, and was employed as a specialist at the organization I was covertly studying. This circumstance also happens to be related to some of the issues I was experiencing in my dual capacity as researcher/employee, which will be discussed in the next section.

On existential aspects

The problem of understanding a 'foreign' culture goes beyond issues that can be resolved through merely learning the language spoken by its members. When we try to interpret the role of a set of customs and beliefs in a foreign culture, we are likely to become biased through the cultural baggage we ourselves bring to the scene, what one might call the risk of fitting the interpretation of foreign cultures in the Procrustean bed of our Western cultural perspective.[1] This phenomenon is often exemplified by the person commonly seen as the father of ethnology, James G. Frazer, and his study of folklore, magic and religion, *The Golden Bough* (Frazer, 1993). Frazer spent most of his working life meticulously compiling an anthology of the myths and religious customs of pre-Christian cultures. What might strike a modern reader as surprising is how – after having spent such meticulous effort on documenting the religious practices and magical rituals of a particular cult – he would always come to the same, abrupt conclusion regarding the role of the myth/cult under study, dismissing it as the irrational superstitions adopted by primitive people who had not yet developed the higher forms of knowledge and understanding of the Western scientific tradition. Such superstitions, Frazer argued, were adopted by frightened savages living under constant fear of the brutal forces of nature that enveloped them, fearing them because they did not properly understand them, and inventing fictive superstitions to assuage these fears. Ultimately then, he viewed myths simply as 'mistakes' that primitives people make about their world, mistakes made in the grip of ignorance and fear (Frazer, 1993).

Bronislaw Malinowski was a student of Frazer, and tried to modify the dismissive perspective of his mentor somewhat in his classical study of cultures of the Trobriand Islands. He focused his interpretation on the economic *function* of the kula trading practice in their culture, arguing that it served its purpose (resource allocation and distribution) just as well as that of the Western economic system of free trade

---

[1]In the classical Greek legend, Procrustes invited some guests to stay the night, and cut off their legs when he saw that they did not fit into the beds he had arranged for them (rather than adjust the length of the beds).

capitalism, thus putting their cultural customs on an equal footing with our own (Malinowski, 1978). Malinowski in turn has been vehemently criticized by the French anthropologist Claude Lévi-Strauss, who argued that Malinowski's function-alist perspective still betrays an interpretive bias shaped by the utilitarian tradition within Anglo-Saxon philosophy, of attempting to understand all cultural customs according to the utility value they bestow on the participants forming part of a trans-action. This is a tautological argument, says Lévi-Strauss (1974), which does not help us to understand the meaning of the specific custom under study, why it has come about rather than something else.

To overcome the interpretive biases that we inevitably bring along with our cul-tural baggage to the study of foreign cultures, Lévi-Strauss suggests that we should practise something he calls *dépaysement*, roughly translated as 'de-countrification', consciously attempting to detect instances of culturally conditioned interpretive bias in our own observations of foreign cultures, questioning them to see if we can adopt an alternative interpretation, which might come closer to a true insider's perspective. As pointed out by Lévi-Strauss (1974) himself, such an attitude runs the opposite risk of losing one's sense of self when venturing to study a foreign culture, by systemati-cally undermining the barrier and distance between oneself as a researcher/observer and the object of study. This is related to the risk of going native, where, having completely adopted the insider's perspective of the culture under observation, one is no longer able to reassume the role of an ethnographic researcher, in order to write down a scientific account of what one has set out to study. There is no longer any cultural vantage point from which such an account might be seen as meaningful. More broadly, immersing oneself in a foreign culture, in an attempt to understand it from an insider's perspective, is associated with mental sanity-related risks, of los-ing a firm grip of oneself as a distinct metaphysical entity, since the undermining of one's own cultural conditioning gradually risks opening up an existential abyss, and a vertiginous sense of the frailty and thinness of the cultural veneer that separates human civilization from the brutishness of nature.

An intriguing example of such risks might be found in the story of Aby Warburg and his study of the Native American Hopi tribes in New Mexico. At an early stage in his scholarly career, Warburg made the discovery of how the symbolism of pagan myth and magic had survived not only in Christian ritual and theology, but in the symbolic repertoire of Renaissance art and sculpture. Prompted by this discovery, he made a somewhat drastic methodological shift, in turning from art historical stud-ies of religious symbolism, to embark on an ethnographic study of the Hopi tribes' serpent rituals, to see whether the structural logic of pagan symbolism he had discov-ered would feature in a wholly separate, primitive culture. As he became gradually convinced of the timeless universalism with which symbolism operates in our cul-tural consciousness, Warburg, in contrast to Frazer, began to lose confidence that Western science and knowledge could supersede pagan symbolism as a way of dealing with human terror and awe of the natural world. At the onset of World War I, and the brutal slaughter of European military troops that ensued, Warburg began having nightmares about the earth slopping in blood. With Germany's defeat, he slid into a state of psychotic depression that landed him in a Swiss mental clinic (Gombrich, 1986). As suggested by Schama (1996), perhaps Warburg's descent into insanity was linked to his zeal in detecting the survival of pagan symbolism in our own culture, that by scraping away the Western cultural veneer and its presumption of rationality, a metaphysical abyss was opened, whereby he was no longer able to hold his object of study at the comfortable distance required to maintain mental stability.

One might thus envisage the risk of Procrustean beds (and the opposing virtues of *dépaysement* and adopting an insider's perspective) on the one hand, and the risk of going native and losing oneself on the other hand, as two extreme points on a continuum which the ethnographer must seek to navigate between, in order to construe a meaningful scientific account of the culture under observation, interpreting it in a way which (ideally) also seeks to remain loyal to the way it is understood by its members. In methodological textbooks dealing with organizational ethnography (see, for example, Ybema et al., 2009), the virtue of adopting an insider's perspective versus the risk of going native are commonly highlighted, much in the same way as they have in classical anthropology. Perhaps because my father was a classical anthropologist, and through my own acquaintance with the works of Frazer, Malinowski and Lévi-Strauss, this analogy initially struck me as a little preposterous. I could not believe that work organizations in Western societies are so fundamentally different from each other, in terms of cultural belief patterns, as are primitive cultures compared to Western culture. The need to consciously strip oneself from culturally conditioned interpretive biases thus struck me as rather exaggerated, and the whole idea of treating work organizations as culturally distinct entities as somewhat ludicrous. Furthermore, as an employed expert in my field, I had very little difficulty in understanding the various goings-on within the organization I worked for, from the perspective of a fully-fledged insider.

What I gradually discovered was precisely how my 'insidership' posed problems for me in terms of the very premise of carrying out covert observations of an organization that I was simultaneously a legitimate member of. The overarching purpose of my observations, how they might fit in with a research agenda and be related to a research problem, was unclear to me during this initial stage of my research, and so the whole premise of what I was doing felt a little uncertain. Compared to my ulterior (and still unclear) research agenda, the non-covert duties I had to carry out as an employee felt like they had a much firmer ontological basis. I performed numerical analyses, wrote, and was consulted as an expert on decisions on matters where my expertise was considered relevant to the outcome. These activities felt much more substantial and real than my role as a covert participant observer. And so I began to lose a firm sense of the reality and substance of my clandestine observations, as well as my plans for future academic pursuits, having immersed myself in a 'real' setting under false pretences, secretly carrying out research according to a covert agenda. Who are you, and who do you become, when you spend your days doing work under false pretences?

Covert research, especially in the context of critical ethnography, thus reawakens and even intensifies some of the issues related to going native in classical ethnography/anthropology, through inverting them, if you will. The ontological barrier between yourself (being a researcher/observer) and your object of study (being something other than you, which you can hold at a comfortable metaphysical distance when you have the role of an overt researcher) is of necessity concealed. You are native, and for all practical purposes have already lost yourself. This means that you must constantly make an effort to distance yourself from the insider's perspective, rather than the other way around. This is perhaps even more difficult, compared to the practice of *dépaysement* in traditional anthropology, since there at least you have an exotic cultural reference point – the primitive culture under study – with which you can seek to align your interpretation of empirical phenomena that you suspect yourself of carrying an interpretive bias against. In covert ethnography, there is a double familiarity – with one's broader cultural reference point (Western capitalist society) as well as the setting under study – which one must seek to distance oneself from, without any directly observable, tangible reference point from which to aim for.

A further issue is that the subject matter of critical ethnography – those deep structures which constrain human behaviour – is impossible to observe directly, and requires intensive interpretive efforts to uncover. The focus of attention is precisely the overly familiar, and the interpretive effort is premised on the inherently somewhat paranoid suspicion that everything is not what it seems: that what passes for ordinary work 'is a thickly layered structure of political struggles concerning power and authority, cultural negotiations over identity and social constructions of the problem at hand' (Forester, 1998: 47). Without any academic colleagues to discuss my hypotheses and tentative interpretations with, these tended to come across increasingly as the feverish brainchildren of a paranoid imagination, when compared to the trivial, mundane reality of my everyday office setting. I began to feel similar to Aby Warburg, who ended up haunted by visions of blood-soaked pagan motifs popping up everywhere, through cultural rabbit holes in the contours of Western social reality.

In this spiral of oscillation between my real, overt role as an employee, and the ulterior (somewhat unreal) role of a covert ethnographer, desperately trying to uncover sinister structures of power and control, I discovered that I could find precious little of interest to say about the object of study: the internal branding project that my employer was running. The project had a clear enough purpose, that of boosting employee morale after the company's image had been tainted through allegations of misconduct in the press. This was to culminate in an external rebranding campaign, whereby the company aimed to reinvent its brand as that of a responsible corporate citizen. My own reaction to this, as well as how I interpreted that of my colleagues, was one of outspoken cynical distancing. It felt like a rather fake and conceited effort. To think that they could repair the brand's reputation and improve employee morale through such superficial window-dressing activities! Much amusement on this subject was shared by my colleagues, in the form of relatively outspoken puns and derogatory comments. On the other hand, I did not feel there was anything particularly interesting to say about this observation. I found the project to be, at worst, naïve and a little silly, but there was nothing particularly sinister or sordid about the intention of wanting to repair the company's image, particularly when employee opposition (at least within my team) to the project was so concerted and outspoken, and management was comparatively resigned and powerless in the face of such opposition, presumably conscious of their own role in the aforementioned allegations of misconduct.

With time, I began to reflect on how my own reaction (and that of my colleagues), as well as my inability to see something interesting about them, was influenced by precisely my own dual identity: that of a fake corporate persona, masking an 'authentic' covert ethnographer, carrying out theoretically informed research about management practices, with a decidedly critical lens. This had precluded any ability of my own to identify with my chosen career-path, in the sense of belonging to a social category I could conceive of as prestigious. My reaction to the project, cynical distancing, was thus predetermined from the outset, being somewhat of a recurring leitmotif in the confused and rather anxious attitude I harboured towards my own career-path – as was, for that matter, my identification with my ulterior role as a critically inclined researcher, an iconoclast that would 'bite the hand' of the very capitalist system that put food on my table.

As these reflections began to temper my cynical attitude toward the project, I began to see how precisely my own reaction was the real mystery of the research project. There was a certain tension between the violence of my own distancing from the branding project, and the relatively innocuous nature of it. Why was it so important for me to conceive of it as fake and lame? As I began my formal PhD training, I started to immerse myself in the literature on identity theory, and began to see how my anxious and conflicting attitudes towards my own business career might be seen in the light of an attempt to identify with alternative social categories, seeing as my social background had affected my ability to identify with my career, in the sense of a social category subjectively carrying any social status/prestige. One might see this realization as a consequence of adopting a discursive perspective on social identity, whereby perceived status is acknowledged as a highly subjective measure and not determined by any internal essence of the social groups people aspire to belong to (Knights and Willmott, 1999).

This interpretive turn was not entirely trivial, and I had much support from constructive discussions with my supervisors, who are keen advocates of reflexivity as a research ideal (Alvesson and Sköldberg, 2009). Briefly put, this may be conceived of as a kind of triple hermenutical process: the first stage involves a basic digestion of the raw empirical material into a meaningful account of those observations made; the second stage attempts to determine whether this initial account might be better understood through the lens of critical theory; and the final stage involves a reflection on one's own constructive role as a researcher – which accounts are given priority or played down, in order to favour the emergence of a particular statement? It was arguably through this final hermeneutic stage that I discovered how my own account was biased by the anxieties of my personal identity struggles. I thus gradually began to shift the focus of my interpretation away from the fakeness of the project, to the over-determination of my own attitudes towards it. However, since the reactions of my colleagues had been similar, I began to wonder what mechanisms might lie behind the commonality of our attitudes, even though most of them did not come from a similar background to my own.

Something they had all commented on was the conceitedness of 'fixing' the company's image through window-dressing activities. It dawned on me how this was rooted in the fact that they themselves had already disidentified with the company, after its image had been damaged by various media scandals, a reaction which might be understood as culturally conditioned by contemporary notions of authenticity and self-expression, which have become commodified as important markers of social status and prestige (Fleming, 2009). This sparked a broader research interest in organizations that have suffered crises of confidence, and how the damage done to the image of the organization affected the willingness of employees to identify with the need for change efforts. In a culture which increasingly turns on the ability to narcissistically identify with a prestigious self-image, of seeing oneself reflected in the social status of the company one works for, or in the profession one has chosen, organizations become increasingly reliant on a prestigious external image, as a cultural steering device. This latter interpretive turn marked a further shift of focus, away from the specific circumstances of the project run by the organization I worked for, towards the broader contemporary phenomenon of social status and identity as a key mobilizing agent for human effort; how publicly disgraced organizations might end up in a state of inertia, where they lose the ability to mobilize employees to improve the company's external image, as well as address and remedy the concrete problems which have caused it to fall into disrepute.

On ethical aspects

Another source of personal discomfort was more moral in nature, in that I felt rather ill at ease about noting down observations about people's behaviour and reactions, without having sought their prior consent. While the method of covert ethnography is certainly not so common as to form an established alternative within qualitative business research, it has a longer history within the broader social sciences, and there is a substantial literature dealing with ethical issues related to it (Beauchamp et al., 1982; Bulmer, 1982; Herrera, 1999; Warwick, 1982). Some would go so far as to completely discourage it, considering it an illegitimate breach of the integrity of those you deign to study. There is, furthermore, a very concrete risk that the jobs, livelihoods and careers of the people you study could be compromised. Regardless of how hard the researcher tries to anonymize case details and the names of participants in the study, it is impossible to fully conceal personal identities, from those that know the organization well. I had similar moral reservations about publishing the results of the study I was carrying out, which were rendered all the more poignant by the circumstance that some of my colleagues were closer to being personal friends (people I profoundly respected and liked).

However, I felt another type of ethical concern about focusing my study on their reactions to the project, which was related more to the hermeneutical aspect of the research process: what I would read into my observations of my colleagues' reactions during the subsequent stage of interpretation. As I came to realize, these reservations were similar to such felt by an earlier generation of anthropologists (and critics of anthropological research), of assuming the voice of others, to speak on their behalf. The historically close association of anthropological research with colonialism and ethnocentricity has been connected with a type of research that provides 'a totalizing description of a certain reality, in which the researcher speaks for the Other and blocks any alternative voices' (Alvesson and Sköldberg, 2009: 199).

As argued by Geertz (1988), many anthropologists have consequently been concerned with ensuring objectivity through some notion that crucial elements in ethnographic description can be made more reliable via the mechanics of knowledge: how empathy and insight can be promoted, how the inner lives of others can be brought out and represented as thoughts and feelings. Geertz contends that this simply constitutes an attempt to legitimate a certain style or genre of ethnographic writing, through dressing it up in a scientific-sounding vocabulary, while ignoring the real issue and substance of ethnography: that of authorship. Geertz argues that the authorial role of the ethnographer is inevitable: the plurality of a culture (and the social world in a broader sense) is impossible to convey, and so the role of the ethnographer inevitably consists of selectively making use of his or her empirical material to craft a textual narrative.

While much of Geertz's criticism is aimed at an earlier generation of anthropologists (the likes of Malinowski and his followers) who he felt had been projecting and legitimating their own ideologically flavoured research agendas on the people they studied, the very ideal of representing natives[2] from an insider's perspective (which one might see Lévi-Strauss and Geertz as providing different articulations of) has also been criticized for its colonial sediments (see Prasad and Prasad, 2002). One might question to what extent Lévi-Strauss or Geertz were really driven by an ambition to gain an understanding of the culture (in the sense of a collective inner representation of the world) of the primitive societies they studied, on their own terms – and not, rather, to project a recurrent Western fantasy of authenticity (in the sense of a primal innocence) which we feel has been lost in our own disenchanted culture. Such attitudes (the condescension of Frazer, or the

---

[2] I use the term 'native' in the classical anthropological sense throughout this chapter – of participants of a culture that is the object of study – although I am conscious that it is part of a problematic terminology within the ethnographic tradition.

romanticization of Lévi-Strauss and Geertz) have arguably spilled over in much of the ethnographic work in organization studies, in that 'researchers often behave condescendingly towards practitioners, giving advice, establishing "best practice", or "emancipating the oppressed"' (Czarniawska, 2007: 21). The concept of critical ethnography is itself premised on an emancipatory agenda, with the ambition to 'describe, analyze and open to scrutiny otherwise hidden agendas, power centres and assumptions that inhibit, repress and constrain' (Thomas, 1993: 3). The presumption that employees in contemporary organizations are invariably oppressed can lead to a condescending attitude on behalf of the researcher, when he or she encounters employees who do not feel particularly oppressed. A typical reaction by the researcher is to brush such reports aside as a result of psychic prisons, false consciousness or communicative distortion, in the larger interest of one's emancipatory agenda.

Such attitudes arguably also represent an instance of what Silverman (2006) calls a romantic conceit underlying much qualitative research: that of the very possibility of obtaining access to the inner lives of others, through invoking some sentimental and idealistic notion of empathy. My own reservations about drawing too sweeping conclusions about what I could observe about my colleagues' behaviour resonated well with the above referenced critiques of the anthropological tradition: I felt uncomfortable about projecting the reasons for my own reaction to the branding project onto them, and while acknowledging (with Geertz) that the narrating role of an ethnographer is inevitable, I felt that the empirical data did not allow me to cast my colleagues as prominent protagonists in the story that was emerging – I had little empirical material in which their own voices (on the subject of the branding project) were allowed to transpire. This is a crucial problem with covert ethnography. While one's role as a covert researcher is less likely to disturb the naturalistic setting being studied (compared to the presence of an overt researcher), one has less opportunity to complement direct observations of cultural behaviour with alternative empirical material, such as interviews, which might serve to corroborate one's tentative interpretations of said behaviour. The reliability and 'naturalness' of ethnographic observation thus comes at the expense of interpretive reliability. In my own case, I found it very difficult to verify to what extent my own reasons for disidentification with the branding project were mirrored by those of my colleagues – other than in a very broad sense, that we were unable to subjectively conceive of our employer's image as having any social prestige value.

My observations in relation to the branding project had originally been taken down as diary entries, which I wrote down after coming home from work, since it was difficult to take running notes of my observations while at work, without betraying my covert agenda. As I began to shift the interpretive focus towards my own reactions to the project, and how they had been influenced (or rather predetermined) by my own social background and consequent view of what would constitute social status/prestige for me, I also began to change my understanding about the methodology I had adopted. Since I was really focusing on my own experiences and reactions in relation to the branding project, I realized how the account and emergent analysis/understanding of these experiences might come closer to what has been labelled auto-ethnography (Strathern, 1987; Goodall, 1994), a more overtly autobiographical form of ethnographic research concerned with researching settings where the cultural background of the observer and the observed is shared. This is a genre of ethnographic research which draws explicitly on the conventions of literary fiction and the novel, a form of 'writing, story, and method that connect the autobiographical and personal to the cultural, social, and political' (Ellis, 2004). I began to see how my own diary entries constituted a distinct narrative, with its own peculiar emphasis on certain narrative tropes – such as a heavily satirical account and representation of top management's role as protagonists in the branding project. I also started to realize how precisely this narrative was linked to my own identity, how the satirical representation of top management was linked to my own disidentification with the branding project, being part of a broader personal life story of anxiety/hesitation about identifying with my chosen career-path. This shift away from assuming the voice of others, of speaking on their behalf, to something which came closer to self-examination, also made me feel less uncomfortable about the covert nature of what I had been doing, and the fact that I had not sought the consent of my colleagues to make observations about their reactions to the project.

Concluding remarks

The above account illustrates some of the difficulties as well as the potential for methods associated with critical ethnography, specifically the covert variety. Much like the problem of going native in classical anthropology, the ideal of insidership poses a risk of becoming blind to the phenomenon one aspires to study, since the need for maintaining a myopic focus on one's daily activities and personal relations at work – in the twin role as a working employee of the company being covertly studied – disables you somewhat from reflecting over the broader cultural setting of which you form a part. You also become inclined to treat your own reactions and attitudes, as well as those of your colleagues, as 'natural' and/or self-explanatory, in the sense of not meriting any further scrutiny or analysis. As you try and distance yourself from the mundane reality of your all-too-familiar role as an employee, trying to convince yourself that everything is not what it seems – attempting rather to reconceive of the ordinary and quotidian as something exotic, potentially sinister and strange – you are likely to start feeling a little paranoid, in more than one sense. Without the possibility of being recognized at work in your ulterior role as a critical researcher, this sense of paranoia is likely to be augmented, since you are forced to keep your interpretive reasoning process and emerging hypotheses entirely private.

The phenomenological process determined by such a constant inner voice, which compulsively insists on trying to interpret every facet of an ordinary work day, in the context of a thickly layered texture of political struggles, is probably not entirely different from the inner life of a paranoid schizophrenic. As a piece of concrete advice, I would recommend maintaining a close line of communication with the academic community you form part of. To vent your thoughts and feelings on a regular basis with someone who recognizes and can confirm your researcher identity is perhaps the best lifeline of sanity in such a situation.

Conversely, I also think that the ulterior role and identity of a critically inclined management scholar might carry the risk of adopting a predetermined empirical and interpretive focus, one that might draw attention away from what is really interesting about the phenomena you are studying. There is an interpretive bias in the core stream within the CMS research tradition that draws on critical theory and the Frankfurt School, and in which critical ethnography has been a method of choice. This can be argued to harbour a certain colonial sediment, in the sense of being guided by an ideal of emancipation, in interpreting the behaviour of 'natives' (viewing them as culturally oppressed), and providing emancipatory guidance. Without recourse to alternative empirical data, such as interviews, to corroborate one's tentative interpretations, there is thus a strong risk that the covert nature of the research effort might strengthen this predetermined bias and force highly subjective interpretations on research objects, in a manner similar to James Frazer's interpretation of pagan myths. I personally have found that reflexivity as a research ideal can serve to temper such a bias, in forcing you to reflect on your own role as a researcher (Alvesson and Sköldberg, 2009).

This is not to say that I hereby wish to discredit the whole notion of critical ethnography. But it lends itself better to micro-studies of power relationships within specific organizational contexts, where there is indeed a strong line of stratification, separating the disempowered from the empowered, and where there is opportunity for a democratization of organizational practices. However, this is not always the case in the organization under study, and sometimes such an interpretive focus might draw our attention from other, potentially interesting phenomena. I still consider my research project as 'critical', but in a broader sense than the specific organizational context of my first case study, one which involves critique in a more dialectical sense, of the way identity is being used as a control device in contemporary organizations, and ways in which such control processes can break down and turn in on themselves.

On a more positive note, I believe that covert ethnography holds out the prospect of producing really interesting research output, perhaps through the very oscillation between a dual set of roles. In the resulting experiential struggle, we might have the chance to distance ourselves from both, as it were, and through the metaphysical cracks opened up by our existential confusion, we might be able to glean something which the fixity of our prior identity position might have made us blind to.

References

Alvesson, M. (2009) 'At-home ethnography: Struggling with closeness and closure', in S. Ybema, D. Yanow, H. Wels and F. Kamsteeg (eds), *Organizational Ethnography: Studying the Complexities of Everyday Life*. London: Sage.

Alvesson, M. and Sköldberg, K. (2009) *Reflexive Methodology: New Vistas for Qualitative Research*. London: Sage.

Alvesson, M. and Willmott, H. (2002) 'Identity regulation as organizational control: Producing the appropriate individual', *Journal of Management Studies*, 39(5): 619–644.

Beauchamp, T., Faden, R., Wallace, J. and Walters, L. (eds) (1982) *Ethical Issues in Social Scientific Research*. Baltimore, MD: Johns Hopkins University Press.

Benyon, H. (1975) *Working for Ford* (2nd edn). Harmondsworth: Penguin.

Bryman, A. and Bell, E. (2007) *Business Research Methods*. Oxford: Oxford University Press.

Bulmer, M. (1982) 'Ethical problems in social research: The case of covert participant observation', in M. Bulmer (ed.), *Social Research Ethics: An Examination of the Merits of Covert Participant Observation*. London: Macmillan, pp. 3–12.

Czarniawska, B. (2007) *Shadowing and Other Techniques for Doing Fieldwork in Modern Societies*. Copenhagen: Liber.

Dalton, M. (1959) *Men who Manage: Fusion of Feeling and Theory in Administration*. New York: Wiley.

Ellis, C. (2004) *The Ethnographic I: A Methodological Novel about Autoethnography*. Walnut Creek, CA: AltaMira Press.

Fleming, P. (2009) *Authenticity and the Cultural Politics of Work: New Forms of Informal Control*. Oxford: Oxford University Press.

Forester, J. (1998) 'Critical ethnography: On fieldwork in a Habermasian way', in M. Alvesson and H. Willmott (eds), *Critical Management Studies*. London: Sage.

Fournier, V. and Grey, C. (2000) 'At the critical moment: Conditions and prospects for critical management studies', *Human Relations*, 53(1): 7–32.

Frazer, J. G. (1993) *The Golden Bough: A Study in Magic and Religion*. Ware: Wordsworth.

Geertz, C. (1973) *The Interpretation of Cultures*. New York: Basic Books.

Geertz, C. (1988) *Work and Lives: The Anthropologist as Author*. Stanford, CA: Stanford University Press.

Goffman, E. (1959) *The Presentation of Self in Everyday Life*. Garden City, NY: Doubleday.

Gombrich, E.H. (1986) *Aby Warburg: An Intellectual Biography*. Oxford: Phaidon.

Goodall, H.L. (1994) *Casing a Promised Land: The Autobiography of an Organizational Detective as Cultural Ethnographer*. Carbondale: Southern Illinois University Press.

Grey, C. and Willmott, H. (2002) 'Context of CMS', *Organization*, 9(3): 411–418.

Hammersley, M. and Atkinson, P. (2007) *Ethnography: Principles in Practice*. London: Routledge.

Herrera, C.D. (1999) 'Two arguments for "covert research" in social research', *British Journal of Sociology*, 50(2): 331–341.

Jermier, J. (1998) 'Introduction: Critical perspectives on organizational control', *Administrative Science Quarterly,* 43(2): 235–256.

Johnson, P. and Duberley, J. (2009) 'Critical management methodology', in H. Willmott and M. Alvesson (eds), *The Oxford Handbook of Critical Management Studies.* Oxford: Oxford University Press.

Knights, D. and Wilmott, H. (1999) *Management Lives: Power and Identity in Contemporary Organizations.* London: Sage.

Lévi-Strauss, C. (1974) *Structural Anthropology,* New York: Basic Books.

Lupton, T. (1963) *On the Shopfloor.* Oxford: Pergamon Press.

Malinowski, B. (1978) *Argonauts of the Western Pacific.* London: Routledge.

Prasad, P. and Prasad, A. (2002) 'Casting the native subject: Ethnographic practice and the (re)production of difference', in B. Czarniawska and H. Höpfl (eds), *Casting the Other: The Production Maintenance of Inequalities in Work Organizations.* London: Routledge.

Roy, D. (1958) 'Banana time: Job satisfaction and informal interaction', *Human Organisation,* 18(4): 156–168.

Schama, S. (1996) *Landscape and Memory.* New York: Alfred A. Knopf.

Silverman, D. (2006) *Interpreting Qualitative Data* (3rd edn). London: Sage.

Strathern, A. (1987) 'The limits of auto-anthropology', in A. Jackson (ed.), *Anthropology at Home.* London and New York: Tavistock.

Tajfel, H. (1974) 'Social identity and intergroup behaviour', *Social Science Information,* 13: 65–93.

Tajfel, H. (1982) 'Social psychology of intergroup relations', in M.R. Rosenzweig and L.W. Porter (eds), *Annual Review of Psychology,* 33: 1–39. Palo Alto, CA: Annual Reviews.

Thomas, J. (1993) *Doing Critical Ethnography.* Newbury Park, CA: Sage.

Van Maanen, J. (1988) *Tales from the Field.* Chicago: University of Chicago Press.

Warwick, D.P. (1982) 'Tearoom trade: Means and end in social research', in M. Bulmer (ed.), *Social Research Ethics: An Examination of the Merits of Covert Participant Observation.* London: Macmillan, pp. 38–58.

Ybema, S., Yanow, D., Wels, H. and Kamsteeg, F. (eds) (2009) *Organizational Ethnography: Studying the Complexities of Everyday Life.* London: Sage.

SEVEN

Critical and compassionate interviewing: Asking until it makes sense

Susanne Ekman

Introduction

The current chapter will place the art of interviewing inside the complex world of organizations and hierarchical interactions and explore some of the challenges which this setting creates for the researcher. Furthermore, it will propose an approach to interviewing which sympathizes with critical management studies (CMS) agendas, yet on important points also recognizes potential blind spots in critical research. Consequently, the aim is to develop and describe in practical detail a form of critically inspired interviewing which is at the same time committed to remedying what it considers to be recurring tendencies in CMS: moral condescension, polarized opposition to mainstream research, and predefined subject positions for many of the key research subjects (for more on this debate, see: Alvesson and Ashcraft, 2009; Brewis and Wray-Bliss, 2008; Reedy, 2008; Wray-Bliss, 2003). I will return to these tendencies later.

Notably, the kind of interviewing proposed here wishes to retain some of the strengths of CMS, namely the sense of solidarity with those on the receiving end of suffering, marginalization or exploitation. In other words, the agenda is to establish a form of engagement with the field which avoids the tendency towards not only prescriptive instrumentalism in mainstream research (Adler et al., 2007; Fournier and Grey, 2000), but also suspicion and moral superiority in CMS. The best way to transcend these two approaches, I suggest, is by means of compassion. In order to succeed with this, it is necessary to ask for and endure a high degree of ambiguity.

This represents a challenging demand for the interviewer who will be required to pursue issues and conflicts more in the mindset of a scrupulous arbitrator than that of a judgmental partisan.

Below, I will start by delineating some of the key aspects of qualitative interviews, including the differences in epistemological approaches. Then I move on to discuss critical interviewing, and more specifically the elements in critical analyses which I believe could benefit from revision. This leads me to my key concept of 'compassion' which I present as the possible source of inspiration for such revision. Through a reading of various classical texts on compassion, I argue that compassion allows us to make sense of every agent in the field while at the same time retaining the ability to point out injustice and suffering. I move on to define a number of concrete interview techniques which allow the researcher to carry out this intention in practice. I conclude the chapter by describing situations of frustration and confusion which interviewing in general and compassionate interviewing specifically may entail.

Qualitative in-depth interviews

Interviewing is probably one of the most thoroughly described, discussed and debated qualitative research methods throughout the social sciences. The subject has been treated in depth by distinguished scholars such as James Spradley (1979), Steinar Kvale (2006), Denzin and Lincoln (2007) and Gubrium and Holstein (1997), just to mention some of the giants in the field. Although there are many different approaches to qualitative interviews, there are a number of characteristics which are generally agreed upon. Most researchers argue that one of the great strengths of qualitative interviews is their ability to generate nuance and detail. Contrary to quantitative approaches, qualitative interviews show the fine-grained qualities of social life in a manner that potentially tolerates a high degree of complexity. Furthermore, interviews are well suited to the study of subjectivity and the minutiae of everyday life (Gubrium and Holstein, 1997).

That said, there are also important variations in the approach to interviews, not least relating to epistemology. In the empiricist or naturalist approach, interviews are seen as a source of 'data' about the world 'as it is', independent of context. Here, the ideal is to capture the rich details of social realities without distorting them through interference or bias. This leads to interviewing techniques concerned with getting behind the façade and reaching the 'true stories' (Alvesson, 2003). Consequently, the naturalist researcher typically generates large quantities of detailed material about the informants' world, making an effort not to taint them with her own presuppositions. This material is then analyzed according to rigorous and systematic guidelines (Alvesson, 2003; Gubrium and Holstein, 1997).

The emotionalist approach to interviewing (somewhat condescendingly called 'romanticist' by Alvesson, 2003) does not attempt to make the researcher as invisible as possible in the process. Rather, it regards the researcher's empathetic and mirroring abilities as an essential tool to generate truthful and authentic accounts from research subjects. Here, the focus is on the intimate and trust-based exchange between two parties in a way that opens up the richness of inner lived experience. Consequently, the interviewer must be 'creative' and move beyond traditionalist techniques. This could involve the willingness to engage in self-disclosure and the extensive effort to form an authentic relation with the interview subject. Furthermore, it might even presuppose a thorough familiarity with one's own psychological patterns, so that unresolved emotional baggage does not obstruct trust and empathy in the interview (Gubrium and Holstein, 1997).

Another, increasingly influential approach is the contingency perspective, or what Alvesson (2003) calls 'localism'. In this approach, the notion of a natural world 'out there' has been left behind. Instead, the focus is on how social worlds are constructed in different contexts and by various linguistic or social practices. This means that the interviewer is no longer seen as a discrete outsider, but rather as a co-constructing participant. Consequently, the interview situation itself is a relevant object of study, rather than simply a vehicle for the generation of data or knowledge. The contingency perspective has been accompanied by a so-called 'crisis of representation' in which social researchers strongly denounced traditional, naturalistic approaches for veiling power asymmetries between observers and observed, and for disregarding the reflexivity which poststructural researchers consider vital (see Clifford and Marcus, 1986). In the wake of this crisis, a variety of experimental representations were developed to ensure 'multiple voices' and critical reflections on the proposed 'truth claims' from researchers. Interviews conducted within this framework embrace an active or possibly even consciously interfering interviewer, as opposed to the unobtrusive or empathetic interviewer in naturalism and emotionalism, respectively (Holstein and Gubrium, 2004).

Critical interviewing

One cannot position CMS squarely within one of the three approaches above. Generally, it is recognized that CMS is a highly diverse movement, both epistemologically and theoretically. It ranges from Marxist, critical realist, and poststructuralist to pragmatist perspectives (Adler et al., 2007). Yet it is surprising how much CMS empirical work tends to accord only minimal attention to research methods (Brewis and Wray-Bliss, 2008). To the extent that it does reflect on methods, it often reproduces surprisingly conventional approaches (Alvesson and Ashcraft, 2009; Alvesson and Kärreman, 2007; Wray-Bliss, 2002). Generally, the critical agenda tends to enter at the phase of analysis, rather than in the design of empirical study (Alvesson and Ashcraft, 2009). The neglect of methodological considerations may risk contributing to a number of the common risks in critical research. CMS researchers themselves have acknowledged these risks in various contexts. They include the reliance on 'usual suspects' such as 'capitalism', 'managers', and 'bureaucracy' (Alvesson and Ashcraft, 2009: 67), the reproduction of preconceived and inflexible subject positions for informants, for example those designated as 'dominated' and 'dominating' (Alvesson and Ashcraft, 2009: 70; Wray-Bliss, 2003: 310), the representation of managers as 'culpable dupes' and employees as 'cultural dupes' (Legge, 2001: 21; Reedy, 2008: 68), or the tendency to use empirical data from local realities as a mere 'illustration' of ready-made universal, critical plots (Alvesson and Ashcraft, 2009: 74). What all these risks have in common is the temptation to 'brandish a critical "hammer"', as Alvesson and Ashcraft put it, without showing any due appreciation of situational complexities (2009: 74).

In recent years, however, an increasing methodological reflexivity in CMS is beginning to surface (see Alvesson and Deetz, 2000; Alvesson and Kärremann, 2007; Alvesson and Ashcraft, 2009; Wray-Bliss, 2003). In these texts, the authors attempt to face the above-mentioned risks head-on while contemplating the recurring tensions and dilemmas involved in empirical research based on a critical framework. Rather than offering easy solutions, they urge CMS researchers to display an increased degree of reflexivity about these tensions when conducting their studies. In this chapter, I will focus on some of these dilemmas, as I describe the compassionately critical interview. First, there is the tension between being understanding and being critical. Second, there is the tension between a focus on 'lived experience' and on more structural aspects such as political frameworks, discourses, and steering mechanisms. Third, there is the tension between various epistemologies and their respective criteria of quality. In their definition of 'critical listening' Alvesson and Ashcraft attempt to address these tensions. They suggest that critical listening involves the ability to hear not only the social realities of participants, but also the dominant discourses and formations of power embedded in them. Furthermore, they propose an exploration of multiple or even competing voices combined with the application of 'alternative and nuanced' theories (2009: 68). I would like to subscribe to these suggestions and develop them further through the notion of compassion. My argument is that compassion indicates a mode of involvement with the field which assists us in navigating the tensions above. Below, I will make a brief presentation of various texts on compassion and then move on to show how this principle can be translated into concrete interview techniques.

From unreflexive instrumentalism or suspicion to compassion

Taking a closer look at the tensions described above, one can see that they have something in common. This something concerns a precarious negotiation of distance and proximity. Should we be close to and intimate with the research subject, or should we apply a structural view from above? Should we engage to the point of defining what The Good Life is, or should we make more modest interventions by pointing out patterns of pain and suffering? These tensions risk generating polarized practices unless we find a way to integrate them. In order for such an integration to succeed, we need to expand our tolerance for ambiguity and complexity. This involves leaving some of the neat dualisms behind and instead entering a territory of contradictions and gray zones. It is precisely the commitment to ambiguity and gray zones, as opposed to polarized dualisms, that characterizes the notion of compassion throughout the very varied texts on the theme. Exploring these texts can help us define an approach to interviewing which steers clear of 'black and white' research practices, whether they be the tendency to non-reflexive instrumentalism in mainstream studies or the tendency to moral condescension in critical studies.

Compassion is a profoundly ethical concept. It has been treated by thinkers from fields as diverse as medicine, psychology, Buddhism, existentialism, and Christianity (Aring, 1958; Dalai Lama and Cutler, 1998; Hendrix et al., 2005; Lévinas, 1991; Løgstrup, 1956; Ricoeur, 1992). Despite their considerable differences, all these texts attempt to formulate an ethical stance from which one can relate to a significant Other without either over-engaging with her or disregarding her suffering. Put differently, the notion of compassion seeks to strike a middle way which allows fundamental separateness to become the prerequisite for and facilitation of fundamental commitment. It thus promises to dissolve the antagonism between distance and intimacy by suggesting that the former actually serves to enhance the latter. This allows us to formulate a critical commitment which is not moralizing, but still engages strongly in the attempt to relieve suffering.

In the existential ethical philosophy of Emmanuel Lévinas this is expressed as a distinction between 'totality' and 'infinity'. He argues that when we claim to know the Other in her totality it equals a form of violence. We commit this kind of violence when we see the Other as the 'same as' me. Instead, we must be able to allow the Other her radical alterity, which Lévinas equates with infinity. Infinity entails 'a relationship with a surplus always exterior to the totality' (Lévinas, 1991: 22). Consequently, the opposite of violence, namely peace or compassion, is a relationship 'where the I both maintains itself and exists without egoism' (Lévinas, 1991: 306). Put more mundanely, the act of peace or compassion means a form of commitment to the Other which intensifies precisely by respecting the radical separateness or alterity, and by practicing compassion without an ego driven desire to steer the Other in a certain direction.

Similarly, Buddhism points out the difference between feeling with somebody and being attached to somebody, arguing that compassion helps us establish the former approach (Dalai Lama and Cutler, 1998). Compassion, in Buddhism, is a deep commitment to the reduction of suffering, yet without desiring or clinging to a specific notion about how the Other should be or not be in this process. In other words, this notion of compassion also emphasizes how engagement is intensified precisely through the preservation of distance and the ability to let go. The point is that when we become attached to a certain notion of how the Other should be 'saved', 'enlightened' or 'emancipated', we are driven by ego concerns and the will to succeed, rather than by an open-minded, moment by moment compassion.

Finally, in the field of medical ethics, Charles D. Aring argues for the distinction between sympathy and empathy. While sympathy involves a fusion with the feelings of the suffering patient, empathy involves the ability to identify while at the same time preserving a clear notion of the Other's alterity. Aring calls this 'one of the most difficult tasks put upon mankind' (Aring, 1958: 448).

Returning to the question of interviews, the points about compassion above help us strike a third way between the potential unreflexive instrumentalism of mainstream approaches and the potential suspicion and moralizing of critical approaches. It does so by insisting on sustained engagement and the attempt to relieve suffering, yet at the same time constantly trying to minimize attachment to specific notions about emancipation and, more importantly, attachment to one's own position as emancipator. The attempt to relieve suffering is always a simultaneous act of letting go, however paradoxical this may sound. In practice, this means that we must let go of our attachment to certain plots about exploitation and liberation, just as we must let go of our attachment to specific subject positions like exploiter and exploited. Notably, this does not mean that we let go of our ability to point out exploitation! But we never assume that the term 'exploiter' can tell the whole truth about a person. Based on the principle of compassion, we must always approach the Other with the assumption that we do not know her in her totality. Our interview, whether conducted with shareholders, managers or employees, is thus an exercise in making sense of an unknown Other, irrespective of her position. Letting go of attachment is the same as increasing tolerance for ambiguity. Thus, the measure of a good, compassionate interview is the degree to which it yields complex, multifaceted results. While it may capture elements of exploitation from, say, a manager, it should preferably capture elements of suffering, vulnerability or dependence too. Similarly, the interview with employees may capture elements of being exploited, but hopefully it would also capture contradictory aspects such as opportunism, immoderate expectations or the like. The analytical plot ensuing from such interview material can point out patterns of suffering without making an overly neat distribution of qualities between the various groups and subject positions involved. And most importantly, it can portray *all* the participants compassionately!

In order for this to succeed, the interview process must be prepared and conducted in a manner that facilitates the researcher's ability to make sense of every interviewee while still staying alert to the structural patterns of suffering and injustice. Below, I will describe in closer detail how this can be done. For illustrations, I draw on my own research experiences as an interviewer.

Principles and techniques of compassionate interviewing

As mentioned earlier, there are three central sets of tensions which pose a challenge to the critical interviewer: the tension between understanding and critiquing;

the tension between a focus on micro-level experience and macro-level structures; and finally, the tension between various epistemological ideals such as naturalism, emotionalism and localism. Compassionate interviewing attempts to handle these tensions through integration rather than polarization. Basically, this is done through various techniques to maximize the tolerance for ambiguity. When ambiguity is permitted, dualistic elements become mutually constitutive, rather than mutually exclusive, as we saw in the section on distance and intimacy. Tolerance for ambiguity is heightened when we systematically pursue multiple perspectives. The principle to be followed is similar to that of a conflict broker: the researcher needs to know and understand the stakes, stories, and experiences of all the primary positions within the social phenomenon being studied, before the analytical plot can be developed. Knowing and understanding means asking *until it makes sense*. If a certain position, say that of a manager, has only yielded unambiguously negative data, it means that the interview technique was not sufficiently tolerant of ambiguity. Below, I will describe how the tolerance of ambiguity can be maximized in various phases of the interview study: formulating the research problem, selecting participants, phrasing interview questions, finding a mode of listening, and developing an analytical plot.

When formulating a research problem the main challenge is to capture an issue where cultural, social and material patterns seem to generate powerful norms, rigidities or sufferings, but at the same time phrasing the question in a manner which allows for actual empirical *exploration*. By exploration is meant that the plot, the structures and the subject positions of the problem field are not known in advance. We generally have to make certain initial assumptions on which our research problem rests; however, we can still attempt to maximize room for surprise and contradiction. If we look at some of the classic empirical studies in CMS, they have a tendency to import the familiar subject positions and dualisms of the critical plot already in the research problem. Just to name one example, James Barker's famous study of teamwork in the company known as 'ISE' was driven by the question of whether this new form of work actually transcended traditional bureaucratic control (Barker, 1993). This research problem has a high risk of reproducing classical CMS plots about (nasty) bureaucratic control versus (nice) autonomy. It also risks important preconceived subject positions involving exploitative managers exercising ever more insidious and subtle forms of control vis-à-vis employees who are cultural dupes. As cultural dupes, employees either helplessly enact the cultural schemes through which managers control them, or they 'resist' from a position of fundamental moral innocence. None of these subject positions are associated with the kind of ambiguity that compassionate critical interviewing aims for. In compassionate approaches, each subject position must 'make sense' to the interviewer and seem like a probable and understandable position, given the stakes. This does not mean that the researcher is uncritical of the actions and consequences ensuing from such a subject position. However, the critique is made on the basis of extensive attempts at understanding rather than condemning.

This leads us on to the question of which participants to recruit for the study. Here, the key principle is *multiple perspectives*. The aim is to look at the research theme through a prism of as many different positions as possible. One way to do this is to recruit based on 'snowballing' rather than a representative sample. Snowballing means that you let one participant lead you to the next. In my study of hierarchical interactions in creative knowledge work, I followed the principle of 'intensity'. For example, several of my participants seemed intensely preoccupied with the feeling that they did not get enough recognition for their work. I would then inquire into whom they wanted this recognition from, which situations they wanted it in, which concrete experiences they could use as an example, and so on. From their answers, I could then gauge who the important 'primary Others' were on this issue. Perhaps it was a certain middle manager, project leader, or colleague – or all of those. Based on this, I then went on to recruit those 'primary Others' in order to hear their perspective on the issue. My focus on intensity ensured that I pursued problems that were significant, and my focus on snowballing ensured that I elicited multiple perspectives on the matter. This form of recruitment is more in line with the so-called multi-sited fieldwork (Marcus, 1995), than with traditional notions of attempting to map units. The multi-sited approach operates in chains of significance rather than in discrete settings. John Law has illustrated the difference as one between a map of traffic and a map of nations: the former concerns networks and connections, the latter concerns bounded fields (Law [personal communication] in Jensen, 2005: 196).

When preparing the interview questions, the ideal about ambiguity, complexity, and multiple perspectives also applies. If we return to the sets of tensions facing the critical researcher, namely understanding versus critique, subjective experience versus structural patterns, and various epistemological ideals, the aim of a compassionate interview is to cover the spectrum, rather than choose between poles. Therefore, the interviewer consciously approaches the same theme from different angles. In my study of creative knowledge workers, I always combined emotional and subjective questions with questions of a more general and normative flavor. For example, when trying to understand the ideals and practices of hierarchical interactions, I would ask employees about managers in two different ways. Early in the interview, I would ask questions such as:

Please name the five most important characteristics of a good manager.

This question mostly elicited normative and general answers which adhered relatively closely to the dominant discourses. The majority of my interviewees mentioned characteristics such as 'giving recognition and feedback', 'being present and empathetic', and 'allowing me autonomy and influence'. These characteristics fit well into the dominant discourse about self-realization and self-management. However, later in the interview I posed the same question from a personal angle:

Could you please tell me about the last time you went home from work feeling really pleased with your manager?

or

> Could you give me an example of an episode with your manager which was really positive?

Interestingly, the two kinds of questions often elicited quite different responses. In the personal and emotional framework, interviewees were less steered by the normative ideals of discourses. Hence, they would mention episodes of satisfaction which did not necessarily fit with the discourse which they preferred to understand themselves through. Several interviewees told me that they had been really pleased with episodes where the manager put them straight or acted authoritatively. Similarly, they told me that they were often frustrated if managers did not give them very clear instructions and direct them towards unambiguous goals. These bureaucratic values were normally sifted out of the more normative answers. In other words, by combining different types of questions, it was possible to capture the ambiguities of norms and practices in hierarchical interactions. Similarly, it was possible to see the dominant discursive trends while also having an eye on the many variations in individual practices.

Combining different kinds of questions also means that the interview approach cannot be neatly categorized into one of the three epistemological frameworks mentioned above. On the contrary, the compassionate interview actively combines types of questions associated with naturalism, emotionalism and localism, respectively. While purists may find this eclectic, the rationale behind such a combination is that it forces the researcher out of preconceived assumptions and epistemological comfort zones. While an emotionalist approach may yield a certain kind of response, the naturalist focus on categorizing and listing may yield another. The way in which these responses differ may actually represent valuable input for the researcher.

During the interview, the compassionate interviewer has an ideal about a certain kind of listening and engaging with the participant. It is through this form of listening that the integration between understanding and critique can come about. For this purpose, the interviewer can draw on techniques developed in marriage counseling which aim to engage the spouses with each other in a manner that defuses their habitual communicative patterns and prejudices (Hendrix et al., 2005). In other words, these techniques, called 'imago dialogue', serve to maximize the understanding of the counterpart's motives and stakes, yet without necessarily aiming for consensus or agreement in the end. In practice, this process of understanding is carried out by paying heed to three different elements in the communication: mirroring, validating and extending empathy. In the mirroring phase, the interlocutor attempts to repeat the message from the counterpart as loyally as possible, thus illustrating that it was perceived in the intended way, and if not, allowing for corrections. In order to move from a purely cognitive to a more compassionate mode, the exchange also needs to involve validation. According to Harville Hendrix (1996: 17), 'validation requires one to look through the eyes of the other, to see the world as it appears to him or her, and to understand the logic of the other's point of view'. However, and quite importantly, validation is not synonymous with agreeing! Validation simply means that one has 'asked for more' until the other person's perspective makes sense. It means 'Seeing the world through your eyes, I understand how you must experience it like that'. The final element in imago dialogues is to extend active empathy by offering comments such as 'I can imagine how sad you must have felt'. This element can be turned up or down in intensity when conducting a research interview, depending on the kind of rapport one aims at establishing with the interviewee. The point of paying heed to the three imago elements is to ensure that one captures ambiguities and complexities, rather than reproducing familiar subject positions. However, the compassionate interview is not exhausted by these techniques, which would make it more or less identical with the emotionalist approach. Rather, they are integrated with techniques from the two other perspectives. For example, from the naturalist approach one can employ the focus on extensive details about the 'natural world' of the interviewee. And from the localist approach one can use the sensitivity towards how discourses and structures are speaking through the subject. Altogether, these integrated forms of asking and listening allow us build criticism on the basis of understanding.

Let me give an example from my study of creative knowledge workers. The publishing house Booker (pseudonym), which was one of my cases, was undergoing a process of extensive restructuring and merger activity. This meant that new hierarchical constellations were established and the assignments of many employees were changing. During this time, I interviewed one of the experienced editors, Karen, for whom a new junior manager had just been appointed, and who had lost some of her old colleagues and gained some new ones. She told me that she was very frustrated with the process so far. In particular, she was displeased with the fact that a set of assignments seemed to have just 'landed on her desk' without any formal notification from her boss. She felt that this omission was a sign of disrespect and a breach of the rules about how to engage with each other hierarchically. Consequently, Karen more or less ignored the assignments, simply telling her boss that she was waiting for a proper introduction to them. I spent a considerable amount of effort trying to understand Karen's point of view in this conflict, including her norms about work, authority, distribution of tasks and so on. Then I followed my snowballing principle of recruitment and went on to interview the manager in question. Without making any explicit prompts about Karen, I ensured that the interview was directed towards the question about subordinates and possible conflicts. The manager soon brought up the relevant conflict and started giving her perspective on the issue. According to her, Karen was an example of a 'modern kind of employee' who lacks an autonomous sense of responsibility. Instead, she needs to be instructed in every little detail before she sets about her work.

As a critical researcher, it is tempting to analyze this situation as an example of exploitation: the manager gets away with pushing a boundaryless work model onto her subordinate, who in turn offers resistance by refusing to work unless she receives instructions. However, such an analytical plot does not live up to the ideals about multiple perspectives and ambiguity driving the compassionate approach. As I delved into the stories, frustrations and legitimations of these two people in conflict with one another, I reached a point where both versions made sense. It seemed to me that Karen interpreted the situation by drawing on bureaucratic norms about formality, clear task descriptions, and asymmetrical hierarchical relations. In this perspective, her manager did not live up to the requirements about explicit distribution of tasks and a quid pro quo renegotiation of Karen's work situation, now that she had received additional assignments. The manager, however, interpreted the situation by drawing on norms about self-management, autonomy and commitment. In this perspective, Karen did not live up to the requirements about showing initiative, ownership and independence. Interestingly, both Karen and the manager seemed to alternate between these two frameworks throughout the interview, depending on the situation they were describing. Apparently, both of them were trying to maximize the advantages of the frameworks while evading the costs. Strategic shifts of framework made such opportunistic maneuvering possible.

In this reading, both Karen and the manager are coping with the daily cross pressures and tensions of their working life by developing hybrid or opportunistic approaches to hierarchical interactions. Considering their situation, such strategies make sense. In turn, both parties feel recurring frustration, helplessness and disbelief as their counterpart acts inconsistently or unreliably. This kind of pattern seemed to repeat itself all the way up through the hierarchical ladder in both my case companies.

Having thus made sense of the individual actors, the next step is to take a critical look at the cultural trends and social structures which generate such patterns. This could be the combination of the current capitalistic focus on short-term growth and shareholder value combined with late modern narratives about individualism, self-realization and freedom through work. Together, they generate patterns of flexibility and optimization strategies which put pressure on moderation, prioritization, and consistency. However, the focus on ambiguity in compassionate analysis means that every subject position is seen as contributing to this pattern in some way or other. While there may be gross inequalities and injustices, there is often some kind of unholy alliance between the parties. In this case, many employees are fierce supporters of the late modern discourse about self-realization and flexibility, because it offers an enticing narrative about freedom without the need to prioritize. Also worth noting is that many managers feel instrumentalized by these demands from employees, because it becomes increasingly difficult to discuss work as a matter of assignments rather than personal development. In other words, the pattern cannot be explicated through neat subject positions of exploiting managers and exploited employees. However, exploitation does take place! Certain kinds of employees and certain kinds of managers become highly vulnerable in this system while others become skillful opportunists and networkers. But skillful opportunists and networkers experience other kinds of vulnerabilities, which the compassionate researcher should preferably capture and make sense of too.

Frustrations and challenges in the compassionate approach

Each methodological approach has its own set of potential pitfalls and challenges. This is also the case with compassionate interviewing. There are three such challenges which I would like to mention and exemplify: the failed alliance with an interviewee, the generation of material which is too sensitive to publish, and the inability to develop analytical narratives due to over-tolerance of ambiguity.

During fieldwork in a hi-tech corporation, I was exploring a drama in the management group caused by a highly unorthodox project manager. This project manager was a star employee in the company, generating both high sales and invaluable new concepts. However, he was an unpredictable player in the internal power game, establishing alliances and challenging the existing power structures to promote himself. In particular, he had attempted to take over responsibility for the overall strategy process, which had hitherto been run by the presales manager. During my exploration of the tense situation, I used the snowballing method of recruitment and talked to all the primary people affected by the maverick employee, not least the presales manager. From all of them, I elicited long, detailed stories. However, as the time came for an interview with the CEO, my interview techniques failed me. The CEO was extremely curt, speaking only in short primary clauses. All my prompts for more detailed stories failed. He would only offer brief, factual information and painted a picture of the management group as a well-functioning unit. My attempts to mirror and validate his perspective did not loosen up the conversation. As I grew increasingly frustrated, I grasped for every straw in the interview which might lead me towards the desired theme. When the CEO mentioned the strategy process and how the maverick employee was gaining more influence in this area, I asked: 'Is it correctly understood that the presales manager was responsible for the strategy process before?' The CEO affirmed this. 'And he is now perfectly happy with the new constellation?', I prompted, to which the CEO responded: 'I assume that he is, but it sounds from your question as if he is not?!' This obviously led to instant backpedalling from the interviewer. The rest of the exchange unfolded more like the CEO's cunning and systematic attempt to gauge what I as an interviewer had heard through the grapevine. Rather than successfully establishing a validating atmosphere which facilitated detailed accounts of personal perspectives, I was reduced to a defensive position in order to reveal as little as possible about my volatile insider information. In other words, this was an example of how the compassionate approach of trying to elicit multiple perspectives on the same precarious issue not only failed, but risked causing ethical problems.

Another example of challenges in the compassionate approach concerns data material which is too explosive to publish. During my fieldwork in a large media company, I soon discovered that there had been an intense conflict between a certain middle manager and a group developing science programs. Following my snowballing principle, I interviewed all the primary parties, and they needed little prompting before the detailed accounts started flowing. During these interviews, both parties made such harrowing remarks about each other and gave such an embittered version of the process that any future cooperation between them would be impossible, if this was published. As a researcher I was left with probably some of the best interview data in my entire career, showing the minute details of an intense psychological drama within the frameworks of self-management and creative knowledge work. However, it was ethically inconceivable that I could ever use it. I made several attempts at veiling and anonymizing the quotes, but either the participants were still recognizable, or the story lost its point and became superficial. The only feasible approach was to use the data as mere background material for my general analytical plot. In other words, when pursuing the intimate accounts of intense and precarious issues from all the key actors, one may end up intractably bogged down in ethical dilemmas. In these cases, I have always chosen to prioritize anonymity above research quality.

The final challenge which I would like to point out concerns the risk of 'losing the plot', so to speak, as a result of one's desire to acknowledge multiple perspectives. Generally speaking, one can say that a research process involves transforming information into knowledge through a systematic and theoretically informed reduction of complexity. The compassionate approach has a distinct inductive flavor, especially due to the focus on multiple perspectives, and it thus tends to generate detailed empirical material. The ensuing analytical process easily risks losing its momentum once all the perspectives have been recounted. Consequently, the result is more like a descriptive mosaic than an actual analytical plot. This is where the researcher must remind herself that distance is as essential as intimacy in the compassionate perspective. We are not taking over the perspectives of the research subjects, but using our respectful understanding of them as a platform for analytical distance and reduction of complexity.

Altogether, the analytical plot based on compassionate interviewing becomes a great deal messier and more confusing than naïve stories about win–win capitalism and moralizing stories about perpetrators and victims. However, if scrutinized with care, patience, and a high tolerance for ambiguity, data from compassionate interviews may provide the opportunity to construct analyses where each research subject makes sense and where the joys, sufferings and inequalities of the larger patterns become apparent.

The willingness to endure ambiguous data and plots requires of the interviewer that she does not feel attached to a certain identity as 'emancipator' or 'spokesperson of the weak'. Instead, she commits to an empirical world of gray zones where there are no neat moral subject positions for either researcher or research subjects. This requires a permanent attention to research reflexivity as the interviewer scrutinizes her own agenda and identity project in relation to the empirical study she undertakes.

Conclusion

In this chapter, I have presented an account of so-called compassionate interviewing. This form of interviewing is intended as a revised version of critical interviewing: it retains the ambition to point out suffering, yet it insists on the extensive attempt to make sense of every research subject in the process. This focus on multiple perspectives and tolerance of ambiguity is meant as a remedy to the risk in CMS of operating with preconceived subject positions and critical plots and of brandishing a default moralizing hammer. I name three key tensions which often face empirical researchers of a critical creed: the tension between respectful understanding and critique, between personal accounts and structural patterns, and between various epistemological frameworks. My claim is that the notion of compassion can help us maneuver in these tensions due to its high tolerance for ambiguity. Through a brief reading on key texts about compassion, I argue that the term offers integration of aspects which critical research often treats dualistically. This ambition about integration is then transferred into the key elements in the interview process in order to illustrate how it can be carried out in practice. The insistence on ambiguity and multiple perspectives involves a specific set of techniques throughout the interview process, including the definition of a research problem, the selection of participants, the phrasing of interview questions, the mode of listening, and the development of analytical plot. In each of these research phases, I try to show how the three sets of tensions named above can be integrated fruitfully rather than being polarized. My claim is that the analyses based on compassionate interviewing can yield critical plots which at the same time manage to make sense of every subject position and illustrate their ambiguities.

References

Adler, P., Forbes, L.C. and Willmott, H. (2007) 'Critical management studies', *Academy of Management Annals*, 1(1): 119–179.

Alvesson, M. (2003) 'Beyond neopositivists, romantics, and localists: A reflexive approach to interviews in organizational research', *Academy of Management Review*, 28(1): 13–33.

Alvesson, M. and Ashcraft, K. (2009) 'Critical methodology in management and organization research', in D. Buchanan and A. Bryman (eds), *The Sage Handbook of Organizational Research Methods*. London: Sage, pp. 61–77.

Alvesson, M. and Deetz, S. (2000) *Doing Critical Management Research*. London: Sage.

Alvesson, M. and Kärreman, D. (2007) 'Constructing mystery: Empirical matters in theory development', *Academy of Management Review*, 32(4): 1265–1281.

Aring, C.D. (1958) 'Sympathy and empathy', *Journal of American Medical Association*, 167(4): 448–452.

Barker, J. (1993) 'Tightening the iron cage: Concertive control in self-managing teams', *Administrative Science Quarterly*, 38(3): 408–437.

Brewis, J. and Wray-Bliss, E. (2008) 'Re-searching ethics: Towards a more reflexive critical management studies', *Organization Studies*, 29(12): 1521–1540.

Clifford, J. and Marcus, G. (eds) (1986) *Writing Culture: The Poetics and Politics of Ethnography*. Berkeley: University of California Press.

Dalai Lama and Cutler, H.C. (1998) *The Art of Happiness*. London: Coronet.

Denzin, L. and Lincoln, Y. (2007) *The Landscape of Qualitative Research*. London: Sage.

Fournier, V. and Grey, C. (2000) 'At the critical moment: Conditions and prospects for critical management studies', *Human Relations*, 53(1): 7–32.

Gubrium, J.F. and Holstein, J.A. (1997) *The New Language of Qualitative Methods*. Oxford: Oxford University Press.

Hendrix, H. (1996) 'The evolution of imago relationship therapy: A personal and professional journey', *Journal of Imago Relationship Therapy*, 1(1): 1–17.

Hendrix, H., Hunt, H.L., Hannah, M.T. and Luquet, W. (eds) (2005) *Imago Relationship Therapy: Perspectives on Theory*. San Francisco: Jossey-Bass.

Holstein, J.A. and Gubrium, J.F. (2004) 'The active interview', in D. Silverman (ed.), *Qualitative Research: Theory, Method and Practice*. London: Sage.

Jensen, T.E. (2005) 'Aktør-netværksteori – Latours, Callons og Laws materielle semiotic', in A. Esmark, C.B. Laustsen and N.Å. Andersen (eds), *Socialkonstruktivistiske Analysestrategier*. Roskilde: Roskilde Universitetsforlag.

Kvale, S. (2006) *InterView – En introduktion til det kvalitative forskningsinterview*. Copenhagen: Hans Reitzels Forlag.

Legge, K. (2001) 'Silver bullet or spent round? Assessing the meaning of the "high commitment management"/performance relationship', in J. Storey (ed.), *Human Resource Management – A Critical Text* (2nd edn). London: Thomson Learning.

Lévinas, E. (1991) *Totality and Infinity – Essays on Exteriority*. Dordrecht: Kluwer Academic.

Løgstrup, K.E. (1956) *Den etiske fordring*. Copenhagen: Gyldendal.

Marcus, G.E. (1995) 'Ethnography in/of the world system: The emergence of multi-sited ethnography', *Annual Review of Anthropology*, 24: 95–117.

Reedy, P. (2008) 'Mirror, mirror, on the wall: Reflecting on the ethics and effects of a collective critical management studies identity project', *Management Learning*, 39(1): 57–72.

Ricoeur, P. (1992) *Oneself as Another*. Chicago: University of Chicago Press.

Spradley, J.P. (1979) *The Ethnographic Interview*. New York: Holt, Rinehart and Winston.

Wray-Bliss, E. (2002) 'Abstract ethics, embodied ethics: The strange marriage of Foucault and positivism in labor process theory', *Organization*, 9(1): 5–39.

Wray-Bliss, E. (2003) 'Research subjects/research subjections: Exploring the ethics and politics of critical research', *Organization*, 10(2): 307–325.

EIGHT

Critical netnography: Conducting critical research online

Jon Bertilsson

Introduction

The proliferation and establishment of the internet as a (new) medium of communication has generated increased possibilities for people and organizations not only to share and obtain information, but also to interact and socialize with each other unhindered by geographical and physical distance. The internet, and the subsequent development of various forms of social media vehicles such as blogs, chat rooms, forums, Twitter and Facebook, have provided communicative platforms where people can interact in real time, enabling them to jointly discuss important aspects of society and their everyday lives. It allows people to form far-reaching networks, virtual cultures and communities centring on those everyday life issues and interests (Bertilsson, 2009). The development of Web 2.0 and social media simultaneously has therefore opened up new opportunities for researchers to collect and analyse data on social interactions, the creation and maintenance of (virtual) cultures, hierarchies, power, status, identity, attitudes and existing social discourses.

In order to capitalize on the emerging research opportunities stemming from the proliferation of internet communications and social media vehicles, the consumer researcher Robert Kozinets developed a method at the end of the 1990s, which is referred to as *netnography*. It is specifically designed to investigate consumer behaviour of cultures and communities existing on the internet, and it provides valuable guidelines and advice to researchers for how to conduct trustworthy and rigorous research online (Kozinets, 2002). However, what is argued here is that the method has a much wider potential than merely being used to study consumer behaviour and consumption communities online. Its potential stretches beyond the field of consumer research, and may with great benefit be used to study phenomena in other research disciplines within the social sciences such as social interaction, hierarchies, power, status, identity and discourse – phenomena that are more commonly associated with the domain of critical management studies. It may thus fruitfully be used to study the practices of organizing, be it the (self) organization of online communities or the traditional organization of public or business corporations.

In this chapter I will describe and illustrate an additional version of netnography, which I refer to as 'critical netnography'. Instead of merely striving to generate a written account or story coming from fieldwork with the aim of investigating the (consumption) communities and cultures emerging from online internet-based communications, critical netnography directs its attention in particular to uncovering and conceptualizing the various forms of domination, asymmetry, hierarchy, conflicts, discourses and status positions prevalent in internet-based communications of both online consumption communities and more established forms of organizations. A critical netnography could then be used by critical management researchers to reveal the existence and reproduction of the underlying hierarchies, strategies of domination and power asymmetries being hidden and/or embedded in regular organizational communication, and in that way identify and give voice to the weak or marginalized members of organizations. However, since the critical version of netnography is a development from its original predecessor, it is impossible not to make strong reference to and describe the original version in my discussion of the research procedures of critical netnography.

The overall aim of this chapter is to provide critical scholars with insightful reflections regarding the conduct of systematic and trustworthy critical research online so that common methodological pitfalls may be avoided. I will start by giving a more detailed description of the ethnographic method and the main principles for conducting rigorous and trustworthy research online. I will then provide an empirical example of how a critical netnography may be conducted, which involves the analysis of text-based interactions of an online forum centring on the interest of fashion and clothing. The chapter concludes with a discussion on the strengths, weaknesses and challenges of this method.

What is netnography?

As previously stated, the method of netnography was developed in order to capitalize on the research potential emanating from internet-based communication, providing researchers with proper methodological procedures for how to conduct trustworthy, credible and rigorous research online. Netnography is often referred to as an interpretive and qualitative method inspired by social anthropological and ethnographic research techniques that has been adapted to online settings and conditions (Kozinets, 1998). It involves participant-observational research grounded in fieldwork conducted in online milieux. It makes use of computer-mediated, often interactional, communications as a source for data collection to arrive at an ethnographic understanding and representation of communal, social and cultural phenomena, in both offline and online settings.

Being inspired by conventional ethnography, netnography naturally shares several characteristics with the ethnographic method. As with most conventional ethnographies, it often includes other and complementary research methods such as interviews (online and offline), archival data collection (documents), descriptive statistics, videographical projective techniques, extended historical case analysis, semiotic analysis, discourse analysis, in addition to an array of other techniques (Kozinets, 2010). Like ethnography, netnography also has an inbuilt and essential flexibility to deal with the naturalistic character of the setting and actors being studied. This means that netnography, like ethnography, involves the undertaking of an immersive, long-lasting engagement in and with the constituents and members of a community or culture, followed by an effort to understand, represent and convey their reality through nuanced, detailed, thick and culturally based description and interpretation (see Geertz, 1973). This requires from netnography (as from ethnography) legitimacy and the trust of its constituents through shared, detailed, trustworthy, and rigorous research practices (Kozinets, 2010).

Although ethnography and netnography have much in common, there are some differences that need to be acknowledged. Kozinets (2002) argues that netnographies are less time-consuming and resource-intensive concerning the choice of field sites, moving and travelling to and between those sites, arranging meetings and introductions, and transcribing fieldwork notes or data. Much of the data is already in written form when it is collected from various social networks or forums online, which substantially reduces the time researchers normally spend on transcribing field notes and interviews. In addition, as netnographies often involve the collection of data from publicly available online forums and as the researcher may adopt a complete observer position, it has the capacity to be carried out completely unobtrusively, that is, without the researcher's presence and the detrimental influence it may have on the research situation and the data being collected. Consequently, netnography may be used to capture informants' 'naturally occurring talk and interactions' – a potential that ordinary ethnography seems to lack (Bertilsson, 2009). Conversely, a potential that ethnographies do have, which netnographies simultaneously lack, is the capacity to actually observe, meet and talk to people face-to-face, in person, and in real life, thereby being able to capture bodily expressions and body language. Instead of focusing on the differences between the methods, however, a more fruitful approach is to regard netnography as a methodological extension of ethnography, where a combination of the two methods together productively may shed light on issues and phenomena within the social sciences.

A critical netnography of a teenage online community

Before moving further into the empirical example of a critical netnography, it is important to acknowledge that doing research at online sites requires the same demand for rigour, trustworthiness, and ethical consideration as with other traditional offline research and methods. Therefore carrying out research on the internet and on social media vehicles implies more than merely downloading a couple of postings and doing a swift analysis. Instead it entails a systematic collection of a substantial amount of text and images, and a diligent analysis grounded in theoretical models or constructs in combination with insightful interpretations, and it should be emphasized that anything does not go.

The netnographic example presented here is greatly influenced by the methodological procedure developed by Robert Kozinets's (1998, 2002, 2010) continuous work on netnography. His ethnographically inspired methodological procedure provides valuable guidelines on how to conduct such systematic, rigorous and trustworthy research online, and is applicable and helpful both for the complete observer and complete participant version of netnographic research. The research procedure involves five main steps: (1) definition of research questions, object of study, or topics to investigate; (2) site or community identification and selection; (3) site or community participant observation (immersion and degree of engagement) and collection of data (ensuring ethical procedures); (4) data analysis and iterative interpretation of findings; (5) writing, presenting and reporting research findings and/or theoretical and/or policy implications. All steps are equally important and all present different challenges. The researcher needs to cope with and handle such challenges if the research is to withstand the same scientific scrutiny as all other offline research. In the forthcoming empirical examples I will mainly treat and discuss the first four steps in more depth.

Defining the research questions and the object of study

Although netnography has been used to study research topics outside the marketing and management fields, such as the sensitive topic of cosmetic surgery (Langer and Beckman, 2005), and how children communicate around and make sense of their illnesses (Eysenbach and Till, 2007), it has predominantly been employed to answer research questions within the consumption field, for example on consumers' behaviour in online coffee communities (Kozinets, 2002), the *X-Files* subculture of consumption (Kozinets, 1997), the meanings of *Star Trek*'s culture of consumption (Kozinets, 2001), the negotiation of personal identities in brand communities in cyberspace (Schau and Muñiz, 2002), the formation and perpetuation of brand communities (Muñiz and O'Guinn, 2001), and consumers' learning and education playing out in online information sites of consumer education (Sandlin, 2007). The studies previously referred to have indeed shed light on crucial elements of consumer culture, that is, the local and temporal social/communal aggregations that constitute, as it were, the very spine of consumer society. However, the anthropological and structuralist underpinnings of that research stream tend to hide the social, symbolic and discursive processes through which various types of communities are locally produced, by and in-between its members in their micro-level interactions. Consequently, the a priori pre-existence of a harmonious and unproblematic social order structuring the social relations and interactions has been overemphasized at the expense of conflict, tensions, the reproduction of hierarchical order, and status positions. What has been lacking in prior studies of online communities is therefore a critical but micro-interactionist approach that can capture and uncover such conflicts, tensions and hierarchical relationships, as these are equally important to our overall understanding of the functioning of online consumption (and other) communities. The purpose of my netnographic study was therefore to bring in a more critical view on the creation, organization and perpetuation of such communities. The intention was to uncover how online consumption community order, hierarchy and status positions are maintained, defended and reproduced on a micro-interactionist and micro-discursive level. This purpose led me to pose the following research questions: In what way are community order and hierarchy accomplished in the members' micro-level interactions? What kind of conflicts and tensions exist in the online community, and how are these handled by its members?

Community/site identification and selection

The next important step in the netnographic research process is to search for, identify and choose online communities or sites appropriate for the intended research. Online sites that fit the research questions and that serve as good illustrations of the phenomenon under study ought to be selected (see Kozinets, 2002, 2010). However, although this may sound natural enough – a methodological truism[1] – it often proves to be quite a challenging task. How does one, in practice, actually handle and live up to such methodological wisdoms, particularly when doing research online?

One way to go about it is to ask oneself a number of fairly basic questions, the answers to which subsequently provide one with valuable guidance. The questions that primarily guided me in my search for and selection of appropriate online community sites were: Which informants might be particularly prone to substantially discuss consumption issues in communal online settings? On which community

---

[1]The character of the research questions is what should guide the appropriate choice of method, which in turn is supposed to generate the type of data that in the end may enable the researcher to credibly and trustworthily answer those research questions (see Silverman, 2001; Alvesson and Sköldberg, 2009).

sites might these informants primarily be found, and where could those sites be located? How rich are the interactions taking place and, subsequently, the data that could be collected from those online interactions, and does the empirical material substantially deal with what you are trying to study and conceptualize? While the first three questions mainly deal with the issue of scanning the online environment, trying to identify a manageable number of relevant online site alternatives, the latter questions deal more with actually choosing the best research site given your research questions.

Teenagers (as potential informants) are often considered as fairly unsure individuals who are avidly striving to become adults and find out who they really are. Consumption, fashion and brands seem to constitute important resources for the often intensive self-image and self-identity construction process (see La Ferle et al., 2001). In such teenage identity-seeking processes, fitting in with peers and conforming to social norms often needs to be balanced with the requirement of expressing individuality. Brand symbols are often brought into play to handle that balancing act, largely because brands (or other forms of symbolic consumption) can be used to symbolize the relation between an individual person and the social group s/he wants to belong to and gain acceptance from. However, if the teenagers are to conduct their identity and image construction competently, in the eyes of both themselves and their peers, they need to gain knowledge and understanding of the meaning of the numerous existing and relevant consumption and brand symbols existing in consumption society. It is not enough for a teenager to love a certain brand and its meanings, s/he still needs and wants approval and confirmation from peers (Elliott and Percy, 2007). Such knowledge, approval and confirmation is extensively obtained in their teenage peer interactions centring on important consumption issues – interactions that are particularly lively and rich in nature. I therefore decided to choose teenagers as my group of informants; and since teenagers nowadays to a large extent interact with each other via various forms of social media, I started pursuing typical teenage online communities.

As there are a wide range of different but discernible types of online sites and communities to choose from, the task of identifying and selecting sites may be experienced as a quite demanding task. Kozinets (1999, 2010) mentions forums, chat rooms and dungeons, playspaces, virtual worlds such as Second Life, web-rings and listservs as eligible types of online research sites. In light of the more recent development in cyberspace, however, he also adds blogs, wikis (e.g. Wikipedia), audiovisual sites (sharing and commenting on audiovisual and photographical material such as on YouTube and Flickr), and social content aggregators (designed to help individuals communally to share and discover online content, e.g. StumbleUpon) to that list of potential online research sites.

What made the identification and selection process somewhat easier for the study at hand was that it was conducted in a Swedish context, narrowing down the scope of the site search quite substantially. At the time of the study there existed two main and dominating web communities for teenagers (13–20-year-olds) in Sweden,

Lunarstorm and *Hamsterpaj*. Both websites had many members, and offered the members a diverse range of activities to engage in and exciting rooms (photo gallery, web radio, film clips, online data games, chat, etc.) or spaces to enter. More importantly, however, there were forum sections where teenagers could interact and discuss important life topics. Forums (text-based interactions organized around particular shared interests and orientations) are, according to Kozinets (2010), the oldest and richest form of online community, and their character has the important advantage of enabling the researcher to capture ongoing, intense and fertile interactions between different internet users and community members. The existence of forum sections on the two web communities therefore enabled me to actually capture rich micro-level interactions and thus the tensions, conflicts and hierarchies prevalent in an online community setting.

The real challenge then became to select one of the two communities as the main and sole empirical online site on which to focus. In the face of that challenge I found it fruitful to make use of the criteria developed by Kozinets (2002) – criteria that serves to help the researcher to evaluate and pick out the most suitable online site for the investigation at hand. He suggests that principally online communities should be preferred that have: (1) a focused and, for the research question, relevant topic, segment or group; (2) a high level of 'traffic' of postings; (3) a greater number of members or message posters; (4) more descriptively and detailed rich data; and (5) significant between-member interactions of the sort required by the research questions. Applying these criteria on the two web communities, it soon became clear that Hamsterpaj had a much higher traffic of postings. It had more community members (around 300,000), a greater degree of between-member interactions where tensions, conflicts and hierarchy clearly emerged, and richer and more detailed data. The interactions and discussions at Hamsterpaj also turned out to be lengthier, more substantial, eloquent and intensive than at Lunarstorm. I therefore chose Hamsterpaj as the sole online community on which to focus.

Community (non-)participation and data collection

Having chosen the most appropriate online community for the research, it is then necessary to decide on what type of role the researcher should assume when performing the netnographic study. This is important as it has implications for how the empirical material subsequently is collected, what type of empirical material is gathered, and the discussion around research ethics online. It is common to discriminate between two major but different types of netnography. One is referred to as a full participant observation, where the researcher adopts a complete participant role and becomes a full and active member of the online community being researched. The other main type is often referred to as a complete unobtrusive netnography. Here the researcher adopts a complete observer role and performs a passive analysis of the community. Both approaches have their individual strengths and weaknesses, and some authors may prefer the one over the other. Langer and Beckman (2005) have argued, for example, that unobtrusive and passive studies are desirable since they allow for the analysis of sensitive content (conflicts, tensions, hierarchy and status are often perceived as fairly sensitive content), the collection and analysis of naturally occurring talk, and the avoidance of researchers affecting the data material being generated. Conversely, Kozinets (2010) has argued that the exclusion of the participative role removes profound cultural knowledge and experiences, leading the netnographer to engage in guesswork on cultural meanings and processes that s/he cannot completely capture and grasp via a complete observation. Ultimately this may lead to the production of a superficial and descriptive analysis.

I decided fairly early on in the research process to use a completely unobtrusive netnography[2] and to assume the role of a complete observer. I therefore refrained from becoming a real cultural member (I did not register as a member on the site), posting comments on the forum, and becoming an active individual inside the community. There were three main reasons for choosing such a completely unobtrusive approach in my critical netnography.

Firstly, my opinion is that capturing naturally occurring talk has great, even unique value per se, and it offers an opportunity that very few research methods can. It would be a pity not to capitalize on such an opportunity. As a consequence, I could not make use of additional research techniques commonly used within a participant-observation netnographic approach such as interviews, e-mail interviews, instant message interviews or chats, to communicate with the members. Irrespective of the choice of approach, however, the researcher has the obligation to learn as much as possible about the community, its participants and the cultural context in order to make a thick description of it, thereby ensuring that an informed and trustworthy analysis of what is going on at the online site is being carried out. I therefore I spent about 2–3 months simply 'hanging out' at the site to gain as a rich and contextualized understanding of the site and the forum as possible.

As the data collection proceeded, it became clear that the challenge for the study at hand lay not in the generation of rich data, but rather in how to limit the amount of it. The choice therefore was between what data to keep for further analysis and interpretation (in light of the purpose of the study), and what data to discard as less relevant. In order to simplify that process, I made a first initial scan in which I filtered out interactions and topics that were not within the focus of the study. I then started to collect what Kozinets (2010) refers to as the archival data. This is data that the researcher copies or downloads from (pre-)existing computer-generated communications at online sites and communities – data that the researcher is not immediately involved in prompting or constructing. I stopped collecting data material when

---

[2]Complete unobtrusive netnographies do not always have to be critical. Researchers may well use unobtrusive versions of netnographies with a different approach and with a different purpose.

I experienced a saturation effect, that is, when the same or a similar type of content appears in the material over and over again, and nothing new of significance seems to come up. The empirical material was pre-dominantly textual, with a lesser amount of pictures. The year-long complete observation of the Hamsterpaj forum resulted in the collection of 46 discussion threads of various lengths, consisting of some 6,370 postings or comments made by approximately 1,650 different users/individuals.

The second main reason for carrying out a complete observational and unobtrusive netnography was that since such an approach is well suited to investigating and capturing more sensitive content (see Langer and Beckman, 2005), such as conflicts, tensions, hierarchy and status, it fitted well with the purpose of the overall study. In addition, an unobtrusive approach involving a complete observation position enables the researcher to balance more easily his/her required analytical and reflexive distance with the closeness needed to produce a rich and trustworthy description of the community under study.

The third main reason relates to the ethical difficulties and complexities associated with doing research online in general, where choosing an unobtrusive approach enables the researcher to avoid some of those difficulties. What makes online research challenging or difficult from an ethical perspective is that there is yet no clear consensus among researchers on the proper ethical guidelines for conducting online research. The debate regarding proper ethical guidelines has, according to Kozinets (2010), centred on two contestable but important interrelated ethical issues: Are online forums and communities to be considered private or public sites? And what constitutes informed consent online? In order for the researcher to realize when informed consent is needed from the informants, he/she must thus first decide whether the postings on an internet site or community are 'public' or 'private' communications.

Eysenbach and Till (2001) have provided three measures that can be used to estimate the perceived level of privacy of an online site. Firstly, if a site or a community requires some form of registration or subscription to gain access to a discussion group, a majority of the subscribers are likely to consider the site or forum a 'private place' in cyberspace. Secondly, the number of members of a community indicates how public the site is perceived to be. The more members there are the more public the space is seen. Finally, and perhaps most importantly, a community's norms, codes, aims (often represented in the type of research question asked and the topics discussed), and target audience largely affect the perceived privacy of a site or community online. Since the Hamsterpaj community at the time of the data collection had about 300,000 members, since people were not required to register in order to observe the ongoing interactions, since the topics being discussed were not judged to be of a sensitive nature, and given my intention to carry out an entirely unobtrusive study, I concluded that the Hamsterpaj site was a public space and that informed consent was not therefore needed. My conclusion is supported by the arguments put forward by Sudweeks and Rafaeli (1995) who consider informed consent to be integrated in the act of posting a message on a public site, and provided that the researchers anonymize the informants, no informed consent is needed. It also gains support from Eysenback and Till's (2001) view that if the researcher conducts a passive analysis and unobtrusive research of retrospectively posted messages on communities, the demand for informed consent may be waived. With the ambition to live up to the ethical guidelines for an unobtrusive netnography, I therefore anonymized the members' identities, and to be on the safe side, I gained informed consent from the founder and the editor of the Hamsterpaj community.

It is important to acknowledge, however, that in spite of all the efforts being made by the researcher to conduct this type of unobtrusive online study with a high ethical standard, one cannot be completely sure that all the informants would perceive the research process accordingly – unless informed consent is obtained from all the research subjects. Just because an online community or website is highly public does not automatically mean that all of the people participating expect or desire to be a part of a scientific study. It is therefore imperative that researchers, prior to a planned unobtrusive critical netnography, both deeply reflect upon and work out a strategy for handling the ethical complexity of the study. As it was impossible to gain informed consent from all of the research subjects in my study of Hamsterpaj, I decided to conduct a passive analysis, to provide the community members with anonymity, and to obtain informed consent from the founder and editor of the website, in order to perform the study as ethically appropriate as possible. It should also be pointed out that it was the text-based interactions, thus the speech acts, and their content that was in focus and of interest, and not the identities and characteristics of the different community members. The fact that the website was a highly public place where the users knew that they were being watched by others (they even seemed to make a point out of it), together with the fact that the topics being discussed at the site were not of a sensitive or private nature, were also important factors that affected my decision to proceed with an unobtrusive critical netnography.

Analysis and interpretation

The most commonly used analytical procedure within netnographic research is the hermeneutic procedure or circle, in which the iteration between the part and the whole of the text reveals the underlying but coherent and non-contradictory meaning of qualitative data (Thompson et al., 1989, 1994; Thompson, 1997). However, the hermeneutic procedure strives to reveal underlying but non-contradictory meanings, while my intention was quite the opposite, to capture, reveal and emphasize tensions, conflicts and asymmetries in micro-interactions. I therefore adopted a more critically oriented type of analytical approach in order to analyse systematically the interactional and text-based empirical material – an approach consisting of a combination of the tenets of critical discourse analysis and tenets from micro-sociology. More specifically, the tools offered by critical discourse analysis helped me to make sense of the discursive strategies members employed to create and maintain hegemonic and asymmetrical relationships, while the micro-sociological approach helped me to analyse how the discursive acts being used in the micro-interactions actually contribute to forming and reproducing a social structure and reality for the community members.

To embrace a critical stance towards the accomplishment of community, I firstly tried to conceive of the Hamsterpaj community through the metaphor of a 'power struggle'. This helped me to regard and understand communities in a different way compared to previous conceptions of online communities from consumer research. It also enabled me, more specifically, to direct my attention to and to observe central and typical aspects of power struggle, such as conflicts, hierarchies, status positions, and the (re)production of order/disorder. Secondly, I brought in explicit theoretical concepts not only in order to be able to make reflexive and informed interpretations of the empirical material, but also because theory helps the researcher, on a more general level, to avoid first-hand and naïve interpretations of the existing empirical material (Alvesson and Sköldberg, 2009; Alvesson and Deetz, 2000).

In order to be able to make such reflexive and critical interpretations I included Bourdieu's concepts of 'language as symbolic violence' and 'social reproduction' (see Bourdieu and Wacquant, 1992; Bourdieu, 1991). Bourdieu uses these concepts to explain dominance and hegemony (particularly masculine dominance). Symbolic violence is a mild/soft and misrecognized type of violence that is practised in a pure symbolic way, through communication and through knowledge. This quiet and soft symbolic violence thus pertains to a violence that does not have to be very clear or obvious, even if it sometimes is. Its softness or mildness lies in its naturalness and self-evidential nature. It is a part of the taken-for-granted order: 'this is just the way it is'. The mildness, naturalness and self-evidence of the symbolic violence are thus what reproduce the taken-for-granted order of dominance. It should, however, be clarified that the concepts borrowed from Bourdieu are not used here in a strict sense but more as sensitizing concepts to inspire the analytical interpretations and to direct attention to interesting and relevant themes which somehow relate to conflicts, hierarchies, status positions and the accomplishment of order.

The reproduction of community hierarchy and order

The year-long observation of the online community clearly illustrated that the Hamsterpaj site displays a rather formalized social structure and hierarchy where certain members retain certain status positions, which are concretized in formal titles. These members have various degrees of authority and power ascribed to their role and title, which may be used to affect the discussions playing out between the members of the community. The members seemed to be very familiar with this hierarchical order and ranking system. The member with the highest formal title and status position was the founder of the entire website and community. The second highest formal status position is held by the administrators. They are responsible for various sections of the community such the forum part (one of the administrators may also at the same time be responsible for the maintenance of the entire site and is then titled 'System Operator' or 'SysOp'). These members have the authority and power to issue directions, restrictions and rules on how people should behave/interact/discuss in the community forum. Third in the hierarchical order are the guards of order. They could be seen as a type of middle manager with the main task of ensuring that the rules set up by SysOps and administrators are enforced and executed. They have the power and authority to lock discussion threads that are considered to be unproductive and slide away from the main topic of the thread. They even have the authority to boot people off the forum if they refuse to follow its rules and guidelines, which is a task that administrators also may perform if necessary. Fourth in the hierarchical order are the assistants. Their task is both to encourage members to stay on the topic being discussed in the thread, and to provide 'newbies' and ordinary members with advice and guidance on how to behave on the forum so that they understand and follow the established rules of interaction. At the bottom of the status hierarchy are the ordinary users who do not have any formal power to affect the interactions and discussions taking place. More experienced ordinary users sometimes also engage in the similar activities of encouraging and helping normally performed by assistants. The different members' formal title and status position is clearly visible on their forum avatar, together with their name, where they allegedly live, their alleged age, and the number of comments they have posted on the forum.

Surprisingly, this social hierarchy and the relations of dominance and power are already integrated in the way the forum and the community is constructed – in its infrastructure. What is perhaps even more surprising, and at the same time interesting, is that this hierarchical order seems to be experienced as legitimate by the members interacting on the forum: 'it is just there, and that is the way it is'. However, this does not automatically imply that there are no conflicts and tensions between members with different status positions as they interact and discuss various relevant topics around fashion, clothing and brands. Ironically, it is in the emergence of these tensions and conflicts that the order, hierarchy, and dominance of the community become most obvious to the observer. This is illustrated in the forthcoming interaction between the lower-ranking assistant 'Knight' and the two high-ranking administrators 'Rock' and 'Number One'. 'Knight' posts recalcitrant comments, creating tensions and conflicts in a discussion thread on the community that deals with the relationship between the price and quality of name brands. 'Rock' and 'Number One' interfere to put 'Knight' straight, to educate him on the proper view and to restore order in the emergent conflict, which is done by making use of their powerful positions and the symbolic violence they have at their disposal.

Knight (assistant):

I paid 150 kronor for my new pants, it turned out to be my best deal ever. Comfortable, nice and durable. You only pay for the brand, just look at Nike and other similar brands, their clothes are sooo expensive, but have pretty much the same quality as other clothes that are 100 kronor cheaper.

Rock (administrator):

Jeans involves much more than what you bring up. Things that no-name brands can't give you.

Knight (assistant):

Sure why don't you believe in that and I will believe in whatever I want. Instead of buying a pair for 1800 I can buy 7 pairs that are as nice and comfortable for the same amount of money.

Rock (administrator):

Believe? What do you mean, believe? That's just the way it is. You have no idea of how many factors that really have an effect on price and quality. That you then lack the necessary knowledge to recognize that is another story. It's also clear that your ignorance shapes your opinion, but to argue against those who know is just stupid. It is like claiming that Mazda and Ferrari are the same shit. The Mazda looks alright, it's also comfortable, and it runs faster than the speed limits. Is that the same thing? No. And if you believe that you always only pay for the brand itself, you're nothing but naïve.

Knight (assistant):

I never said that it is ALWAYS like that. But expensive is overrated, and I don't think you should call anyone ignorant, just like that. If I have found a nice and comfortable pair of jeans for 150, 450 or 1000 kronor, it really doesn't matter which ones I bought, right? I found a nice and comfortable pair of jeans and I bought them. I therefore think that expensive is overrated. End of story!

Rock (administrator):

Why shouldn't I call you ignorant when you obviously are?

I couldn't help noticing that you play the guitar so let's apply your logic on guitars:

I bought a guitar for 95 kronor. It's awesome and beautiful, it has six strings and it works well to play on. Claiming that a Fender is better is just ridiculous because expensive brands are just overrated.

Knight (assistant):

If you buy a guitar for 95 kronor you have no one else to blame but yourself.

Rock (administrator)

If you buy a pair of Jeans for 150 kronor you have no one else to blame but yourself.

Don't you realize that you're just stubborn and ignorant? In addition you're most welcome to answer the question I posed in my previous posting.

Number One (SysOp/administrator):

Knight! That is exactly what we say if you buy a pair jeans for 200 kronor (unless they are not on sale).

We like jeans, you like guitars, we know jeans, you know guitars, we don't know guitars, and you don't know jeans.

As the assistant 'Knight' put forward his idea and view concerning higher-priced name brands, arguing that they overcharge for their products and that the high price is not at all reflected in a corresponding quality, he attracts the attention from the high-status members of the forum, 'Rock' and 'Number One'. To him it appears as irrational or even stupid to pay a high price for a brand when there is a weak correspondence to the functional quality of the physical product. He uses the price–quality ratio as way to show the absurdity of paying so much money just because it has a certain brand name on it. One could, from his perspective, get several additional pairs of jeans for the same amount of money. When 'Knight' puts forward his view he draws upon the consumption discourses of a modernistic consumer culture where the rationality in consumer purchase decisions is defined by time and resource allocations, costs and benefits (see Firat and Shultz, 1997). It is the functional quality of the physical good in relation to its price that is considered crucial, rather than, as in a postmodern consumer culture, the quality of the brand's symbolic meanings, and what it communicates to other consumers (Holt, 2002). However, as fashion (clothing) and name brand aficionados, the high-status members, 'Rock' and 'Number One', cannot let such a critical view just slip by. It has to be firmly countered because it attacks the area of their interest and expertise (even deeming it as irrational and stupid), and thereby their authority as highly titled members and the power hierarchy as such.

In order to defend and reproduce themselves as status members and the existing hierarchical order 'Rock' (and to some extent 'Number One') start to exercise the mainstay of what Bourdieu calls symbolic violence – pedagogical action (Jenkins, 2002). Firstly, 'Rock' discredits the competence and knowledge of 'Knight' by claiming that he fails to recognize the true nature of the name brand phenomenon since he lacks the proper interest in and knowledge of all its complexities. It has nothing to do with what 'one believes'. One has to be a competent expert and knowledgeable of all the complexities (for example, concerning the design, quality and manufacturing process) regarding name brands in order to put forward a credible view. As 'Knight' is considered to have neither an interest nor expertise ('Why can't I call you ignorant when you obviously are?'), he therefore lacks the ability to appreciate the complexity and value of name brands and has no right to make such strong claims regarding those types of brands. Secondly, 'Rock' uses an example from one of 'Knight's' favourite areas, guitars, to illustrate the absurdity in his reasoning concerning name brands, their price and (functional) quality. 'Rock' educates 'Knight' in the proper way of thinking regarding name brands by rejecting his ideas as wrong, absurd, and illegitimate. He exerts a type of discursive censorship, which according to Bourdieu is one of the most effective modes of pedagogical action practised to reproduce uneven cultural capital and an uneven social structure. 'Number One' makes this really clear in the last posting where he states that as 'Knight' lacks legitimate expertise regarding fashion and name brands (and it is of course status members such as 'Rock' and 'Number One' who decide the ideas and knowledge that are legitimate and credible) he has no right to put forward those kinds of ideas – in precisely the same way as

'Number One' and 'Rock' do not have the legitimacy to put forward correspondingly absurd ideas regarding guitars as they lack expertise within that particular area.

The preceding empirical quotes and the subsequent interpretations, however, merely constitute one of several examples and ways in which hierarchy and asymmetry are created and maintained in the micro-interactions at the Hamsterpaj online community. Unfortunately, space considerations preclude an empirical illustration of all these examples. On some occasions this hierarchical order is maintained through the ordinary and lower-ranking members' consent to the existence of a hierarchy per se – both explicitly acknowledging and accepting it. In some instances the power asymmetry is manifested in the low-status members' 'sucking up' to the high-status members. This is commonly illustrated when these members heap exaggerated praise on ideas, views and knowledge put forward by high-status members, although these views and ideas are ordinary, rudimentary and common/obvious to everyone in the community. However, perhaps the most striking example of hierarchy and power asymmetry on the Hamsterpaj community is expressed in the quietest form of symbolic violence – the complete silence sometimes greeting comments posted by low-ranking members. Being completely and silently ignored is paradoxically a very clear sign of one's insignificant position. Although 'Knight' was 'educated' by high-status members through the exertion of pedagogical actions and symbolic violence, the status members at least acknowledged his existence and his views. He was not met with complete silence – perhaps because he, at least, was in possession of the title 'assistant'.

Concluding discussion

Inspired by Kozinets's five-step methodological procedure for netnographies, I have tried in this chapter to illustrate how a critical and complete unobtrusive netnography may be employed as a plausible and credible method to conduct research at/on online sites by critical management scholars. Although the previous example of a critical netnography was conducted within the field of consumer research to unravel the reproduction of an online consumption community order and hierarchy on a micro-discursive level, I would argue that a similar methodological approach may be used to study hierarchy, power asymmetries, inequalities and the production of order, as practices of organizing, within social aggregations and organizations outside the consumption sphere. It could therefore serve as a viable tool for those who see themselves as critical management scholars and strive to uncover forms of domination and exploitation embedded in organizational communication, in order to acknowledge, illuminate or give voice to the less powerful and marginalized organizational members.

A critical netnography may be conducted separately and on its own merits. However, due to its limitations of not enabling the researcher to actually meet and interact with people in person, or just to observe human behaviour and body language in real life, its full potential would probably only be reached if it were combined with a traditional critical ethnography, and integrated in a larger offline–online methodological approach. In addition, since both consumption communities and other forms of social aggregations and organizations often exist in both offline and online settings, such a combined methodological approach may also be preferred in order to fully capture and understand, for example, the production and negotiation of hierarchy, asymmetry, order, discourse and identity playing out in micro-level interactions. Business and non-profit organizations most certainly make use of intranets and other social media vehicles and tools to communicate internally, employer to employer, and superior to subordinate. Getting access to and doing unobtrusive observations of the micro-interactions playing out there may generate important insights concerning hierarchy, power and identity for critical organization scholars – insights that may not be gained by exclusively conducting traditional critical ethnographies.

When considering employing a traditional netnography or a completely unobtrusive netnography as a plausible research method, one of course needs to reflect on the methods' limitations and possibilities. Yet both time-saving and quick ordinary participant-observation netnographies and complete-observation (unobtrusive) critical netnographies largely lack the ability of ethnographies, that is, observing, meeting and investigating human behaviour (such as body language) in real-life situations. In addition, while ordinary netnographies involve the participation of the researcher and the ability to interact with the cultural members being studied (for example, through instant messaging and e-mail interviews), they simultaneously lack the ability to capture naturally occurring talk and the ability to perform a completely unobtrusive netnography. Which type of method or combination of methods appears most sensible to the researcher ought, given their strengths and weaknesses, to be governed by the character of the research questions and the aim of the research. Here the researcher often needs to make a methodological trade-off, where he/she has to decide whether to prioritize the ability to fully participate in community life and to be able to interact with the cultural members, or to be able to capture naturally occurring talk and interactions by assuming a complete observational role. In the previous empirical example I prioritized the latter, mainly because an unobtrusive approach sits well with more sensitive research aims, and a complete observant position also makes it less difficult to keep one's critical, reflexive and analytical distance from the community, site and research subjects being studied.

Besides considering relevant and illustrative online research sites, one of the most important considerations when planning to perform any form of netnographic study is the ethical principles of online research. Since there is no firm consensus yet established on what constitutes ethical research online this may constitute quite a challenging task for the researcher. A fruitful guiding principle, however, is whether the site is considered or perceived to be a private or public space. If it is perceived as a private space, informed consent is probably needed from the online site or community when performing a participant-observation netnography. However, if a complete unobtrusive netnography is conducted where the researcher assumes a complete observation position, merely collecting existing conversations (archival data) and performing a passive analysis, informed consent can be waived. The trickiest part in this process is often to evaluate whether the online site is perceived as a private or public space. The number of members of the community, the sensitivity of the subject around which the community centres, and whether registration is needed to be able to follow/observe the community activities together give a valuable indication of the online site's degree of privacy. When conducting netnographies of official organizations, however, this problem may be more easily resolved as informed consent could be integrated in the overall access granted to the researcher by the organization and its key representatives.

Despite its challenging elements, particularly concerning research ethics, I would argue that an (unobtrusive) critical netnography may serve as a fruitful and credible means to collect and analyse data (both textual and pictorial) on several relevant phenomena within consumption studies, critical management studies and other fields within the social sciences. This chapter has hopefully illustrated the fruitful potential of this method and provided interested scholars with some valuable reflections on how to perform credible and trustworthy research online.

References

Alvesson, M. and Deetz, S.A. (2000) *Doing Critical Management Research*. London: Sage.

Alvesson, M and Sköldberg, K. (2009) *Reflexive Methodology: New Vistas for Qualitative Research*. London: Sage.

Bertilsson, J. (2009) *The Way Brands Work: Consumers' Understanding of the Creation and Usage of Brands*. Lund: Lund Business Press.

Bourdieu, P. (1991) *Language and Symbolic Power*. Cambridge, MA: Harvard University Press.

Bourdieu, P. and Wacquant, L.J.D. (1992) *An Invitation to Reflexive Sociology*. Chicago: University of Chicago Press.

Elliott, R. and Percy, L. (2007) *Strategic Brand Management*. Oxford: Oxford University Press.

Eysenbach, G. and Till, J.E. (2001) 'Ethical issues in qualitative research on internet communities', *British Medical Journal*, 323: 1103–1105.

Firat, F. and Shultz, C.J. (1997) 'From segmentation to fragmentation: Markets and marketing strategy in the postmodern era', *European Journal of Marketing*, 31(3): 183–207.

Geertz, C.J. (1973) *The Interpretation of Cultures: Selected Essays*. New York: Basic Books.

Holt, D. (2002) 'Why do brands cause trouble? A dialectical theory of consumer culture and branding', *Journal of Consumer Research*, 29(1): 70–90.

Jenkins, R. (2002) *Pierre Bourdieu*. London: Routledge.

Kozinets, R.V. (1997) '"I want to believe": A netnography of the X-Philes' subculture of consumption', in M. Brucks and D.J. MacInnis (eds), *Advances in Consumer Research Volume 24*. Provo, UT: Association for Consumer Research, pp. 470–475.

Kozinets, R.V. (1998) 'On netnography: Initial reflections on consumer research investigations of cyber culture', in J.W. Alba and J.W. Hutchinson (eds), *Advances in Consumer Research Volume 25*. Provo, UT: Association for Consumer Research, pp. 366–371.

Kozinets, R.V (2001) 'Utopian enterprise: Articulating the meanings of *Star Trek*'s culture of consumption', *Journal of Consumer Research*, 28(1): 67–88.

Kozinets, R.V. (2002) 'The field behind the screen: Using netnography for marketing research in online communities', *Journal of Marketing Research*, 39(1): 61–72.

Kozinets, R.V. (2010) *Netnography: Doing Ethnographic Research Online*. London: Sage.

La Ferle, C., Li, H. and Edwards, S.M. (2001) 'An overview of teenagers and television advertising in the United States', *International Communication Gazette*, 63(1): 7–24.

Langer, R. and Beckman, S.C. (2005) 'Sensitive research topics: Netnography revisited', *Qualitative Market Research*, 8(2): 189–203.

Muñiz, A.M. and O'Guinn, T.C. (2001) 'Brand community', *Journal of Consumer Research*, 27(March): 412–432.

Sandlin, J.A. (2007) 'Netnography as a consumer education research tool', *International Journal of Consumer Studies*, 21(3): 288–294.

Schau, H.J. and Muñiz Jr., A.M. (2002) 'Brand communities and personal identities: Negotiations in cyberspace', in S.M. Broniarczyk and K. Nakamoto (eds), *Advances in Consumer Research Volume 29*. Valdosta, GA: Association for Consumer Research, pp. 344–349.

Silverman, D. (2001) *Interpreting Qualitative Data: Methods for Analysing Talk, Text and Interaction*. London: Sage.

Sudweeks, F. and Rafaeli, S. (1995) 'How do you get a hundred strangers to agree? Computer-mediated communication and collaboration', in T.M. Harrison and T. Stephen (eds), *Computer Networking and Scholarship in the 21st Century University*. New York: SUNY Press.

Thompson, C.J. (1997) 'Interpreting consumers: A hermeneutical framework for deriving marketing insights from the texts of consumers' consumption stories', *Journal of Marketing Research*, 34(4): 438–455.

Thompson, C.J., Locander, W.B. and Pollio, H.R. (1989) 'Putting consumer experience back into consumer research: The philosophy and method of existential-phenomenology', *Journal of Consumer Research*, 16(2): 133–146.

Thompson, C.J., Locander, W.B. and Pollio, H.R. (1994) 'The spoken and the unspoken: A hermeneutic approach to understanding the cultural viewpoints that underlie consumers' expressed meanings', *Journal of Consumer Research*, 21(3): 432–452.

PART III

OUT OF THE FIELD

NINE

Motifs in the methods section: Representing the qualitative research process

Karen Lee Ashcraft and Catherine S. Ashcraft

Introduction

This chapter reconsiders how to compose the methods section of an empirical paper – a ritual that can be especially vexing for organization researchers with interpretive and critical leanings. Journals increasingly oblige authors to elucidate and justify the qualitative research process. Yet conventions for doing so cannot readily accommodate the ambiguity, intuition, and sensuality endemic to much qualitative practice. Moreover, the typical tone of methods accounting – neutral rigour – sanitizes the moral and political process of knowledge production. Many interpretive and critical scholars therefore castigate the methods section as excessive professional regulation. Rarely is this ritual the subject of explicit reflection.

We commence reflection by sketching the key ingredients of a 'good' qualitative methods section. The composite we present stems from our combined 30 years of experience reading, conducting, publishing, reviewing, editing, teaching, and supervising qualitative research, and from considering others' counsel regarding methodological accounts (e.g. Golden-Biddle and Locke, 1993; Tracy, 2013). We then unravel the implications of this common recipe. To accommodate layered and contradictory readings, we suggest how we might celebrate, debate, censure, and transform elements of the ritual. Our argument is that the qualitative methods section is a routine 'disciplinary' practice that both facilitates researcher accountability and negotiates pivotal institutional realities. It is thus a consequential site of struggle best tackled conscientiously. As we make this case, we integrate matters of ethics and reflexivity throughout the discussion, on the grounds that such critical issues are better interwoven than left to a separate section.

How to compose a qualitative methods section: A recipe for persuasive accounting in organization and management studies

Several clarifications are in order before we begin. Our focus is on qualitative empirical research that involves interactive fieldwork with human participants (e.g., participant observation, interviews). We are especially concerned with research from interpretive and critical orientations. The formula offered here presumes that one is attempting to translate such research into the normative format of a scholarly journal article, wherein theoretical framework and literature review precede discussion of method, followed by presentation of analysis, discussion, and conclusion. We also assume that the normative format, derived from the deductive and linear conventions of quantitative social science, sits at some odds with the inductive and embryonic character of much qualitative research.

The formula we present is meant to capture expectations across the leading journals of organization and management studies that publish qualitative scholarship. Of course, this sweeping profile risks minimizing significant variation among venues. We might observe, for instance, that 'mainstream' journals tend to favour the deductive, linear article genre and enforce stringent norms of methodological accounting. Typically, interpretive and critical scholars seeking to publish in these outlets must respond to such rigid standards. Critical-leaning journals, on the other hand, tend to permit more flexibility. Lest this be read as a claim for superior mainstream rigour against comparatively lax critical venues, we hasten to remind the reader that mainstream journals often make demands that violate interpretive and critical assumptions and reflect the enduring hegemony of 'normal science'. In this light, the flexibility afforded by critical journals is a vital form of resistance. We take care to mark such distinctions among venues where relevant to our standard recipe.

We claim that the formula presented below is *widely regarded* to yield strong methodological accounting. We are less concerned with whether it *actually* does so, though we make no effort to conceal our take. The discussion is guided by a spirit of conversation, not of certainty or closure. We acknowledge our own participation in enforcing the formula, even as we have felt ambivalence in doing so. Indeed, it is our own experience of opposing impulses that motivates our attention to contradiction in this chapter.

Finally, the instrumental reader may find here a handy set of do's and don'ts to be applied strategically, with little regard for broader implications. To be clear, we regard critique of the recipe as an equally practical skill. Those who cultivate a nuanced understanding of competing forces at play are best equipped to engage with the formula deftly, enacting the sort of reflexivity that moves the field forward rather than replaying tired scripts. We ask readers to remain mindful of these qualifiers as we turn to articulate, in a direct and prescriptive voice, a recipe for composing a 'good' qualitative methods section.

#1: Provide an overarching position statement and rationale

Begin by characterizing, precisely but succinctly, what kind of qualitative research you claim to have conducted, as well as why and how this way of knowing is appropriate given the ontological stance, theoretical framework, and research question(s) established earlier in the paper. How you depict your overall methodology depends on the relationship between the type of research you claim and the journal's audience: if the audience is less familiar with your approach, you must paint in broad and clearly bounded strokes; if they are more familiar, you have more licence to assume common ground and assert sophisticated distinctions.

An example can help to illustrate, drawn from a paper published by the first author in *Administrative Science Quarterly* (Ashcraft, 1999: 249), a North American management journal whose customary readers were not well acquainted with qualitative methods of a critical variety:

> The ethnographic methods I used reflect a critical, participatory bent. A critical approach seeks knowledge of social action in the service of social change; it asks researcher participant and reader to assess and transform the taken-for-granted contexts in which we define and solve problems (Mumby, 1988; Alvesson and Willmott, 1992; Thomas, 1993). My methods illustrate participatory research in various ways: (1) my research problem originated in the participants' community; (2) the community consisted of a traditionally oppressed group; (3) participants affected the research process; (4) the project prompted participants to reflect on the consequences of their actions; and (5) I became a participant of sorts (Mumby, 1988; Heron and Reason, 1997).

Evident in this excerpt is the 'broad and clearly bounded strokes' approach prescribed above. The generic level of distinctions (e.g., 'critical' versus all other approaches), as well as the sharpness with which they are drawn (e.g., five features), would likely be read as simplistic in the context of a critical journal like *Organization*. There, a finer-grained reading of specific critical epistemological influences, in relation to larger 'families' of critique, would be necessary. Multiple references to precedent might also be seen as surplus protest in a critical-friendly venue, whereas *ASQ* urged extensive citation to relieve reader doubts regarding the legitimacy of critical methods.

Finally, it is worth noting that the label 'critical, participatory' was first suggested by *ASQ* reviewers and only retrospectively adopted by the author, as a means to help readers recognize a mode of qualitative research she herself had not yet branded as such. This sort of reviewer–author negotiation illustrates our later point (see #7) that, while one should never fabricate research activities to satisfy reviewer preferences, the techniques we employ can be fairly characterized in a number of ways. In other words, the identity of a research practice is evolving, co-constructed, and contestable; it is not predetermined, merely awaiting report.

#2: Provide a descriptive profile of research participants and sites

The second ingredient entails describing key characteristics of the population(s) and location(s) studied. 'Key' features are those commonly expected by readers of the journal (at minimum, how many participants and their basic demographic profile), as well as features crucial to contextualizing and evaluating your subsequent analysis. The latter category varies widely with the nature and focus of your study. Beyond additionally relevant demographics, this category should include any contextual factors significant to the study, factors that may have shaped participation in the study, or factors that may distinguish your participants from others who could have partaken in such a study. For example, the second author (Ashcraft, 2008: 640) includes the following description:

> The [peer educators (PEs)] also represented a wide range of experiences with academic success and engagement. Approximately one-third of the PEs reported a history of average/above average grades, with two of them being enrolled in some honours classes. Another third reported having had significant difficulties with school. The final third experienced one or more criteria that would place them in traditionally labelled 'at-risk' categories (e.g., significantly below grade level in literacy, dropped out of high school).

While detail about participants' academic records may not be of general interest, it is vital to anticipating reader queries in this case (e.g., if all participants were 'high-achieving' students from the outset, are the findings applicable to other populations?). To be sure, expectations for 'generalizability' are quite different in qualitative research. Providing this kind of contextual detail helps enact the difference by allowing readers to develop a nuanced appreciation for your setting and consider other contexts in which your findings may be relevant.

Beyond participant characteristics, it is also important to describe the research site(s) where the study occurred. At minimum, this includes characterizing geo-locality (often kept general and confidential by necessity), organizational or occupational context, and other unique or significant features of the site relevant to study processes and outcomes. Particularly in the case of ethnographic research, sophisticated descriptions of site move beyond list-heavy renderings such that readers can imagine 'being there' (Golden-Biddle and Locke, 1993).

Finally, it is helpful to explain how and why you selected the site(s) as appropriate and promising. The second author, for instance, describes how her site enabled meaningful engagement with silences in previous research (Ashcraft, 2012):

I also chose this program because these educators saw themselves as sex educators who were explicitly attempting to involve students in critiquing ... the social inequalities affecting their lives ... In addition, this program worked with urban teens diverse in race, gender, class, and sexual orientation. These features made ESPERANZA a particularly rich site for exploring these issues and distinguish it from previous research.

#3: Detail the process of data collection

The goal of the third ingredient is to give the reader a precise sense of what data you generated and how exactly you went about doing so. Be sure to describe the time period for gathering data, detail every data-generating technique you employed, and describe how you carried those out.

For observation methods, it is helpful to indicate the forums you observed (e.g., which meetings attended, activities shadowed) and for how long. If you observed multiple contexts, briefly describe each and your relative time spent among them. A rationale for why you privileged certain contexts in your site(s) over others (i.e., why they were more important to answering your research questions) is also advisable. Equally important is what you intended to observe in each context (e.g., decision-making processes, relational dynamics, non-verbal cues); how these intentions link directly to your research questions and prior research); and how actual observations lived up to (and/or failed) your expectations of what you would witness. If your goals for observation changed over the course of the study, clearly indicate how and justify why this evolution was appropriate. Finally, describe how you recorded and reflected upon field notes (e.g., did you scribble on site, enhance detail afterward, reflect and pre-analyse periodically, keep any sort of reflective journal – and why?).

For interview or focus groups methods, describe how many you conducted, of what sort (e.g., open-ended, self-guided, semi- or highly structured), with which participants, and how long the sessions lasted (i.e., average length and shortest-to-longest range). Indicate whether you audio- or video-recorded and transcribed interviews and focus groups; if not, provide a compelling rationale for that decision. Also include information about the questions you asked, recognizing that the expected level of detail varies by journal. Some request a sampling of the range of questions, whereas others require that you append your entire protocol. In any case, make it clear how your interview and focus group questions serve the study's larger research questions.

Generally speaking, we notice that mainstream journals tend to emphasize information about data quantity or volume (e.g., how many pages of field notes or interview transcripts?), whereas critical-leaning journals tend to stress instead the quality of research practices (e.g., how did the sessions proceed and feel, and how does this suit your claimed epistemology?). The distinction does not entirely hold, however, as journals can be concerned with quantity and quality in varied and simultaneous ways (e.g., did you conduct enough interviews to warrant your claims, and was their tenor in keeping with your philosophical stance?).

Finally, if you employed any innovative data generation techniques, describe these – specifically, how you arrived at them (e.g., building on methodological calls or in conversation with participants); what you designed them to discern and how they differ from similar methods; how you implemented them; the contributions they make to existing research methods; and 'lessons' (e.g., pros and cons, necessary refinements) your study recommends for their further development.

#4: Detail the process of data analysis

The fourth ingredient asks you to make accessible and sensible the analytic process you actually followed. The crucial question here is how exactly you moved from a large pool of transcripts and field notes to the specific findings presented in the paper. Typically, the process is laid out in a series of steps, which tend to be 'iterative' or cyclical (e.g., repeated reading and coding) rather than linear. Authors often invoke a formal procedural vocabulary when describing such steps. The following excerpt is especially heavy-handed in this respect (Ashcraft, 1999: 251–252):

> [T]he iterative, inductive character of grounded theory … analytic memos … recurring patterns … continued a textual dialogue between data and memos until I could articulate a local logic that lent coherence to the cases … constructed a timeline of evidence to build a logical chain … subsumed particulars into periods…revised and refined the character of each phase … comparisons and contrasts with sensitizing concepts … a form of narrative analysis.

This passage also contains, at the behest of reviewers, illustrations and citations meant to assure readers of 'appropriate' application and precedent. We reduced it to snippets of terminology here in order to accentuate how recognition and credibility can be achieved by linking your own analytic practice to shared procedural vocabularies. At minimum, you are expected to provide a semi-technical description of process in keeping with both the general attitude of qualitative inquiry and whatever specific strand(s) you claim (see #1 above). Again, differences among journals become relevant. Not surprisingly, descriptions that sound highly technical tend to be more compulsory and compelling in mainstream management journals, whereas critically oriented journals tend to emphasize coherence with your declared epistemological spirit.

In any case, it is tangible examples from your project that will make your use of common vocabularies accessible and persuasive. The more vividly you can demonstrate to readers how the themes you are soon to present resulted from the professed procedure(s), the better. To the extent possible, *show* us how you used an analytic device in the specific context of your research; do not merely *tell* us that you did so. Consider this extended example (Ashcraft, 2006: 64–65):

> I analysed the data in three basic steps, following Craig and Tracy's (1995) model of grounded practical theory. First, I sought to foreground tensions stemming from the

merger of feminist and bureaucratic control as experienced by RMS participants. For this paper, I narrowed my focus to one acute tension: how to promote and curtail ideological diversity. This tension was difficult to miss at RMS, for – as elaborated in my analysis – members openly addressed it as a constant struggle ... Second, I reconstructed their tactics for coping with the diversity tension. This step too was relatively straightforward, since participants managed the dilemma by developing an ideological policy of sorts ... I thus tracked the formation of the policy across a series of meetings devoted to that purpose.

Third, to detect emergent organizational forms, I combed the evolution of the policy for tacit assumptions about 'appropriate' control mechanisms. I began by conducting a preliminary reading of relevant meeting and interview data, during which I recorded subtle assumptions implied by participants' discourse and decision making. I then went back through the data several times, adjusting my rendition of these assumptions until they better encompassed nuances (i.e., brief conflicts and other 'blips') in the policy formation process. Finally, using the tensions theorized in Table 1 as 'sensitizing concepts' (Jorgensen, 1989), I collapsed the assumptions into three principles of practicing paradoxical control at RMS. Although all three analytic steps involved grounded theorizing in that themes were derived from member perspectives and activities, the third step particularly reflects the inductive, iterative analytic process common to interpretive work.

Notice how abstract terminology from the first excerpt assumes a project-specific dimension here. As readers learn how you applied available qualitative procedures in context, they are better equipped to evaluate these appropriations. As a general rule, then, references to formal technique and precedent are insufficient on their own. A lucid, precise account of their interaction with the project in question is indispensable.

Three related pitfalls are worth considering. One involves short-changing the description of analytic process relative to other aspects of method. Most authors appear to be more comfortable describing 'data collection' than 'data analysis'. How they produced and interacted with the material to 'make it speak' often remains a mystery, a declared transformation that defies transparency. A major part of the difficulty is that intuition is integral to interpretive and critical analysis yet resists the conventions of formal accounting. Nonetheless, we see it as our obligation to trace and render as accessible as possible how our 'hunches' and 'senses' arose and evolved in context, why we believe others should find them reasonable and credible, and what important ambiguities persist. In other words, we urge you *not* to approach this responsibility as an exercise in conformity with 'normal science' by stretching or manufacturing systematic procedures and closure. Instead, we urge you to frame this as a duty integral to the larger effort to redraw the norms and boundaries of so-called normal science. Through the contours of a particular project, that is, you are helping others to cast intuition as a scientific technique or procedure, a 'new normal' vital to qualitative science.

A second and related pitfall entails trotting out boilerplate text to describe one's analytic process (not unlike the earlier snippets of terminology, had they actually appeared in isolation). While references to 'grounded theory' and 'inductive', 'iterative', or 'thematic' analysis are in stride with much qualitative inquiry, on their own such references reveal little about the research in question. Such encompassing terms unite a wide range of actual techniques, and wielding them in abstraction flouts one of the distinguishing features of qualitative inquiry: a commitment to contextual sensitivity (e.g., immersion). Almost invariably, the burning question is less *which* technique and more *how* and *why* exactly did it work in this project?

A final pitfall involves erasing the researcher from the analytic process, as in the common claim that 'themes emerged'. As a journal editor, the first author has been struck repeatedly by a tendency to shift from active to passive voice as authors transition from discussion of data collection to data analysis. A pressing question for interpretive and critical scholars is thus not only *how* themes unfolded, but especially how *you* as researcher massaged the empirical material to yield those themes. As we elaborate next, it is incumbent on you to bring your role into the open rather than hide in the shadow cast by formal procedure.

#5: Describe the role of the researcher

A fifth ingredient involves characterizing your role as researcher and accounting for your positionality (for more on this, see the discussion of 'vulnerable' voice in #7 below). Adequately performing this task is often difficult due to journal space restrictions, and journals vary widely in their expectations. Critical journals, for instance, tend to expect greater reflexivity from the researcher, whereas some mainstream journals allow the researcher to all but disappear from the account, resulting in a detached 'god's-eye' view. Because we find such permission contrary to interpretive and critical impulses, we focus on feasible ways for authors to resist the 'normal science' practice of erasing researcher presence.

A first and fairly straightforward set of tips includes: writing your methods section in the first person ('I'); rectifying moments when you slip from active to passive voice (e.g., 'I interviewed … themes emerged'; see the discussion of third pitfall in #4 above); and changing verbs that imply neutral discovery to those that explicate researcher agency (e.g., rather than 'I found theme X', try 'I generated theme X by applying these techniques').

Beyond these basic tips, we urge you to explore how your subjectivity affects at least three aspects of the research process: your interest and investment in the research; data generation, and data analysis. Our sense is that organization scholars tend to feel relatively uncomfortable with all three, but that the third remains most challenging.

Speaking to the first, describe briefly what led you to and through your study (e.g., curiosities related to your own identity and experience, felt participant reactions). An abbreviated example from the second author's research (Ashcraft, 2012) helps to illustrate:

> As a former literacy teacher, I first became interested in studying teen sexuality as I witnessed its pervasive influence in adolescents' lives … it seemed an important topic to address … but I often felt ill-prepared to do so … This background influenced

my perspective throughout this study. For example … I was always interested in how 'lessons learned' in this context might be brought back to literacy and other classrooms.

This excerpt offers just a taste of how you might talk about the relation of self and project. The point is not to confess personal detail for its own sake but, rather, to show how your partialities are relevant to knowledge production. The question is: how do your interest and investment in the research, your role in the various scenes comprising the field, and your analytic stance enhance the findings and arguments in specific ways?

Exploring your investments in the research can also enhance your formulation of arguments and contributions, as in this case where the second author's own experience brings an emotional exclamation point to a dilemma under analysis (Ashcraft, 2008: 659):

an important concern arises regarding the preparation of teachers in addressing such issues. As I noted earlier, I often found this difficult in my own classroom and, indeed, many other teachers are worried about how to conduct such efforts.

Weaving researcher experience throughout your claims, even briefly, can yield a richer, more embodied set of conclusions.

Turning to the researcher's role in data generation and analysis, two sets of questions become pressing. First, what role did you play in producing and analysing the empirical material, how did this vary during the project, with what significance for your analysis, and how does this role suit your epistemology? An example of how you might engage with this question follows, but discerning readers will notice that only data generation is addressed (Ashcraft, 2000: 359):

As this account suggests, my role changed with field setting. For instance, I gathered volunteer data from a complete participant perspective, whereas my role in staff meetings fit that of immersed observer. Such ongoing shifts engendered a unique perspective on SAFE life – outsider and insider, expert and subordinate, and researcher and participant at once. This dual stance reflects a feminist preference for research conducted through active participation, not aloof observation … it supports a feminist view of all researchers as situated, implicated participants, not autonomous, objective observers.

Second, how did your subjectivity in relation to participants lead you to recognize and privilege certain information and interpretations? For instance, the second author (Ashcraft, 2008: 642) acknowledges contradictory influences when she notes that, 'My previous teaching experience … served me well in building rapport'. She continues:

As a white, middle class woman in her mid-30s, I differed from many of the participants, especially in terms of race and class. This certainly made me an 'outsider' to many of their life experiences and circumstances. At the same time, there were also points of intersection with participants in terms of gender, class, and religion. These … certainly predispose me to understand some experiences more than others.

Although this excerpt acknowledges that researcher positionality shapes the selection, production, and analysis of data, it also reveals the challenges of limited space, in that the qualifiers remain relatively general (for an extended, nuanced account, see Kauffman, 1992).

Given our earlier treatment of pitfalls in accounting for data analysis (see #4 above), it is not surprising that accounting for the researcher's role in analytic activity also appears to be the most difficult. One popular way of accomplishing this is by claiming to have conducted 'member checks'. While these checks can be practised and reported in ways that honour the relational, contextual spirit of interpretive and critical qualitative inquiry, we caution that they also can take a deferential tone to 'normal science': namely, validity through bias minimization. The second author navigates this tension in her account of conducting fieldwork and analysis side-by-side (Ashcraft, 2012):

> I used several methods to acknowledge my subjectivities as a researcher and how they shaped the research. I conducted frequent 'member checks,' discussing my findings with and getting feedback from both adult facilitators and PEs ... I also waited to conduct individual interviews until after I had spent significant time building initial relationships. This helped to ensure that participants would feel comfortable talking with me in interviews and in providing genuine feedback during member checks. I also spread the interviews over the course of the study so that I could initially analyze the first transcripts, refine questions, and get additional feedback from participants.

#6: Summarize the legitimacy, novelty, and/or contribution of your method

Although it need not consume much space, it is vital to bring home your methodological case. As should be clear by now, the essential act of a 'good' qualitative methods section is formulating a persuasive methodological argument, not – as many seem to treat it – merely reporting on your research activities. At minimum, your summary of that argument should: remind readers why the articulated methodology is suited to your conceptual and empirical project; clarify anything innovative about your approach (e.g., do you claim to chart new terrain or induce movement in an epistemological debate, or do you mostly use available techniques toward specified ends?); and explain how your methodology offers something to the intellectual conversations that your paper has opened. Consider this example (Ashcraft, 1999: 252):

> This unique blend of grounded theory and narrative analysis allowed me to tell an informative, engaging 'realist' tale that also allows my influence on it ... My research methods respond to recent calls for innovative, qualitative approaches to succession ... which may enrich our understanding with complex, local accounts of succession as constituted in the discourse of organizational members. Importantly, qualitative methods are not merely heuristic tools in the service of objective, generalizable knowledge. They engender a different, salient form of understanding. Qualitative methods enable us to investigate situated action, to illuminate the meanings and practices that constitute actual succession events, and, thus, to facilitate fuller awareness of context and process.

In this summary, the first author makes the case for novelty and contribution in terms of a phenomenon (leadership succession) largely studied through quantitative measures that limit understanding in certain ways. Adapting to the context of *ASQ* at the time, the argument is pitched to an audience sceptical of qualitative research. The argument would shift dramatically in friendlier venues or in the case of phenomena already examined extensively through qualitative means. It would, for example, read less self-consciously, less defended against predictable attacks from a stance of 'normal science'. It would not suffice to depict qualitative methods as a homogeneous category, or to claim their sheer application as a contribution unto itself. It would trade the wide-angle lens for a finer-grained zoom, acknowledging nuanced relations among qualitative approaches. It would – in a critical journal, especially – need to justify the claim to a 'realist' tale rather than the author's influence on it.

#7: Walk a fine line among scientific, artistic, personal, and political voices

Finding an authorial voice that satisfies the spirit of interpretive and critical inquiry, adequately captures the actual research experience, *and* meets editorial and reviewer demands is – in our experience – the most delicate dance of the ritual. Different moves suit different audiences, but most variations entail striking an appropriate balance among three voices.

The first we dub 'methodical' voice – disciplined, rigorous, precise, procedural, systematic, and meticulous. This is *the* voice privileged by most mainstream management and organization journals. But some measure of this voice, particularly demonstration of qualitative consistency and rigour (along the lines detailed above), tends to be a minimum requirement for critical-leaning journals as well. In our view, this voice is most productive when it does not fetishize order and procedure to the point of *rigor mortis* – that is, when rigour serves a purpose, accomplishing something for the research beyond a glorification of itself (e.g., enhancing the researcher's care with participant voices, establishing confidence in the researcher's interpretations).

The second we call 'aesthetic' voice, which honours artistry amid ambiguity – the dynamic, creative, evolving, adaptive, sensual, embodied, and situated knowing that renders interpretive and critical qualitative scholarship as much craft and art as science (Kvale and Brinkmann, 2009). This voice tempers (or even counters) methodical voice by opening representational space for intuition and imagination, beauty and affect, doubt and uncertainty (e.g., Locke et al., 2008), resourcefulness, unresolved tension, impressionistic reading, and so on (for an example of application, see the discussion of the first pitfall in #4 above). In our observation, few journals require this voice, but the most compelling methods sections tend to deploy it, respecting the inevitable ambiguity and untidiness of actual qualitative research experiences.

A third voice we deem 'vulnerable' in a few senses. At the least, it invokes the researcher's presence and influence (e.g., with the use of the first person and active voice), particularly in orchestrating the generation and analysis of data (see #5 above). Going further, it can embrace the notion that researchers are fallible subjects replete with identities, investments, anxieties, and limitations that invariably shape knowledge production (e.g., 'confessional' tales à la Van Maanen, 1988). Gesturing toward a stronger critical orientation, a vulnerable voice can also interrogate how such partialities are neither merely personal nor idiosyncratic. Rather, they are political subjectivities that interact with one another, with those of participants, and with the symbolic materialities of scenes to produce the relations of power that inevitably constitute knowledge production (Kauffman, 1992). Vulnerable voice in the latter two senses remains rare in the methods sections of organization and management studies, though it is arguably in step with reigning ideals of critical reflexivity (Wray-Bliss, 2004). Meanwhile, researchers and methodologists in other fields provide poignant demonstrations that can inspire bolder accounts on our part (Behar, 1996; Kondo, 1990).

What constitutes the 'right' balance of voices is of course the priceless question. It is also a contextual one, entailing a complex negotiation among your epistemological commitments, your evolving understanding of the research experience, and journal expectations and audience. We have heard some say that altering accounts of one's research process – during a review process or across different articles published from one data set – signals a lack of authenticity or, at least, an overly performative orientation to representing methodology. We do not think this is necessarily so. Done well, after all, the review process involves conversation and intersubjective sense-making. Such exchange yields an evolution of understanding as well as situated knowing and adaptation (for an example of this, see the end of #1 above). That said, we have also experienced moments as authors where we felt compromised by editorial requests, as if 'Who do you want me to be?' is the only permissible response. As an editor, the first author has occasionally wondered if she or reviewers are asking for something an author did not in fact do, and whether the author would admit this and risk rejection if so. We hope that willingness to bear the consequences of integrity remains the rule, and we urge sensitivity to the meaningful difference between joint sense-making and fabrication in the review process. The following excerpt from the second author's research (Ashcraft, 2008: 643) demonstrates how such tensions can be navigated in print:

> In this article, I do not aim to make large-scale claims about increases in traditional measures of academic achievement, such as grades, test scores, or graduation rates. I did not have access to these data sources for the participants in my study, nor is large-scale data of this sort readily available for students in the few similar programs that exist. I do, however, include other evidence of academic benefits ... I would certainly encourage more qualitative studies into the differing effects of various programs as well as larger-scale, quantitative studies of other measures of academic achievement or civic engagement. Indeed, one purpose of providing this in-depth look at ESPERANZA is to increase the prevalence of such programs so that these issues could be studied on a larger scale and from a number of different perspectives.

#8: Know that methods sections are judged in part by the quality of your analysis

It would be a mistake to assume that the methods section is the only place in and from which readers evaluate methodology. In our experience, questions or reservations not initially flagged in the methods section crop up as readers engage with the actual analysis. Below, we identify five common signs of trouble in the presentation of findings that tend to prompt misgivings about methodological adequacy.

The findings are too 'neat and clean'. Organizational life is messy, and analyses that override this complexity raise suspicion as to whether sound analytical work has occurred. Examples include findings that suggest agreement or interpretive convergence among all participants, fail to explore doubts or tensions evident in participant accounts, neglect apparent contradictions in the research setting itself, or are supported with little actual data (e.g., few participant voices). On rare occasions, of course, participants may speak in unison, or relations may be seamlessly oppressive; but such conclusions are more convincing if the author demonstrates sustained effort to probe for alternate, contested, and nuanced readings.

The findings are 'obvious' and fail to extend past research. While analyses should build on previous efforts, they should also say something substantively novel. Simply illustrating that established patterns also occur in your research site, no matter how flavourful the story, provokes readers to wonder whether your analytic efforts were sufficiently diligent or you simply saw what the literature conditioned you to see.

The findings are contextually 'thin'. If readers struggle to grasp a sense of the broader *and* specific situations in which findings occurred, they are likely to question whether the study itself is adequately contextualized for qualitative research. Be sure to provide not only enough empirical excerpts to support your claims, but also sufficient surrounding detail that readers feel vicariously 'immersed' in the scene.

The findings are imprecise about pattern prominence. It is vital to address whether the empirical patterns you identify are dominant, rare, limited to certain participants, times and spaces, and so forth. Helping readers understand how a pattern fits in with other participant realities can be done in a number of ways (e.g., providing frequencies, qualifiers, or contingencies that enhance nuance and precision), though which of these are accessible to you may depend on your claimed epistemology (e.g., without great care, frequency counts can be conflated with positivist leanings).

The findings do not 'hang together'. It is equally crucial to show readers how the strands of your findings interrelate and inform the research questions. Findings that read like a disjointed laundry list of themes raise suspicion that more careful analysis is needed. As noted earlier, contradictory findings are welcome, but such tensions demand thoughtful articulation and exploration. Incoherent analyses can result from poorly organized findings too, which also tend to spark doubts about analytic technique.

We include this final ingredient to underscore that methodological challenges often stem from reviewer uneasiness about the analysis itself. Note how this reverses the usual premise that a strong methods section supplies the warrant for analysis; it is also the case that a strong analysis authorizes methodology.

Unravelling the standard formula: Initiating layered reflection

We wind down our analysis with some vital complications and potential contradictions. In an effort to stimulate a larger, ongoing conversation in the field – not only reforms in individual practice – we successively entertain reasons to celebrate, debate, censure, and transform the above recipe for methodological accounting.

What's to like: An appreciative reading

We begin with reflections on what seem to us valuable features of current accounting protocol. Specifically, we applaud the twin goals of transparency and accountability – the quest to render the research process accessible as one way to interpret the quality of findings. Though we later challenge conventional vocabularies for pursuing this, we find the quest itself at least as important for critical researchers as it is for more traditional social scientific researchers. As others have argued (e.g., Code, 1993; Roman, 1992), critical scholarship maintains a commitment to empirically backed knowledge claims; simultaneously, it insists that the test of these claims lies in a turn back to practice, in conscious exchange about when and why certain truths resonate and fail. It is difficult for readers to join in this conversation without understanding how researchers arrive at their claims. Failure to achieve transparency thus arguably weakens critical commitment to ongoing interrogation of what counts as knowledge.

The methods section can also be read as an important ritual that calls us to account for the politics of our own labour. As we noted earlier and elaborate below, the methodological demands of mainstream journals often exasperate interpretive and critical scholars, prompting resistance on epistemological and moral grounds. It is worth noting, however, that a core tenet of critical research is to illuminate relational positionalities and politics, to rupture brittle dualisms like that of observer–observed and subject–object. Toward this end, critical scholars have developed numerous strategies for facilitating and acknowledging participant influence on the research process (e.g., Roman, 1992). Subjecting our own field conduct and interpretive practices to the gaze of others is another way to rupture problematic dualisms and power relations. In this light, the methods section ritual aligns with the norms of critical research.

What's to debate: A conflicted reading

We become more cynical when we grant the regularity with which goals such as transparency and accountability are enforced and achieved through the logic and language of quantitative social science. We have felt this pressure ourselves, to be complicit in the sort of retrospective sense-making that sanitizes qualitative research into a linear, structured, and systematic process more palatable to 'normal science' tastes. In this sense, methodological accounting becomes a compulsory dance of seduction in which authors are obliged to satisfy reviewers through compromising moves.

On the other hand, we have at times confronted this pressure as an invigorating challenge that elicits inventive forms of translation. In these more optimistic moments, we wonder if the push to play across boundaries and speak in foreign tongues strengthens methodological understanding and dexterity, fostering qualitative-friendly logics and languages that may eventually find equal footing. Perhaps the bigger problem, then, is one of asymmetry – that only qualitative researchers tend to face this push.

Qualitative researchers can struggle for adequate vocabulary even when traditional social scientific constraints are loosened, as when writing for journals sympathetic to creative and critical aims. As noted earlier, this struggle tends to be especially acute when accounting for one's positionality in the research process. It may be that this vocabulary is particularly stunted for lack of pressure or opportunity to play across epistemological boundaries in this way. Because mainstream journals rarely hold researchers to this burden, in other words, we are out of practice, invention muted by the absence of necessity. In any case, we advocate a methods section ritual that invites and cultivates new accounting logics and languages, on the grounds that the presence of competing systems tends to surface the partiality of all.

What's to condemn: A critical reading

Without doubt, the standard methods recipe is 'disciplinary' in multiple senses. As hinted earlier, it constitutes the discipline of organization and management studies through political relations that police the conduct of individual scholars, assert the dominance of editorial voices, and place authors in a compromising position where accommodating those who control key resources (i.e., access to publication) can feel like the only option. On a larger scale, the recipe can be said to privilege constructions of validity and rigour derived from 'normal science', thereby marginalizing humanistic and radical orientations. At the outset, for example, this chapter capitulated to the normative deductive, linear journal format – a form of surrender understandably objectionable to some (e.g., Tracy, 2012). Consider, too, our earlier discussion of voice, where we grant the reign of methodical voice but urge authors to cultivate as well their capacities with aesthetic and vulnerable voices. Because the latter have yet to be institutionalized in the methods section ritual, an extra burden falls to interpretive and critical qualitative scholars: translation or 'code-switching' into a foreign tongue, inventing vocabularies that maintain epistemological integrity while persuading sceptical audiences. Rarely are traditional social scientists asked to do the same. As such, they are likely to overlook the privilege enjoyed when a journal speaks in one's native tongue.[1]

In the context of organization and management studies, this is not just another instance of social science tradition trumping interpretive and critical epistemologies. It is also a matter of international disciplinary relations and, arguably, the colonization of organization studies elsewhere by North American management studies. For example, many times in her role as a US associate editor for a European-based journal of organization studies, the first author encountered related concerns from European organization scholars. Accustomed to greater epistemological and methodological flexibility in critical-friendly European journals, these authors described an intense and rising pressure, enforced by state and institutional regulatory systems, to publish in leading North American management journals, which lean heavily towards quantitative social science conventions. Such concerns suggest the consequential politics of a seemingly mundane technical ritual and, we believe, merit collective reflection and action.

What's next: Towards a transformative reading

Holding together these competing readings of the methods section ritual, we propose three key steps towards fostering more equitable relations in the nearer term. First, we urge *individual* interpretive and critical scholars to prioritize the approximation of transparency as they compose qualitative methods sections. We say 'approximation' in an effort to recognize the impossibility of full transparency. The point is rather to strive for creative renderings that convey alternative epistemological spirits, do justice to the actual research process, *and* are amenable to reader assessment. This is a call to phase out a current tendency to reiterate crusty accounting scripts, which pay homage to abstract qualitative slogans (e.g., 'grounded, inductive, thematic analysis') but tell us little about the situated project in question. Reviewers and editors have a hand in this well, as they too can resist persuasion by empty buzzword.

Second, we urge qualitative organization scholars *as a collective* to leverage these individual inventions in transparency towards the development of shared vocabularies that render the ambiguous, sensual, intuitive, emotional, aesthetic, ethical, and political sensibilities of interpretive and critical epistemologies accessible to

---

[1] Of course, this point and those advanced in the next paragraph become all the more evident with regard to the official language of most management journals: English. Although this matter is beyond the scope of this chapter, it warrants collective reflection, alongside the increasingly decried methodological hegemony of North American management studies, as serious forms of advantage and disadvantage in the evolving global relations of our field.

communal review and reflection. Our sense is that, especially in management and organization studies, the challenging task of accounting is largely left for individuals to tackle, when the formulation of common terminology could go a long way to easing the isolating experience of speaking in a foreign tongue.

Finally, we urge *all* organization scholars to begin requiring translation work in unexpected directions – for example, by asking those who conduct conventional social science to account for their techniques in qualitative-friendly ways, perhaps even as if qualitative modes of knowing were dominant. In spreading and parodying the translation burden, we seek to dislodge the hegemony of partial accounting standards privileged to masquerade as 'normal science'. Qualitative journal editors, reviewers, seasoned researchers, and/or quantitative allies in these roles can lead the way in this regard.

We have pursued two main goals in this chapter: first, to guide curious interpretive and critical qualitative scholars through an intricate understanding of what constitutes a 'good' methods section at this moment in our field; and second, to stimulate explicit critique and conversation about the larger political functions of the methods section ritual. Ultimately, we argue that the qualitative methods section is a consequential site of struggle in the context of organization studies. It is a routine 'disciplinary' practice aimed at achieving research transparency and accountability, which exceeds (and sometimes evades) that purpose to negotiate other institutional realities defining our field. Among these are hierarchical relations between 'observer' and 'observed', between editorial forces and authorial voices, among social scientific, humanistic, and critical epistemologies and methodologies, and between North American and European scholarly traditions. Becoming aware of what is at stake in writing a qualitative methods section can foster critical reflection on the functions served by this ordinary ritual and help us all to engage with it in more thoughtful, humane, skilful, and even playful ways.

References

Alvesson, M. and Willmott, H. (1992) 'On the idea of emancipation in management and organization studies', *Academy of Management Review*, 17(3): 432–464.

Ashcraft, C. (2008) 'So much more than "sex ed": Teen sexuality as vehicle for improving academic success and democratic education for diverse urban youth', *American Educational Research Journal*, 45(3): 631–667.

Ashcraft, C. (2012) 'But how do we talk about it? Critical literacy practices for addressing sexuality with youth', *Curriculum Inquiry*, 42(5): 597–628.

Ashcraft, K.L. (1999) 'Managing maternity leave: A qualitative analysis of temporary executive succession', *Administrative Science Quarterly*, 44(2): 240–280.

Ashcraft, K.L. (2000) 'Empowering "professional" relationships: Organizational communication meets feminist practice', *Management Communication Quarterly*, 13(3): 347–392.

Ashcraft, K.L. (2006) 'Feminist-bureaucratic control and other adversarial allies: How hybrid organization subverts anti-bureaucratic discourse', *Communication Monographs*, 73(1): 55–86.

Behar, R. (1996) *The Vulnerable Observer: Anthropology that Breaks Your Heart*. Boston: Beacon Press.

Code, L. (1993) 'Taking subjectivity into account', in L. Alcoff and E. Potter (eds), *Feminist Epistemologies*. New York: Routledge, pp. 15–47.

Craig, R.T. and Tracy, K. (1995) 'Grounded practical theory: The case of intellectual discussion', *Communication Theory*, 5(3): 248–272.

Golden-Biddle, K. and Locke, K.D. (1993) 'Appealing work: An investigation of how ethnographic texts convince', *Organization Science*, 4(4): 595–616.

Heron, J. and Reason, P. (1997) 'A participatory inquiry paradigm', *Qualitative Inquiry*, 3(3): 274–294.

Jorgensen, D.L. (1989) *Participant Observation: A Methodology for Human Studies*. Newbury Park, CA: Sage.

Kauffman, B.J. (1992) 'Feminist facts: Interview strategies and political subjects in ethnography', *Communication Theory*, 2(3): 187–206.

Kondo, D.K. (1990) *Crafting Selves: Power, Gender, and Discourses of Identity in a Japanese Workplace*. Chicago: University of Chicago Press.

Kvale, S. and Brinkmann, S. (2009) *InterViews: Learning the Craft of Qualitative Research Interviewing* (2nd edn). Thousand Oaks, CA: Sage.

Locke, K.D., Golden-Biddle, K. and Feldman, M.S. (2008) 'Making doubt generative: Rethinking the role of doubt in the research process', *Organization Science*, 19(6): 907–918.

Mumby, D.K. (1988) *Communication and Power in Organizations: Discourse, Ideology, and Domination*. Norwood, NJ: Ablex.

Roman, L. (1992) 'The political significance of other ways of narrating ethnography: A feminist materialist approach', in M. LeCompte, W. Millroy and J.P. Goetz (eds), *Handbook of Qualitative Research in Education*. San Diego, CA: Academic Press, pp. 556–594.

Thomas, J. (1993) *Doing Critical Ethnography*. Newbury Park, CA: Sage.

Tracy, S. J. (2012) 'The toxic and mythical combination of a deductive writing logic for inductive qualitative research', *Qualitative Communication Research*, 1(1): 109–142.

Tracy, S.J. (2013) *Qualitative Research Methods: Collecting Evidence, Crafting Analysis, and Communicating Impact*. Chichester: Wiley-Blackwell.

Van Maanen, J. (1988) *Tales of the Field: On Writing Ethnography*. Chicago: University of Chicago Press.

Wray-Bliss, E. (2004) 'A right to respond? Monopolisation of "voice" in CMS', *Ephemera*, 4(2): 101–120.

TEN

Thickening thick descriptions: Overinterpretations in critical organizational ethnography

Peter Svensson

Introduction

Ethnographic work involves a number of epistemological challenges and ethical queries. Being close to the objects of study (the members, the natives), trying to represent their worlds in a fair and meaningful way is anything but a straightforward task. At the heart of the ethnographic enterprise lies the *interpretation* of symbols, social interactions, rituals, norms, ceremonies, cues and artefacts. The aim of the ethnographer is often to translate everyday and mundane phenomena into meaningful and significant aspects of the ongoing construction of social reality. Alvesson and Deetz (2000: 34) describe the interpretative task as one of showing 'how particular realities are socially produced and maintained through norms, rites, rituals and daily activities'. The theoretical lens offered by anthropology and the notion of 'culture' provides the analytical gaze and the research questions needed for this to happen. Anthropological theory enables us to see culture when we are searching for it, whether on the street corner, in the festival, the market place or in the organization.

The aim of this chapter is to discuss the role of *overinterpretations* in critical ethnography. It is my contention that overinterpretations are of utmost importance in critical organizational ethnographies since they allow us to attend to the silent and hidden forms of power/politics that contribute to the structural stability of organizational culture.[1] I will argue that overinterpretations should not be seen as a weakness of critical ethnographies, but rather, and more importantly, as one of the prerequisites for making *critical* interpretations of organizational culture. Overinterpretations make it possible to transgress the positive data (i.e. all that which can be heard, observed and perceived on the field) and established ways of representing social reality. In order to discuss the role of overinterpretations in critical ethnography I will in this chapter try to revitalize the notion of 'thick description' by means of returning to one of its origins, the semiotic conception of ethnography (Geertz, 1973).

My hope is that this chapter can contribute to the development of the critical researcher's reflexive sense of 'criticality' – a sense of of what it might mean to be engaged in critical interpretations of society. As I will argue in what follows, there are reasons to be much more suspicious of the notion of 'empirical support' than seems to be common within critical management studies (CMS) oriented research. Many CMS researchers would probably have very few problems with the *idea* or *principle* of overinterpretations. After all, transcending hegemonic representations of organizational and business life seems to be one ambition that unites different strands of critical studies of management today. However, in everyday research practice – in review processes, supervision of theses, editorial work, seminar discussions and so forth – there appears to be much less acceptance of interpretations that are not supported by positive observations in the empirical material, that is to say, observations based upon presence and visibility in the data.

Bold and radical analyses of empirical material are not only about connecting familiar themes such as 'oppression', 'exploitation', 'identity work', 'discursive closure' and so forth to visible and identifiable phenomena in organizations. The critical interpretation also strives beyond all that is said and done in the empirical field. I hope this chapter will provide some food for thought, not necessarily models, recipes and tools but ideas that can help the aspiring critical researcher to break free from what I experience as an empiricist straitjacket within the field of CMS (although there are some glowing exceptions from this rule). Arguably, the reflexive researcher is one who not only subjects the world to critical analyses but also allows the critical gaze to reflect back on his/her own research practice. Hopefully this chapter can be of some assistance in this regard.

The remainder of the chapter is structured as follows. In the next section I will discuss the 'critical' aspect of critical ethnography. I will then suggest that overinterpretations are of particular importance for the critical interpretations of organizational culture. Then I will discuss two forms of overinterpretations: the overwriting of natives' own experiences and the illumination of organizational silence. These forms will be exemplified by Rosen's critical ethnography of a business breakfast (Rosen, 1985) and my own study of IKEA catalogues (Svensson, 2010).

---

[1]In another text – and context – Dag Stenvoll and I have argued for the importance of overinterpretations and, more specifically, of *speculative* interpretations in political discourse analysis (Svensson and Stenvoll, 2013).

The chapter concludes with some reflections on the violent and ethical aspects of overinterpretations in critical ethnographies.

Reading culture suspiciously: The critical task of critical ethnography

Interpretations become particularly interesting in the case of critical ethnography. In a somewhat similar vein to Nyberg and Delaney (Chapter 4, this volume), I refer to critical ethnography as a research enterprise that focuses primarily on the relation between meaning and politics/power (see also Duberley and Johnson, 2009). Thus, critical ethnographies, or what Alvesson (1993: 46 ff.) refers to as the 'emancipatory approach to organizational culture', typically take an interest in the various ways in which power operates within and between organizations through the construction and establishment of meaning. Forester (1992: 47) captures the task of critical ethnography nicely when he observes that ordinary action 'is a thickly layered texture of political struggles concerning power and authority, cultural negotiations over identities, and social constructions of the "problem" at hand'. Given this, Forester suggests that 'the purpose of critical ethnographic work is to reveal the politics of this multilayered complexity'. Characteristic foci of critical ethnography include discursive closure (Deetz, 1992), distorted communication (Forester, 1992), the socio-cultural reproduction of hegemony (Rosen, 1985) and naturalizations of representations and worldviews (i.e. ideology critique: Rosen, 1988).

All of these topics seem to share an interest in the politics of meaning and the ways in which power operates through symbols, texts, artefacts and ritualized communication. This 'soft' power is not always easy to identify since it infiltrates the most intimate spheres of subjectivity and identity – often in silence. As has been acknowledged by many critical scholars, from Foucauldians, critical theorists, and Marxists, to Lacanians, critical discourse analysts and postcolonial writers, the most efficient power is the one operating in silence. Silent power works through the production of consent and common sense. Thus, silent power should not be understood as extraordinary and palpable manifestations of 'formal' authority, such as prime ministers' speeches, dictators' violent interventions in revolutionary protests and judges' formulations of sentences in the court. In contrast, when I write about soft and silent power in this chapter, I am referring to something very mundane that structures our everyday lives, often without us even noticing it. There are at least three ways in which soft and silent power operates in society (as well as within organizations).

First, soft power operates when the ideas we take for granted – and seldom or never question or challenge – shape who we are, what we want and how we relate to other people. These are the commonsensical ideas that – silently – enable us to see and understand certain things in the world. Organizational culture is full of such naturalized ideas that are difficult to formalize and represent in corporate documents.

They are, as it were, just there. This just-being-there-ness is what makes these ideas very influential – and indeed powerful. Hence, knowledge and 'truth' are intimately interconnected to power. The ideas that we treat as established truth are the most powerful ones since they do not need arguments in order to be accepted.

Secondly, soft power is not imposed upon us from outside, by an external force, but is an internalized part of how we understand ourselves as active and, indeed, free subjects (Butler, 1997). The internalized power makes us want, desire, yearn and hope. As pointed out by Butler, power produces us and our sense of free will and agency:

> Subjection consists precisely in this fundamental dependency on a discourse we never really chose but that, paradoxically, initiates and sustains our agency. 'Subjection' signifies the process of becoming a subject. Whether by interpellation, in Althusser's sense, or by discursive productivity, in Foucault's, the subject is initiated through a primary submission to power (Butler, 1997: 2).

Thus, Butler reminds us that this is a seemingly paradoxical situation. The 'discourses we never really chose' produce us as choosing subjects. To my mind, this is the essence of soft power.

Thirdly, the silent and soft forms of power are also embedded in the network of social relations and therefore contribute to the orderliness and predictability of everyday life. An organization consists of a myriad of social relations within which organizational members navigate on an everyday basis: relations between managers and subordinates, employers and employees, between different functions (administrative staff, marketing people, human resources and so forth). This is a kind of power that links people to each other and that contributes to the reproduction of cultural stability. A new working day does not need to start with a negotiation of the roles and internal relations of the organization. These structural arrangements are already there when we arrive at work in the morning. Silently they structure our professional lives.

Silent and soft forms of power, exerted in everyday politics of meaning, are not easily captured in terms of empirical observations since this power is already part of who people are, what they think, feel and know, and how they, often unreflectively, relate to each other. In order to shed light upon this power and the role it plays in organizational culture, we need *critical interpretations* that enable the critical ethnographer to penetrate the surface of organizational culture in order to, in Forester's words, 'reveal the politics' undergirding the everyday production and reproduction of meaning in an organization. My suggestion is that the 'critical' interpretation is a specific *kind* of interpretation, one through which the political interests and power relations underlying texts, symbols and social life are unmasked. The critical interpretation is guided by what Ricoeur (1970) has referred to as the hermeneutic of suspicion, the ambition of which is to expose the political functions of the construction of meaning (Itao, 2010). The critical interpretation is not an interpretation that seeks the authentic, true, plausible or sensible meaning of a text, but one that paves the ground for new ways of seeing and talking about the world:

> The goal of interpretation, Ricoeur repeatedly reminds us, is not some world *behind* the text, neither a subtext nor an Urtext, but a world *in front of* the text, a world that opens up new possibilities of being. (Stewart, 1989: 306)

'Opening up new possibilities of being': therein resides the emancipatory potential of critical interpretations. Whereas 'conventional ethnography describes what is, critical ethnography asks what could be' (Thomas, 1993: 4). In order to enable critical interpretations that are suspicious of the surface of organizational culture, there are reasons to revisit and revitalize the notion of 'thick description'.

Thickening thick descriptions: Critical interpretations as overinterpretations

Thick description is a central term in ethnography. However, as with many other popular concepts (Roberge, 2011), it appears to have developed into a clichéd term in ethnographically oriented organization studies, and seems to be 'somewhat overused, often denoting little more than a compulsive attention to detail in any field setting' (Prasad, 2005: 80). Bryman and Bell (2007: 413), for instance, refer to thick descriptions as 'rich accounts of the details of culture'. In a similar vein, Creswell and Miller (2000: 129) suggest that:

> The process of writing using thick description is to provide as much detail as possible. It may involve describing a small slice of interaction, experience, or action; locating individuals in specific situations; bringing a relationship or an interaction alive between two or more persons; or providing a detailed rendering of how people feel.

However, if we return to the origin of the notion of thick description, that is, the semiotic conception of ethnography as famously represented by Clifford Geertz (1973), we soon discover that thick descriptions should not be confused with (or reduced to) rich and detailed descriptions of empirical material (see also Schwandt, 2001: 255). Even though rich empirical accounts of organizational life may be useful for the ethnographer, this is not what Geertz seems to be talking about when he discusses thick description. Drawing upon Gilbert Ryle, Geertz suggests that the thick description should rather be conceived of as the ethnographer's main 'intellectual effort' in his or her attempts to *read* culture (1973: 6). Whereas the *thin* description is the naked, plain description of an act or interaction[2] (to use Ryle's own example, 'the boy rapidly contracts his right eyelids'), the *thick* description aims to discern what Geertz (1973: 7) refers to as the 'stratified hierarchy of meaningful structures' in relation to which actions are 'produced, perceived, and interpreted' (e.g. 'practicing a

---

[2]However, it is hardly possible to produce such an account given the interpretative character of even the simplest observation.

burlesque of a friend faking a wink to deceive an innocent into thinking a conspiracy is in motion').

The semiotic conception of culture highlights that cultural analysis is a way of reading social life that aims at disclosing the 'stratified hierarchy of meaningful structures' (Geertz, 1973: 6). Put differently, the ambition is: 'to read (in the sense of "construct a reading of") a manuscript – foreign, faded, full of eclipses, incoherencies, suspicious emendations, and tendentious commentaries, but written not in conventionalized graphs of sound but in transient examples of shaped behaviour' (Geertz, 1973: 10). The notion of thick description thereby draws attention to the *vertical* dimension of cultural analysis. Whereas a rich description – which, as mentioned above, should not be confused with thick description – is a horizontal reading of culture that takes place on the surface of the hierarchy of meanings, the thick description is about digging through the layers of cultural meaning.

Geertz (1973: 6) suggests that all interpretations of cultures are – or should be – thick descriptions in the sense that they should aim for the 'stratified hierarchy of meaningful structures'. The thick description is particularly interesting for critical ethnography since it penetrates the surface of social and symbolic life, not necessarily in order to arrive at the root or core of cultural life, but so as to unfold the different layers of meaning in the cultural manuscript governing organizational life. Unfolding cultural manuscripts is a way of denaturalizing everyday life and opening up new ways of being, seeing, thinking and talking. But what, then, characterizes the critical interpretation. What is it that makes it 'critical'?

In order to approach these questions, let me return to Forester's definition of critical ethnography. According to Forester (1992: 47), critical ethnography sets out to illuminate the 'thickly layered texture of political struggles concerning power and authority, cultural negotiations over identities, and social constructions of the "problem" at hand'. This is an approach to critical ethnography that, like Geertz's understanding of ethnography, acknowledges the vertical character of the cultural reading. To read organizational culture is to dig through layers of meaning. The critical interpretation seems to involve a *thicker* thick description than other interpretations, one that it is targeted towards the very deepest layers of culture. Thus, the thickened thick description, the critical interpretation, shares Geertz's focus on the layers of meanings undergirding culture, but it proceeds further than this. The critical interpretation pursues also the layers of meaning that are not even indirectly present in the empirical material (e.g. in the form of symbols, rituals and artefacts), but that have been repressed from the field material. These layers are, paradoxically enough, simply not there to be found. When the thick description is thickened, the most established norms as to empirical support and validity are challenged, and alternative interpretative strategies to reach these deep layers of cultural meaning are called for.

One way of thickening the thick descriptions in cultural interpretations of organizational life is to engage in *overinterpretations*. To move through and between the hierarchies of meaning of a culture (or cultural life) is in many ways a violent interpretative act that persistently tries to see through the most superficial levels of meaning – i.e. what people say and what seems to happen in an organization – in order to get down to the layers of soft and silent power of social life. 'Violence' is a strong but nevertheless an apt term for describing the nature of the overinterpretation. Classical examples of overinterpretations are psychoanalytical interpretations of clients' accounts in therapy or Marxist analyses of false consciousness. The psychoanalytical interpretation treats the clients' verbal accounts as symptoms of hidden, psychological processes, whereas Marxist analyses often view individual experiences as products of structural and socio-political forces.[3]

The very term 'overinterpretation' indicates a point beyond that which can be justified in terms of what is seen as empirical evidence or support. To engage in overinterpretation is to do *too* much, like talking or eating too much: 'there is proper eating or interpreting, but some people don't stop when they should. They go on eating or interpreting in excess, with bad results' (Culler, 1992: 111). To overinterpret the empirical material is to impose *too much* of the analyst on the material. However, what is 'over', 'right on the spot' and 'under' are indeed relations constructed and negotiated in specific research communities and within certain established ideas of what constitutes the normal science of the field (cf. Kuhn, 1962). Moreover, established and accepted interpretations change over the course of history. What is a reasonable interpretation today could have been a radical overinterpretation some years ago. A good example is perhaps gender-oriented interpretations that are hardly considered as radical today as they once probably were. The gender category (and analytical lens) has today become very much an established part of the theoretical arsenal of serious critical social research. In so far as critical ethnography deals with the politics of meaning, and given that much of this politics takes place in the form of soft and silent power, the act of overinterpretation can help us illuminate hidden forms of power and reveal meaning structures that organizational members do not talk about or simply have forgotten.

Arguably, the overinterpretation is the *only* meaningful interpretation in critical ethnographies. In his defence of overinterpretations, literary theorist Jonathan Culler (1992: 110) points out that:

> Many 'extreme' interpretations, like many moderate interpretations, will no doubt have little impact, because they are judged unpersuasive or redundant or irrelevant or boring, but if they are extreme, they have a better chance, it seems to me, of bringing to light connections or implications not previously noticed or reflected on than if they strive to remain 'sound' or moderate.

Culler touches upon something here that might be relevant to critical ethnographers. Interpretations can have impact; they can *do* something, e.g. contribute to social change and emancipation. By means of illuminating and analysing power in

---

[3]As it happens, according to Ricoeur, Freud and Marx were, alongside Nietzsche, the masters of suspicion.

organizations, the critical ethnographer can contribute to an increased awareness of how power operates in organizations, and thereby pave the ground for different forms of social change.

Two examples of overinterpretation: Overwriting the natives' interpretations and studying silence

There are different kinds of overinterpretations, all having in common that they go beyond the empirical material. For the sake of the argument, I will in this chapter restrict myself to the distinction between two basic kinds of overinterpretations: the overwriting of natives' own experiences and language; and the illumination of silence.

These overinterpretations are particularly interesting as they, in different ways, violate the emic approach to human behaviour and culture that has become one of the central tenets of ethnography. Coined by Pike (1967), the emic approach to the study of human behaviour refers to the ambition to acknowledge the natives' own local interpretations and conceptions of their lives. The emic approach is based upon the 'discernment of culture from an endogenic rather than an exogenic standpoint' (Prasad, 2005: 78). Whereas emic interpretations are 'regarded appropriate by the actors themselves', etic interpretations are 'judged appropriate by the community of scientific observers' (Harris, 1976: 334). Emic interpretations emerge from inside the field, whereas etic interpretations are imposed from outside. It is my contention that this is in fact what makes etic interpretations potentially critical; they transcend the natives' point of view.

Overwriting the natives' experiences: Disregarding the emic approach

The overwriting of natives' experiences and language use can be seen as a strong violation of the emic approach. The overinterpretation – at least the one I am arguing for in this chapter – is based upon an explicit ambition to render the familiar strange by means of pushing the interpretation far beyond organizational members' own perceptions and interpretations. To the advocates of the emic approach in ethnographic work (e.g. Morey and Luthans, 1984; Jackson, 1993), this aspiration is most likely seen as a violent treatment of empirical material.

I do not agree. I am not a hermeneutic pacifist, at least when it comes to critical ethnographies. To my mind, the violence involved in overinterpretations is needed in order to reach the most silent and hidden forms of power governing or framing organizational culture.

A good example of this kind of overinterpretation is one of my favourite critical ethnographies: Rosen's (1985) study of a business breakfast at the advertising agency Spiro and Associates. Starting from the premise that culture is a control mechanism, Rosen offers a cultural analysis of this breakfast in which he particularly stresses the political function of this event. According to Rosen (1985: 48), the social drama played out during the breakfast at the advertising agency is one way in which social order is maintained and political control is sustained. During the breakfast, a variety of symbolic techniques are used 'in such as way as to influence ideas, thus influencing action, thus shaping experience, consequently shaping ideas' (1985: 33). For instance, a sense of what Rosen refers to as 'commensality' is produced by the very fact that the agency members 'break bread' together (1985: 33). Dress codes signal and reproduce the power hierarchies in the agency. The business people were obliged to wear suits whereas the creative people were free to dress in any way they found appropriate. Rosen (1985: 34) explains this situation as follows:

> [T]he clerical workers and, by and large, the creative people, are not in the main contest for wealth, influence and power, and are hence not as socially constricted in their behavior. By contrast, the behavior of those vying for the larger rewards of power, the business people, is highly circumscribed.

Furthermore, Rosen suggests that the speeches delivered by the managers at the breakfast reproduce and reinforce certain images of the advertising agency, e.g. the image of an important, prestigious, altruistic and a place for personal growth.

It seems to me that Rosen's interpretations effectively overwrite the natives' own interpretations of what happens during the breakfast. In fact, the natives' own interpretations of what goes on are not central to his argument. The natives appear in his ethnography as social actors in the drama he tries to read; they say and do things but they are never asked to share their own interpretations of the social drama in which they act. For a dedicated believer in the emic approach, this is a cause for critique. How is it possible to say something about the social functions of symbolic techniques without taking into account the natives' own experiences and interpretations? How can an ethnographer claim to have anything to say about the webs of significance structuring organizational culture without taking into account the natives' viewpoints?

To my mind, this is, among other things, what makes Rosen's study interesting, provocative and critically sharp. Put differently, this is in fact what makes Rosen's interpretation *critical*. The purpose of Rosen's study is to 'explicate the dimensions and processes involved in the recreation of the bureaucratic form as a mechanism of control' (1985: 33), and the most efficient forms of control are perhaps those which we cannot perceive or talk about. As Rosen declares in another paper, 'participants themselves cannot explain the full effects of rituals on them' (1988: 477).

The thick description of a critical interpretation requires the researcher to redefine the role of the natives' points of view: from a *source* of ethnographic insights to a *symptom* of the politics of meaning. This not to say that the natives' accounts, experiences and interpretations are irrelevant to a critical ethnographer, but they are treated as outcomes of the politics of meaning constituting organization culture.

Obviously all kinds of interpretations are produced by individual researchers with certain conscious and unconscious interests and agendas in mind; the interpretation is the product of the interpreter. The focus on positive data and empirical support that seems to characterize a great deal of contemporary research on organizational culture (including that considered to be 'critical') involves a fear of allowing the interpreter to become too powerful in relation to the empirical material, an anxiety of imposing too many a priori ideas, models and conceptions on the data. However, as already said, there are reasons for the critical ethnographer not to be afraid of going beyond – and in some cases also against – the natives' own interpretations, discourse and experiences.

The illumination of organizational silence

Another example of overinterpretations of relevance to critical ethnographies is the interpretations that focus on the silent aspects of organizational culture. Silence is particularly interesting in critical ethnography, not least so since the most intricate and effective forms of power are exercised in silence. Hence, 'subjectivity and action should also be understood in relation to what is barred from performance, what is not or cannot be performed – the not-there, the unsaid traces, the absent presences, that structure the said and done' (Kulick, 2005: 616). Thus, the incessant production of organizational culture resides not only in the production of positive manifestations (such as the rituals explored by Rosen) but also in the production of *negative* culture, i.e. silence. As suggested by Dendrinos and Ribeiro Pedro (1997: 216):

> The production of silence, like the production of speech, can realise an ideological struggle. It follows that to arrive at an understanding of how ideology expresses itself will involve us in systematic research of who remains silent, about what and in what situations.

Dendrinos and Ribeiro Pedro here emphasize the ideological manifestations in the form of silence, and I would like to suggest that a similar argument can be made for organizational culture. Thus, a thorough exploration of the everyday production of organizational culture would need to take into account a study of silent voices and themes.

The silence of organizational culture can manifest itself in at least two ways. The first form of silence, the *unsaid*, comprises those things we take for granted, the common sense that we never really talk about. The second form of silence, the *not-said*, comprises all that which has been excluded and repressed from everyday life: all the themes, topics, metaphors, motifs, discourses and images that have been excluded from the conversations that occur in the organization. Some themes and topics are actively, and consciously, excluded from social interaction in the daily life. Put differently, people may use silence strategically in order to save a situation, themselves or someone else. Silence can also be used as a way of diminishing another person's authority or political influence. The collectively repressed topics in an organization belong to what Fromm refers to as the 'social unconscious', that is:

> [T]hose areas of repression which are common to most members of a society; these commonly repressed elements are those contents which a given society cannot permit its members to be aware of if the society with its specific contradictions is to operate successfully (Fromm, 1962: 70).

A large portion of the critical potency of critical ethnography resides in the attentiveness of the silence of culture, and the interpretation of silence is, arguably, the thickest of thick descriptions. Silence is, by definition, not positively manifested in the empirical material (it cannot be spotted) but needs to be *imported* by a creative analyst with a certain theoretical gaze and some degree of imagination. To be able to give voice to the silence of discourse, the interpretative efforts need to go over and beyond the manifest text as well as the common-sense assumptions of what the silence is silent about.

My study of repressed themes and topics in IKEA catalogues (Svensson, 2010) is an attempt to study silence empirically. Even though my study is not an ethnographic study in its own right, it could (and should) be seen as a part of a broader ethnographic approach to consumer culture, in particular the consumption of the home. IKEA catalogues are in many ways an interesting cultural artefact that plays a significant role in contemporary consumer culture in Sweden and, to some extent, in the rest of Europe. They seem to express a vast array of ideas and moral points. The annual catalogue presents colourful images of the ideal home, but these images comprise many other ideals, norms and ideologies concerning cultural categories such as 'the family', 'the friend', and 'work'.

As a way of exploring IKEA's role in the politics of meaning, I subjected the annual IKEA catalogues to a series of what I would like to see as overinterpretations of silent themes in the images of homes presented in the catalogues.

In my study I suggested three silences in the IKEA catalogues: silence on aging, silence on pain and conflict, and silence on solitude. Let me by way of illustration cite my discussion on the silence on pain and conflict (see Figure 10.1).

My study of IKEA catalogues is clearly based on my overinterpretations. What I see is obviously *not there*. And that is the point of my analysis. In order to illuminate absent themes in the catalogues, I had to (re-)create the absence on the basis of what I actually can observe. Silence is not easily identified in the midst of all the noise of the positive (present, manifest) world. Thus, the sound of silence is a negative sound; it becomes manifest, and thus empirically observable, only when the volume of the surrounding noise has been turned down. In order to listen to silence we need to go beyond what we can hear.

The homes displayed in the IKEA catalogues are devoid of pain, tension and conflict. A psychoanalytic scrutiny or Marxist analysis of the calm and harmony permeating the pictures in the catalogues would probably interpret this as a repressed state of conflict and aggression. An example of silenced pain is the absence of sadness in the home settings represented in the catalogues. There is simply no explicit sadness in the catalogue homes. No tears, no disappointment, no crying. The catalogue inhabitants are generally happy, shiny people holding hands. Consider this image:

Picture 4: Happy, shiny people in love (IKEA 2007, p. 8), used with the permission of Inter IKEA Systems B. V.

This is the most obvious example of the remarkable silence on sadness in the IKEA catalogues. Love and joy permeate this picture. The brightness of the room is not only a result of candles and white walls. We are here confronted with the happy couple in love. A photo of two children is hanging on the wall to the right. Perhaps the couple are experiencing one of the first times on their own since they became parents. Perhaps the children are sleeping safely in another room. Maybe the children are with their grandparents.

Arguably, it is hard to interpret this picture as a story about a couple who have lost their two children in a car crash a couple of years ago, and now, after years of mourning are slowly getting back to life with hope for a brighter future. Such an interpretation is most likely seen as little more than grotesque, perhaps even offensive, and more a result of the reader's traumatic life history than of the picture per se. There is simply no, or very little, room for these kinds of painful biographies in the IKEA home. Love and happiness seem to be the only accepted scheme for how to read the images in the catalogues.

Figure 10.1 Calm and harmony in the IKEA catalogue

Conclusion: The violent critical ethnographer

In this chapter I have argued for a more forgiving, and perhaps even a more encouraging, approach to overinterpretations in critical ethnographies. To me it seems as if much of the critical potential of critical research depends upon the researchers' willingness to engage in extreme and somewhat violent interpretation of empirical material. Acknowledging the value of overinterpretations may also entail a firm scepticism towards sound, moderate and so-called 'reasonable' interpretations. The moderate interpretation is always situated on the verge of common sense and therefore runs the risk of reproducing already naturalized and hegemonic representations of social reality and relations. Social change, in particular that which is considered radical, often requires denaturalizations of the 'given' and the 'natural'.

One of the implications of the argument presented in this chapter is that we need to rethink the idea of the cultural interpretation, especially so when the ethnographic work has critical ambitions. Like many other forms of 'qualitative research', ethnography is embedded in empiricist notions such as empirical support, validity and trustworthiness. Even though these terms are not always used explicitly, they lurk behind the idea of empirical support in *positive* data.[4] Clearly the overinterpretation implies a violation of the idea of empirical support. In fact, the point of the overinterpretation is – for political and critical reasons – to go beyond that which is empirically justifiable in the empirical material.

In so far as critical ethnography involves the attempt to highlight the hidden, soft and silent power in organizational life, it seems to me that the chief problem of sound and moderate readings of culture is that they do not challenge the established puzzle of normal science. Neither do they suggest new puzzles, new questions and problematic aspects of the political life of organizations. Quite the contrary, the moderate interpretation easily becomes an *under*interpretation that tends to do little more than reproduce representations of work, capitalism, and managerialism.

However, acknowledging the value of overinterpretations does not mean that anything goes. The notion of overinterpretation should not be exploited as a justification for sloppy (or non-existent) empirical research. That would be missing the point. The empirical material disciplines us, perhaps even more so when we are striving for creative readings targeted towards the subtle operation of power. The overinterpretation could be seen as an instance of what Prasad (2005: 7) refers to as 'disciplined creativity'. It requires creativity, fantasy and a suspicious gaze, but it is simultaneously constrained – albeit not determined – by the empirical material. To acknowledge creativity, fantasy and suspicion as central aspects of the critical interpretation of ethnographic material is to take *reflexivity* very seriously. Engaging in reflexivity boils down to the willingness and capacity to look oneself in the mirror and face oneself as an active –and powerful – producer of empirical material and interpretations (cf. Alvesson and Deetz, 2000: 113). The reflexive researcher manages to operate in the tension between creativity and discipline, between violence and sensitivity.

---

[4] The reliance on positive (or present) data is prevalent not only in positivist research. All research that in one way or another is based upon representations of social reality seems to rely on the idea of 'empirical support'.

For instance, the violation of the emic approach is also, in effect, the violation of the native's right to formulate his/her own experiences. This is not unproblematic and calls for political sensitivity. Nyberg and Delaney (Chapter 4, this volume) offer some insightful comments on the importance, as a critical ethnographer, of being aware of what you do to the field, for example the organization subjected to study. The overinterpretation could then be seen as the construction of 'a position of privilege and power for the critical ethnographer' (Katz, 2004, cited by Nyberg and Delaney). I do not want to downplay these ethical problems, but I do want to take the opportunity to reflect upon them.

First, in a general sense, all research can be considered exploitive. Arguably, treating someone as a source of knowledge turns him/her into an object of study rather than a subject with a self-value. In the role as observer and interpreter, it is difficult if not impossible for the critical ethnographer to escape power. The last word always, willingly or not, belongs to the researcher, the one responsible for the interpretations.

Secondly, and more importantly, the production of overinterpretations could be seen as one of the *duties* of the critical researcher. To the extent that critical research is to take the critical ambition seriously (revealing multilayered politics and scrutinizing relations between meaning and power), the transformation of 'natural' states of affairs into strangeness seems to be a crucial research task. Thus, critical research on organizational culture cannot rely solely on emic representations of everyday life in organizations. This would in fact – at least in some cases – be to contribute to the reproduction of common-sense and hegemonic accounts of work life. Disregarding the emic approach to organizational culture should therefore not be seen as stepping away from the 'critical' ethos, but rather as a part of what it means to be 'critical'. Turning the familiar into something extraordinary is probably not painless for the native. The denaturalization of culture does not necessarily confirm the natives' sense-making or support organizational stability but may, on the contrary, lead to insecurity and volatility. Nevertheless, despite potential pain and anxiety, being violent (in terms of overinterpreting culture and natives) could be seen as one of the main tasks of a critical ethnographer. In fact, this is what makes a critical ethnography critically meaningful in that it 'opens up new possibilities of being' (Stewart, 1989: 306).

References

Alvesson, M. (1993) *Cultural Perspectives on Organisations*. Cambridge: Cambridge University Press.

Alvesson, M. and Deetz, D. (2000) *Doing Critical Management Research*. London: Sage.

Bryman, A. and Bell, E. (2007) *Business Research Methods*. Oxford: Oxford University Press.

Butler, J. (1997) *The Psychic Life of Power*. Stanford, CA: Stanford University Press.

Creswell, J.W. and Miller, D.L. (2000) 'Determining validity in qualitative inquiry', *Theory into Practice*, 39(3): 124–130.

Culler, J. (1992) 'In defence of overinterpretation', in U. Eco (ed.), *Interpretation and Overinterpretation*. Cambridge: Cambridge University Press, pp. 109–124.

Deetz, S. (1992) *Democracy in an Age of Corporate Colonization: Developments in Communication and the Politics of Everyday Life*. Albany: State University of New York Press.

Dendrinos, B. and Ribeiro Pedro, E. (1997) 'Giving street directions: The silent role of women', in A. Jaworski (ed.), *Silence: Interdisciplinary Perspectives*. Berlin: de Gruyter, pp. 215–238.

Duberley, J. and Johnson, P. (2009) 'Critical management methodology', in H. Willmott, T. Bridgman and M. Alvesson (eds), *The Oxford Handbook of Critical Management Studies*. Oxford: Oxford University Press.

Forester, J. (1992) 'Critical ethnography: On fieldwork in a Habermasian way', in M. Alvesson and H. Wilmott (eds), *Critical Management Studies*. London: Sage.

Fromm, E. (1962) *Beyond the Chains of Illusions: My Encounter with Marx and Freud*. New York: Continuum.

Geertz, C. (1973) *The Interpretation of Cultures*. London: Fontana.

Harris, M. (1976) 'History and significance of the emic/etic distinction', *Annual Review of Anthropology*, 5: 329–350.

Itao, A. (2010) 'Paul Ricoeur's hermeneutics of symbols: A critical dialectic of suspicion and faith', *Kritike*, 4(2): 1–17.

Jackson J.F. (1993) 'Multiple caregiving among African Americans and Infant attachment: The need for an emic approach', *Human Development*, 36(2): 87–102.

Kuhn, T. (1962) *The Structure of Scientific Revolutions*. Chicago: University of Chicago Press.

Kulick, D. (2005) 'The importance of what gets left out', *Discourse Studies*, 7(4–5): 615–624.

Morey, N.C. and Luthans, F. (1984) 'An emic perspective and ethnoscience methods for organizational research', *Academy of Management Review*, 9(1): 27–36.

Pike, K.L. (1967) *Language in Relation to a Unified Theory of the Structures of Human Behavior*. The Hague: Mouton.

Prasad, P. (2005) *Crafting Qualitative Research*. Armonk, NY: ME Sharpe.

Ricoeur, P. (1970) *Freud and Philosophy: An Essay on Interpretation*. New Haven, CT: Yale University Press.

Roberge, J. (2011) 'What is critical hermeneutics', *Thesis Eleven*, 106(1): 5–22.

Rosen, M. (1985) 'Breakfast at Spiro's: Dramaturgy and dominance', *Journal of Management*, 11(2): 31–48.

Rosen, M. (1988) 'You asked for it: Christmas at the bosses' expenses', *Journal of Management Studies*, 25(5): 463–480.

Schwandt, T.A. (2001) *Dictionary of Qualitative Inquiry*. Thousand Oaks, CA: Sage.

Stewart, D. (1989) 'The hermeneutics of suspicion', *Journal of Literature & Theology*, 3(3): 296–307.

Svensson, P. (2010) 'Silent IKEA', in S. Burt, U. Johansson and Å. Thelander (eds), *Consuming IKEA: Different Perspectives on Consumer Images Of a Global Retailer.* Lund: Lund Business Press, pp. 131–154.

Svensson, P. and Stenvoll, D. (2013) 'Risky readings: The virtue of overinterpretations and speculations in political discourse analysis', in K. Fløttum (ed.), *Speaking of Europe: Approaches to Complexity in European Political Discourse.* Amsterdam: John Benjamins, pp. 171–188.

Thomas, J. (1993) *Doing Critical Ethnography.* London: Sage.

ELEVEN

Conceptually grounded analysis: The elusive facticity and ethical upshot of 'organization'

Hugh Willmott

Introduction

Contributors to this volume were invited to 'focus on the *practical realities* of the research process and how challenges faced can be negotiated' (Jeanes and Huzzard, 2011: 1). What might those 'practical realities' be? Here I consider two.[1] First, there is the practical reality of conducting empirical research, including its writing up. Specifically, I reflect upon my experience of undertaking a PhD. Second, I consider the practicalities of invoking 'organization' as a central concept in management and organization studies (MOS). These two 'practical realities' are connected. The experience of producing my thesis – especially the conduct of fieldwork and the translation of my data into an account of the people and agencies that I researched – provoked reflection upon the basis of social scientific authority and, more specifically, upon how concepts are practically invoked and mobilized in MOS.

The *'practical realities* of the research process' include deliberations over the specificities and scope of the research topic and the methods used. Another kind of consideration, which frames such deliberations and informs responses to them, is the *perspective or approach* to be taken. In turn, this may prompt the posing of

[1] I am grateful to the editors and to Martin Parker for providing comments on an earlier draft of this chapter that enabled me to make substantial improvements.

another deeper question concerning the ontology of the 'practical realities' (e.g. of 'organization') being studied.

My observation from attending many MOS conferences is that researchers, whether at an early or late stage of their career, are comparatively comfortable when discussing their research *topic* or even their research *methods*. Comfort levels tend to drop when we are asked to explicate our theoretical *approach* to the topic. Issues and problems of theorizing, I will suggest, are at the heart of the 'practical realities of the research process'.

The distinction between 'theory'/theorizing and 'practice'/practical realities is an appealingly neat heuristic device as it implies that these elements are separable and perhaps even antithetical. In common with other dualisms (e.g. rhetoric–reality) widely entertained within common sense and social science, its use can obscure an entanglement of the poles. Developing theory is a form of embedded practice; and most practice is conditioned by some kind of background theory that silently renders that practice relevant or legitimizes its pursuit. Without an appreciation of the entanglement of theory and practice, the attention given to 'theorizing' in this chapter might seem deaf to the editors' invitation to explore 'practical realities'. That disjuncture, I suggest, is indicative of how 'theory' and 'practice' are, unhelpfully, conceived as split rather than enmeshed. When addressed more holistically, theory is represented as integral to 'practical questions', such as those that concern the specification of topics and the relevance of methods. What do I mean?

I mean that *how* 'practical questions' – such as how the 'research topic' is defined, or how the research sample is specified – are posed and addressed is theory-dependent. Recognition of theory-dependence is hardly new.[2] Indeed, much stress is placed in MOS scholarship on demonstrating the 'theoretical contribution' of research submitted to journals. Yet, at the same time, there is a widespread tendency to overlook or marginalize the *constitutive role of theory* in the production and interpretation of research. Whether engaged casually or deliberately, theory endows our research topics with significance; it warrants our selection of methods; it informs our interpretation of the status and meaning of empirical data, and so on. To consider and illuminate this theme, I begin by reflecting upon the significance of theory as a departure point for addressing some 'practical realities' experienced in undertaking my PhD and in invoking the concept of organization in contemporary practices of organization analysis.

---

[2]Notably, it was strongly signalled in Burrell and Morgan's (1979) *Sociological Paradigms and Organizational Analysis*, even if the central role of theory, as distinct from the assumptions on which different paradigmatic stocks of theory are based, is largely implicit. *Paradigms* demonstrates the diverse ways in which 'organization' is represented, and thereby invites reflection and debate on the politics of representation (see Burrell, 1999), albeit that, in *Paradigms*, 'politics' is framed largely apolitically in terms of choices between competing sets, or paradigms, of ontological and epistemological assumptions.

The significance of theory

When identifying and presenting a topic of study, researchers necessarily depend upon some ideas, in the form of (an often embryonic) theory, to represent that topic. Theory enables us to define, articulate, explicate, elucidate, interrogate, affirm or transform how we make sense of our topic. As we reflect upon our initial understandings, we engage in further rounds of theory-dependent representation (Tsoukas and Knudsen, 2005).

Where, then, do the empirical data analysed by researchers stand in relation to this cyclical process? From the perspective taken here, the standing and significance of the empirical material resides less in the testing of theory (or hypotheses drawn from theory) than in its contribution to ongoing conversations or dialogues on the topic. In this process, there is respect for what 'common sense' makes of the topic, but this sense is also problematized as it is deconstructed and potentially revised and/ or enriched. Where this position differs from parallel contributions – by journalists, novelists and commentators –is in the relative degree of self-consciousness and transparency in how social scientific narratives are assembled, analysed and presented. Privileging the importance of reflexivity reverses the emphasis found in many PhD theses and research proposals where, for example, previous research is reviewed from an apparently impartial, God-like position, and where accounts of methods used are idealized as they are dressed up in the seductive but disingenuous finery of tests of validity and reliability. Neglected, in comparison, is the role of theory in delineating, and even constituting, the topic of research and/or in lending authority to the methods used to generate and interpret empirical data.

What are ostensibly 'factual' data do not produce themselves or speak for themselves. They are always generated and interpreted by reference to some theory which lends them purpose and significance. That said, an exclusive emphasis upon theory may signal an over-precious retreat from empirical study, with unfortunate consequences – as when, for example, theory development becomes (dogmatically) self-referential, in part because of a lack of opportunity for theory to be challenged by unexpected findings (even when allowance is made for the basis and credibility of those findings to be doubted). The greater danger, though, is to overlook or devalue the import of theory-dependence. This risk is most acute where excessive emphasis is placed upon the careful application of robust methods and the generation of empirical material. This weight can displace adequate appreciation of how claims to falsify (or to confirm) a theory, as well assertions that data serve theory, or vice versa, are theory-dependent.

Topic, method, theory

Consider the *topic* of my PhD: 'the management of single homelessness' which I started in 1972 after completing an undergraduate degree in management sciences at University of Manchester Science and Technology (UMIST)[3]. During my undergraduate studies, I was drawn to the social science elements of the degree – psychology, sociology, labour economics, industrial relations, etc. (no 'HRM' in those days!) .

My interest in studying the single homeless was stimulated by two formative experiences. First, as an undergraduate, I ran a mobile soup kitchen mainly for single homeless people; and, second, an interest in 'deviancy' developed when preparing my undergraduate dissertation. The soup kitchen experience led me to appreciate the existence and work of a number of agencies – the police, social services, hospitals, charitable bodies, etc. – in 'providing for', or 'managing', the single homeless in central Manchester. In my final year, I elected to write a dissertation based upon my experience of taking a group of relatively 'deprived' young teenagers on holiday to a hostel in Europe, one of whom differed or 'deviated' from the other members of the group by evidently having 'Down's syndrome' and having significant learning difficulties. Preparing the dissertation confirmed a preference for substantial projects, rather than fragments of coursework, and further stimulated an interest in the possibility of pursuing a research-based career.

Note how, when referring to my early research experience, I am inclined to focus upon the topic (single homelessness) and, to a lesser extent, the methods (participant observation). To refer to my research primarily by reference to theory – for example, theories of deviance – would seem a little awkward and incongruous, if not pretentious. That, as I suggested earlier, is because greater value, in terms of comfort and relevance, tends to be placed in the topic of research and also, to a lesser extent, the methods of its investigation. Referring to them is easier, more familiar, engaging and unthreatening, at least in comparison to explicating theory and attending to its role in identifying, scoping and examining specific topics.

The fieldwork for my PhD involved interviewing staff from various agencies as well as single homeless people, conducting a survey among staff of one of the major charitable bodies, attending meetings convened within and between the agencies, and so on. The PhD was, in short, a rather typical qualitative study, loosely informed initially by a symbolic interactionist perspective (Blumer, 1969) and then supplemented by more radical theories of deviance (Taylor et al., 1973). The study was designed to collect a large volume of different kinds of data (obtained through surveys, interviews and observation), with the anticipation that this could be 'triangulated' to produce a fresh and robust account of the role of various agencies in the management of single homelessness. The intention was to make a distinctive contribution to knowledge that, potentially, might inform what today would likely be termed 'evidence-based' policy. Two episodes, among others, were important in prompting me to reflect upon these ambitions.

---

[3]The Department of Management Sciences was rebranded in the 1990s as Manchester School of Management. UMIST was subsequently merged with the University of Manchester to become part of Manchester Business School.

First, as a quid pro quo for allowing me access to one of the agencies, part of my data was (with the benefit of hindsight) naïvely and without sufficient safeguards made available to the agency. It was then deployed, highly selectively, to justify and promote the work of the agency to the media and to a central government department from which it received substantial funding. Although this did not, to my knowledge, have adverse effects upon any of my interviewees, it was a hard lesson. I felt used or violated by the conversion of my research into policy-based evidence production.

A second episode involved another key agency relevant to my study, the police, which refused to provide any meaningful cooperation with my research. This refusal made it difficult, or indeed impossible, to produce the inclusive, wide-ranging analysis of the 'management' of single homelessness that I had envisaged.

In retrospect, these practical concerns and frustrations proved to be instructive and helpful in provoking critical reflection upon the conduct and viability of social scientific research. More immediately, they induced some paralysing doubts about the 'scientific' credentials of my study, including notions of 'generalization', 'triangulation' and 'getting close to the phenomenon'. In what sense did the data enable me to 'capture' the phenomenon or even illuminate certain aspects of it? Even if all the agencies had granted me full access, what significance or weight could I give to what I had collected?

Recall that this was the early to mid-1970s. There was limited discussion in social science, let alone in management studies, of issues of reflexivity, including the relevance of the philosophy of (social) science for studying organization(s) and management. When preparing to write up my thesis, not only was I unsure of how to marshal my data to provide a distinctive contribution to existing knowledge of the relationship between single homeless people and (some of) the agencies that cared for/controlled them, I was also uncertain of what theoretical perspective or perspectives I should adopt in order to do justice to my empirical material. Was my initial attraction to symbolic interactionism – in line with many fieldwork studies of 'deviance', including several US-based studies of 'hobos', etc. – viable or defensible? Would its adoption not omit, obscure or mystify broader 'structural' considerations and 'forces' – forces that, arguably, contributed to the sense of dislocation and abuse experienced by my 'research subjects' whose actions I had been studying, and which I had also experienced when my findings were selectively used by one agency and cooperation was refused by a second agency?

The question of how to take account of 'action' in relation to 'structure' or 'system' had been taken up, albeit rather obliquely, in Silverman's *The Theory of Organizations* (1970). Still, in the mid-1970s, the narrowly defined field of organizational behaviour, as it was then known, had yet to morph into the more inclusive domain of organization studies. The 'structure'–'action' issue was only just beginning to surface as a 'central problem of social theory', as Giddens (1979) later characterized it. It was, however, an issue of direct concern to me as I could see merit in action-focused symbolic interactionism (which is the direction of travel of Silverman's 'action frame of reference' before taking his ethnomethodological turn) *and* in structure-sensitive analyses, such as those inspired by the European founders of sociology – Marx, Weber and Durkheim. The question of how to connect 'action' and 'structure' was to become a recurrent theme of future work, including the poststructuralist 'crusade', conducted with David Knights and others during the 1980s and 1990s in which we sought to incorporate substantive considerations of identity and subjectivity into the politico-economic analysis of labour processes (Knights and Willmott, 1990).

Back in the mid-1970s, when preparing to redraft chapters of my thesis, it was not so much the 'subjectivity issue' that detained me. Although it figures in my thesis, what was troubling me most were misgivings, or angst, about how a(ny) presentation of data could stack up as 'social science'. What exactly would I be claiming for my 'findings'? What was the basis of the authority ascribed to my claims? Looking back, I was perhaps taking my research, and myself, a tad too seriously. On the other hand, the grounding of social science seemed to be the 'elephant in the room'. In the end, my angst surfaced in the main title of my PhD thesis: 'The Commitment of Social Science'.

If I was ever going to produce a thesis, I first had to find a remedy for my misgivings. I had put aside, and then abandoned, the draft chapters prepared for the submission of an empirically based thesis. They were no longer of any use once I had become preoccupied by, and indeed obsessed with, a single question: what underpins the authority attributed to social scientific knowledge? Caught in this deadlock, I was unable to 'write up' my work by marshalling the substantial volume of empirical data into what I could present as a credible (?) account of my research. I felt confused, ashamed and guilty. Confused because I did not know how to proceed as I lacked sufficient clarity even to articulate my problem. Shame because I believed that I *ought* to be capable of producing an empirically based thesis. Others were doing it, why couldn't I? Guilt because I had believed, perhaps romantically, that my study of 'the management of single homelessness' might make a small difference to the lives of a particularly disadvantaged and often maligned group of people. Not only was I contemplating discarding a thesis that was substantially drafted; I was also abandoning a strong part of what had motivated me to undertake the research on which it was based. Those were the 'practical realities' of my 'research process'.

Today, I would say that the impasse was symptomatic of my limited awareness of the role played by theory in the production and, especially, the justification of knowledge; and, relatedly, of my faltering and perhaps too abstract understanding of how power, for want of another term, inescapably conditions knowledge. Relations of power between myself (as a naïve researcher, dependent upon others for continuing research, access, etc.) and the agencies responsible for 'managing the single homeless' made it possible, indeed very easy, for one to appropriate my data for self-promotional purposes; and for another to refuse involvement in my study. The particular form of my theory-dependence had not prepared me for grappling with what, in effect, had became a crisis of confidence in whatever truth I might claim for my study, and what responsibility I should take for whatever impact this truth might have. Existentially there was no way of rebooting to return the genie to the bottle. From once being a daunting but probably doable task, completing an empirically based PhD in good faith had become an impossibility. Slowly, it dawned upon me, assisted by a merciful lack of pressure from others to simply 'get the job done!' (the ESRC were not counting completions at that time), that there was perhaps a thesis that I might be able to write. Or at least there was only one thesis that I could even attempt to write. That was a thesis in which I would begin to interrogate my quandary. In conventional terms, the resulting thesis was a retreat from the street to the cloister – from the demanding field of 'practice' to the cosy armchair of 'theory'. Yet, it was of course the 'practice' of doing empirical research that provided the material for theoretical reflection, and this reflection was the practice that produced the thesis. In theoretical practice, and with supportive friends and colleagues, I was able to make the transition from panicking about my thesis to grudgingly accepting my confusion, and slowly dealing with the shame and guilt by letting go of the expectations that had produced those disabling feelings.[4]

Once I got going on Thesis Mark 2, it proved remarkably quick and easy to write. It was as if a subterranean stream of thought which had been welling up for some years came flooding to the surface. An introductory chapter tells the story of what I characterized as 'the false start', reflecting a failure of confidence in social science, and the remaining chapters explore the meaning of this failure and possible ways of addressing it.[5] It was a happy coincidence that, during the next decade or so, many of the issues and debates explored in my thesis became more central to the study of management and organizations, especially following the publication of Burrell and Morgan's *Paradigms* (1979). [6]

Nothing was ever published directly from my thesis which, in contrast to *Paradigms*, made little direct reference to organizations or even to management. I found it difficult to pull out elements as discrete articles, and the late 1970s was a lean time for book publishers in a stagnant higher education market. Completing my thesis

---

[4]Around this time, there was a further complication as David Knights himself registered for a PhD and so was no longer allowed to act formally as my supervisor. Into the breach stepped Peter Halfpenny (a sociologist with a specialist interest in the philosophy of social science) who very generously took on a pretty confused student with an abandoned draft thesis and few sociological credentials. I owe them both an enormous debt.

[5]In addition to my supervisors (see footnote 4), and my closest research student colleagues Frank Daniel and Jeff Simm, I also owe a great debt to Maurice Roche, the external examiner of my thesis. He was willing to consider my rather unconventional thesis and passed it without corrections. Then, after the viva, he very generously sent me numerous pages of closely typed comments that subjected it to more detailed scrutiny than it merited or could withstand.

[6]When visiting the Department of Behaviour in Organizations at Lancaster University in 1978 I recall being intrigued by draft chapters of *Paradigms*. The affinity with issues explored in my thesis later led me to offer a number of commentaries on *Paradigms* (Willmott, 1990, 1993a, 1993b).

coincided with taking up a lectureship at the University of Aston Business School (or Management Centre, as it was then called) where I became absorbed in teaching. At that time, prior to the competitiveness and work intensification engineered by the research selectivity exercises and declining staff–student ratios, there was no great pressure to produce 'research outputs'. With the support of my immediate colleagues – John Child, Peter Clark and Godfrey Williams – I had the luxury of time to reflect on how issues and ideas explored in my thesis might be reworked to engage and foster developments in MOS. This comparatively benign research environment, which also nurtured the writing of *Paradigms*, supported an extended period of reflection.[7] It enabled me to address and, to a degree, exorcise some of the doubts about empirical work that had besieged me during my PhD research. During almost a decade that I worked at Aston, I undertook several empirical studies – an observational study of decision-making at Friends of the Earth in Birmingham, a survey-based study of the Association of Corporate Treasurers and a longitudinal case study of 'Pensco', a mutual pensions and insurance company, with David Knights and a number of his PhD students.

Some of the misgivings that I harboured as a PhD student are echoed today in critical commentaries on 'evidence-based' practice, policy-making and management. Mark Learmonth[8] has shown how evidence-based management (EBM) relies upon an unjustifiable dichotomy of facts and values; and how, as a consequence, it dissembles its theoretical presuppositions, disregards its top-down formulation of problems, and naturalizes its neo-positivist conception of scientific knowledge production (Learmonth, 2006, 2008; Learmonth and Harding , 2006). What proponents of EBM are disinclined to accept is that 'evidence is never just there, waiting for the researcher to find. Rather it is always necessary to *construct* the evidence in some way – a process that is inherently ideological and always contestable – not merely a technical, "scientific" task' (Learmonth, 2008: 285–286; emphasis added). If evidence is *not* simply waiting to be uncovered by the researcher, then there is an issue of what commitments – political and ethical, as well as ontological and epistemological – inform how social scientific evidence is 'constructed', and what status and truth claims are then attributed to it, and with what consequences.

I now believe that 'science', in its plurality of manifestations, can provide powerful ways – negative as well as positive – of (dis)engaging with what it seeks examine. In these (dis)engagements, the role of scepticism, or the hermeneutics of suspicion, is critical to minimize the risk of a dominant scientific narrative becoming entrenched as a dogmatic truth. As Learmonth notes of EBM, its devotees claim that professional decisions can be 'based on the best available scientific evidence' (2008: 286, citing Rousseau, 2006: 256), with the consequence that managerial actions can be justified

---

[7]During this period (1977–1982), David Knights and I were writing much, submitting it to journals and succeeding in publishing almost nothing.

[8]A professor at Durham Business School who is a former National Health Service executive. Coincidentally, I was the external examiner of his thesis.

by reference to 'an "evidence-base" that is (apparently) independent of political, social or moral considerations' (2008: 286). In this way, 'the prestige of science' – common-sensically conceived as an objective, neutral, independent body of knowledge – is mobilized, whether cunningly or naïvely, to 'further a particular set of interests and values in organizational life' (2008: 286) that become naturalized as the prerogative and expertise of managers. The value of critical social science, including critical management studies (CMS), resides in a commitment to developing narratives that can, at least in principle, be enriching and transformative – on condition, of course, that their dissemination is facilitated and that they are not selectively appropriated to bolster what they seek to challenge or problematize. Contributions to CMS, exemplified by Learmonth's commentaries on EBM, show how forms of scientific as well as common-sense knowledge operate either to naturalize and contentedly reproduce, or to problematize and potentially diminish, socially unnecessary suffering manifest as practices of domination and oppression. The production of knowledge of management, including theorizing of organization, supports the reproduction of unnecessary suffering, or contributes to its removal. It is to this issue – of theorizing organization – that I now turn.

Theorizing 'organization'

When considering my PhD, I referred to a number of 'agencies' – social services, hospitals, charitable bodies – that had contact with single homeless people and effectively took social responsibility for their management. I might, instead, have characterized these agencies as 'organizations', or as forms of 'organization'. This begs the question of what marks them out as 'organizations'. Is it credible to suggest that they possess equivalent properties?

Typically, 'organization(s)' are conceived, or theorized, as *entities* that are more or less explicitly differentiated from other smaller (micro) or greater (macro) entities, such as 'individual(s)' or 'society'. In MOS, a 'Levels' metaphor is widely, and more or less reflexively, invoked. When commending the conceptual framework of institutional logics (Thornton et al., 2012; see also Friedland and Alford, 1991), Delbridge and Edwards (2013), for example, write that the framework is 'valuable because it is built upon an integrated conceptual architecture that works at three levels of analysis (i.e. the individual, the organizational and the societal)'. They later underscore this ascription of an ontological status to the three levels when they contend that 'the challenge is to link but not conflate these levels'. The 'meso' scoping of 'organization'(s) which is positioned between the 'individual' and 'society' is defended by reference to distinctive properties ascribed to each level. Research narratives are then generated in which, for example, 'Organization X' is presented as comprising a hierarchy of offices in which priority is given to the goals that 'X' aims to achieve. When this claim is taken to be self-evident, studies of organization proceed by selecting and applying theories and methods which are assumed to be capable of disclosing what, I suggest, they retroactively construct.

Where there is a stronger emphasis upon reflexivity as an integral feature of critical analysis, this *entity view* of phenomena, whether identified as 'individuals', 'organizations' or 'society', is reconstructed as a performative manifestation of a *particular kind of theorizing*. This theorizing might be termed 'objectivist' but is frequently self-referenced as 'realist'. Its 'objectivism' becomes more apparent when its claims are contested by alternative approaches – such as forms of analysis in which organizations are conceived as ongoing *processes*, emergent from 'the relentless arresting, fixing, and stabilizing of an intrinsically wild, fluxing, and changeable reality' (Chia, 2003: 100). From this process perspective, the entity view of 'organization' exemplifies such 'fixing' activity.

As a leading advocate of process theory, Chia (2003) conceives of organizations as 'stabilized patterns that *we* impute to phenomena via the influence of language' (Chia, 2003: 107; emphasis added). Note how unproblematized reference is made to 'we'. In common with the entity view, 'organizations' are assumed to exist as 'islands of relatively stabilized order' (Chia, 2003: 107). This emphasis upon consensus and stability indicates, from the perspective advanced here, the abstraction of organization(s) from the relations of power and domination through which processes of organizing are (re)produced – relations where, for example, the notion of 'organization' as a *social object* is invoked to solidify and legitimize a particular reality (e.g. of impersonalization where entities act, and processes stabilize).

The *social object*[9] view *radically* refuses to subscribe to the 'impression that reality is stable, preorganized and lawlike in character' (Chia, 2003: 107). Rejecting the objectivism of the entity view, it emphasizes the political or power-invested quality of the processes of 'fixing' and 'stabilizing'. Accordingly, its focus is upon how, in practice, social realities, such as 'organization' that convey a sense of order and stability, are constructed *inter alia* through the exercise of power-in-language. Issue is taken with how the process view regards 'fixing' as a manifestation of *universal*, 'generic organizational impulses' (Chia, 2003: 98) that fashion something 'predictable and liveable' from an 'otherwise intractable and amorphous life world' (Chia, 2003: 98).

---

[9]It is relevant to stress that this 'social object' is not an entity but a concept whose meaning is differentiated from other concepts (e.g. 'individual', 'group', 'society') and is invoked to (re)construct or perform (reproduce or transform) social realities in a manner that is intended to be congruent with the favoured meaning. I consider this to be consistent with Bohm's (1980) thinking, cited by Chia (2003: 107), where concepts and theories are understood to offer 'a way of looking at the world, and not a form of knowledge of how the world is' (Bohm, 1980: 4; emphasis omitted). Where the 'cultural construct' view develops that of Bohm is by locating the production and diffusion of particular 'ways of looking' within power relations that these 'ways' articulate and serve to legitimize or indeed destabilize. Their dominance is inescapably incomplete not only because there are countervailing 'ways of looking' but also because reality always confounds the efforts of language to represent it.

While acknowledging the process of creating and maintaining a meaningful world to be universal, 'organization' is conceived as a historically particular, *politically* constructed and contested social object. In the contemporary context, 'organization' is widely invoked to constitute and convey a particular form of fixity in which, for example, power relations are depersonalized and so are ostensibly depoliticized.

Consider, for example, a paper published in *Organization Science* titled 'Finding the Organization in Organization Theory' (King et al., 2010). It begins with the observation that 'Organizational scholars purport to study a unique *entity* in society – the organization – yet we rarely take the time to reflect on what makes an organization unique from other social *entities*' (2010: 290; emphases added). Note how these authors *assert* that *all* organizational scholars conceive of their object of study as a distinctive social entity: 'the organization'. In a sense, they are right. It is 'normal', in modern organization scholarship as well as in common sense, to conceive of 'organizations' as 'entities' and/or as '"*actors*" possessing "*unique properties*"' (2010, emphasis added). But it is the kind of 'normality' or 'normal science' that I was unable to sustain when undertaking my PhD. According to King et al. (2010: 298), organizations qua 'actors' also have a 'self-view'. King et al. insist that this 'self-view, allegedly manifest in the identity and goals of an organization, underlies decision making and deliberation within the organization, thus forming the basis of intentionality' (2010: 298) as organizations 'deliberate and choose particular actions' (2010: 301).

The attribution of 'actorhood', 'intentionality' and 'deliberation' as well as 'identity' and 'goals' to organization(s) is broadly consistent with accounts of business and management in which views and actions are routinely ascribed to corporations such as Apple or the National Security Agency (NSA) as if they were unitary as well as purposive beings. It is unsurprising that theory which builds upon such common-sense understandings enjoys mundane legitimacy and, of course, preferential access to the funding which affirms its 'good sense'. But do 'organizations' have the capabilities ascribed to them by many organization scholars (as well as spokespersons and commentators)? Doubts surface when it is recalled that 'organization' is a *concept* that retroactively constitutes what it ostensibly describes. Yet, despite being a 'mere' concept, or social object, it clearly can *appear* to reflect the reality of its referent, and so mobilizes action based upon this (fetishistic) power.

On the performative facticity of 'organization'

Once 'organization' – like 'individual' and 'society' – becomes established and sedimented as a commonsensical entity, it is then 'experienced as possessing a reality of [its] own, a reality that confronts [us] as an external and coercive fact' (Berger and Luckmann, 1966: 76) such that it effectively exercises a 'coercive power' (1966: 78). In Marxian terms, it 'weighs like a nightmare on the living'. Such 'coercion' is a medium and outcome not only of 'facticity' but also of the '*control mechanisms that are usually attached to the most important of* [institutions]' (1966: 78; emphasis added).

The everyday, taken-for-granted sense of facticity associated with 'organization(s)' becomes buttressed and legitimized by forms of 'theoretical knowledge', such as that advanced by King et al. (2010), which endorse its ostensibly good sense. Within their theory, membership of an organization is assumed to imply a commitment to its 'cause, rules, etc' (King et al., 2010: 293). Organizational membership is considered to encompass an obligation of its members to subscribe to its purpose and rules, irrespective of 'personal preference' that might 'suggest an alternative course of action' (2010: 293). This is an instance of the reality ascribed to 'organization' acting as a 'control mechanism' that demands, yet does not necessarily secure, 'the joint commitment to uphold certain principles' (King et al., 2010: 293).

To the extent that we, as citizens or scholars, relate to 'social objects' – such as 'organization', 'society' and 'individual' – as 'objective facticities' that are capable of 'deliberation, self-reflection and goal-directed action' (King et al., 2010: 292), we vest power in those entities instead of recognizing our participation in, and responsibility for, their ostensible possession of such powers. Such 'complex theoretical systems' (Berger and Luckmann, 1966: 107) contribute to 'the conceptual machineries of symbolic universe maintenance' (Berger and Luckmann, 1966: 126) which are partisan, yet appear to be neutral as their primary effect is to affirm and sustain the status quo. The symbolic universe being maintained is 'the organization as a social actor'. It is a notion which carries a requirement of organizational members to 'uphold certain principles', such as deference to those who have the authority of the organization vested in them as office holders, and a broader 'commit(ment) to the organization's cause, rules, etc' (King et al., 2010: 293).

This oppressive effect has been thematized by Bittner in his 1965 classic 'The Concept of Organization' (see Bittner, 1973). There he appreciates how for 'purposes of sociological inquiry' (1973: 265) the use of common-sense ideas (e.g. the idea that organizations are entities, or the notion of levels) is 'to a certain point unavoidable' (1973: 265). This attentiveness to the entanglement of common sense and social inquiry anticipates the first moment of what Giddens (1987) later calls the 'double hermeneutic' of social scientific analysis. Where 'the use of common-sense concepts becomes a transgression', Bittner (1973: 265) argues, is the point at which 'such concepts are expected to do the analytical work of theoretical concepts'.[10] This contention speaks to the difficulty encountered when writing up my thesis as I questioned the basis of my account of the management of single homelessness, given that I employed common-sense terms to do analytical work. Bittner's favoured (ethnomethodological) solution is to study how common-sense terms, such as 'organization' or 'single homeless', are 'methodologically used' (1973: 271) to *construct* (rather than describe or reflect) social realities. The focus of such analysis is upon

---

[10]So, for example, Weber is admonished for his 'fail[ure] to explore the underlying commonsense presuppositions of his theory' (Bittner, 1973: 269), such as its invocation of 'formalization', that are assumed to be analytically adequate but are spared reflexive scrutiny.

how references to 'organization' (or to 'individual' or 'society' or 'level', etc.) are routinely made for purposes of 'direction', 'justification' and so on, while appreciating how common-sense notions of such entities are themselves increasingly inflected by social scientific representations of them (the second moment of Giddens' 'double hermeneutic').

Bittner usefully flags up a problem. Social scientists do indeed routinely rely upon unexamined common-sense presuppositions and understandings ('attitudes of everyday life' as well as 'socially sanctioned typifications') in order to delineate and analyse these very understandings (e.g. 'bureaucracy'). King et al.'s (2010) work is illustrative of this reliance. But it is less clear how the problem can be solved. This is not least because, as Bittner concedes, it is 'unavoidable', at least up to 'a certain point' – a point that is unspecified. His preference, to repeat, is to engage in ethnomethodological studies that address how particular concepts are 'use(d) in *real scenes* of action' and how such concepts are 'assigned to *real objects and events*' (1973: 270; emphases added).

Bittner's incisive commentary on the limitations of common-sense-bound knowledge is to be welcomed. But I question whether it is necessary or credible to abandon such knowledge on the grounds that it falls short of proper 'analytical work' (1973: 265). Bittner's judgement implies that there is a single, authoritative 'scientific' way of studying the social world (i.e. ethnomethodology), whereas arguably there are diverse discourses and schools of social scientific analysis with distinctive strengths and limitations, albeit that evaluations of their merits are limited by the bounds of self-referentiality. I do not find Bittner's appeal to 'real' scenes, objects or events (1973: 270) credible if they are supposed to be knowable independently of researchers' common-sense-inflected representations of them.[11] Instead, I am more inclined to embrace his call to interrogate the preconceptions of common-sense knowledge (e.g. 'bureaucracy') and everyday invocations of its contents;[12] *but also* to consider their *performative consequences*, with regard to the practical (political) effects of adopting a particular 'commonsense perspective' (1973: 265).

That is what I have sought to do when reflecting upon King et al.'s (2010) 'metatheory of the organization as a social actor', which I have taken as an example of conventional theorizing in MOS. As King et al. themselves acknowledge, albeit in passing and without further reflection, the attribution of agency to organizations is dependent upon 'social conventions' (2010: 298) – such as the conventions which

---

[11]It must be acknowledged that embracing Bittner's (ethnomethodological) call does not overcome dependence upon common sense. It makes common sense a *topic* of inquiry rather than its unscrutinized *resource*; but the interrogation of common sense as a topic continues to rely upon common sense as this is 'to a certain point ... unavoidable' (Bittner, 1973: 265).

[12]For example, Bittner (1973: 272, 273) proposes the study of usages of such terms by managers and others to show how, in practice, they are invoked *inter alia* as a 'gambit of compliance', and so have the capacity to exert some 'determining power over action' by enlisting some 'normative expectation'.

enable 'member-agents' to act *as if* it is the organization that wills their action to realize the identity and goals ascribed to it (see 2010: 295). King et al. adopt and legitimize this convention. But there is no obligation upon analysts uncritically to reproduce common sense – and thereby perpetuate what Berger and Luckmann (1966: 107) term a reified modality of consciousness where there is a 'total identification of the individual with his socially assigned identifications' (1966: 108) and for which 'individual(s) may [then] disclaim responsibility' (1966: 108). Instead of inquiring into how the specific contents of these conventions become established and reproduced by (unidentified) 'other actors in society' (King et al., 2010: 298), and 'within the bounds of authority granted by key stakeholders' (2010: 293), King et al. treat them as facticities. The alternative is to ask how the reified notion of organization(s) adapted and uncritically endorsed by King et al. – which presumes and demands the commitment of its members to the organization's cause, rules, etc. (2010: 293) – has become so established and commonsensical, and how this notion is maintained, including by advocates of forms of organization theory, as it's good sense is assumed by being performed, amplified and legitimized.

In commending a consideration of the performative consequences of the adoption of common-sense thinking when undertaking analysis, I share Bittner's (1973: 265) assessment that relying upon common sense is 'to a certain point unavoidable'. Accepting this dependence, and then paying attention to how concepts such as 'organization' are mobilized in everyday and scientific activity, is commended for (reflexively) raising our awareness of the limits of (social) science. That said, Bittner's interrogation of 'the concept of organization' places common sense in a negative, rather than ambivalent, space. Instead of appreciating how common sense is itself highly variegated, as it contains elements that are more or less 'open' (capable of self-doubt) and 'closed' (capable only of self-affirmation), common sense is positioned by Bittner as 'the other' of social science. An alternative is to accept the impossibility of reflecting or distilling elements of the empirical world, or rendering these elements more accountable, even by deploying theory that aspires or claims to transcend common sense.[13] It is possible to conceive of theory (or, better, theories) as offering different and potentially challenging accounts of social relations, including the relations that are (commonsensically) identified as comprising 'organizations'. In addition, and as I have endeavoured to show, it is possible to consider, and to reflect critically upon how, when it is more or less partially reproduced in social scientific analysis (e.g. King et al.'s 'meta-theory of the organization'), common-sense thinking exerts performative effects that invite critical scrutiny rather than unquestioning endorsement.

---

[13]With regard to the second moment of the double hermeneutic, Giddens notes 'the double hermeneutic' signals how 'the concepts of the social sciences are not produced about an independently constituted subject-matter, which continues regardless of what these concepts are. The "findings" of the social sciences very often enter constitutively into the world they describe' (1987: 20).

The politics of representation: Becoming a 'pig'

Law (1996) commends an understanding of 'organization' which resonates with elements of Bittner's (1973) argument and my commentary on King et al.'s entity view of organization. Law observes how, in all but the most reflexive accounts of organization(s), there is 'an object that appears to be real, to be solid, and to be out there' (Law, 1996: 298). Signalling the relevance of a processual perspective, he notes that seemingly solid social objects are *'created* in the process of representation and accounting' (1996: 298; emphasis added); and that this is a process of 'creation' which presumes a subject–object distinction which it retroactively (re)produces. The 'process' to which Law refers is one that identifies 'out there' objects that are thereby made available for analysis. Inquiring subjects – practitioners as well as social scientists – then interrogate those objects – such as 'bureaucracy' – but without nec-essarily acknowledging how their apparent solidity is a product of power-invested (and unscrutinized) processes of representation.

For such a form of knowledge production to occur, Law argues, 'the processes of forming a knowing subject and the objects to be known by this subject are *necessarily* concealed' (1996: 297; emphasis in original). To suggest that such pro-cesses are *entirely* hidden is, of course, implausible. Otherwise, it would not be possible to point to this concealment, as Law claims to do. What I understand Law to mean is that, in social analysis, priority is routinely given to pre-serving the object. The researcher's sense of (ontological) security is thereby affirmed. Not to conceal the processes of objectification is to invite ontological doubt by acknowledging how 'knower and known ... might be made in quite other ways' (1996: 297); and such an invitation may also prompt reflection upon how rela-tions of power are engaged and institutionalized in both objectifying practices and their concealment.

As an example, consider the following reaction of a manager of a chemical plant, studied by Nichols and Beynon (1977) – a manager who reportedly was widely iden-tified by 'nearly everyone' as a person who would 'do anything for you personally' (1977: 39). What, then, of this manager's reaction to the contents of a left-wing leaflet, published at a time when workers were being made redundant, in which managers were referred to as 'pigs' (1977: 39)? The identity at issue here is that of an 'individual' (a manager) but its analysis is readily applicable to the identity of an 'organization'. Consider, for example, another leaflet that includes a small image of a poster that presents an organization widely promoted and regarded as 'cool' and 'family-friendly', such as McDonald's, as unhealthy and life-threatening. The image, taking a semi-circular shape, mimics the colours of McDonald's red, yellow and black, with the Golden Arch symbol being rotated horizontally to form an E in the slogan 'Єat Fast, DiЄ Young'.

Returning to Nichols and Beynon's example, the manager is reported to say:

> '*Us* they mean' ... 'It's us they're talking about. I'm no pig. I bloody well *care* about what I'm doing.'

This manager, I suggest, forcefully resists the claim of the union leaflet which invites its readers to reflect critically upon a widely held, common-sense representation of him as a caring person. Like the parody of a McDonald's poster, readers of the union leaflet are urged to look upon managers at the chemical plant 'in quite other ways' – perhaps as *apparatchiks* of capitalism, or as functionaries comparable to the pigs in *Animal Farm* who were ostensibly the brightest but least productive of its residents. If this manager were to be persuaded by the analysis offered in the union leaflet, not only would he change as a 'knower' but also what was 'known' would change – out of all recognition. And the same can be said for the McDonald's customer when reading the leaflet containing the parody image.

Neither I, nor John Law, I believe, is suggesting that 'manager', 'caring person' or 'pig' is the more accurate representation of the ChemCo manager, any more than we are arguing that those of us who occasionally 'eat fast' will necessarily 'die young'. Instead, we are pointing to the *politics* of representation – in the sense that representations do political work: representations either affirm and naturalize, or challenge and destabilize, established wisdoms and associated realities. With an attentiveness to the 'political' work of representation, there comes a theoretical shift. The shift is *away from* approaches preoccupied with the question of whether theory A better captures 'organization(s)', or a subset of 'organization(s)', than theory B. The shift is *towards* a concern with questions oriented to the defensibility of the *assumptions* that inform and justify theories A, B, C, ... *And, beyond that,* the shift extends to a concern with the probable, performative consequences of adopting theories A, B, C, ... With this shift, the epistemologically-centric aim of developing or applying the most accurate or revelatory theory is no longer privileged. Space then opens up for more ethically-centric processes of critical reflection where research and scholarship are animated by a different agenda that asks, for example, which theory makes the most ethically defensible suppositions and/or has the most justifiable consequences. Of course, this shift brings its own problems and questions – notably, how is what is counted as 'most defensible' or 'most justifiable' itself to be justified? The point of this shift is not to pre-empt answers to such questions or to become paralysed by them but, rather, to make them more central to social scientific analysis without necessarily rejecting the contribution of analysis that ignores, excludes or brackets such questions. It is also relevant to note that conditions of knowledge production are no less difficult to impute than its consequences are difficult to predict. Concerns about the 'defensibility' of suppositions and the justifications of theorizing in terms of its anticipated consequences do not exclude involvement of scholars who insist upon the normality, virtue and/or expediency of research dedicated to determining whether theory A better captures the focal topic than theories B, or C. Findings drawn from such empirical research may usefully inform conversation and debate so long as they are recognized to be theory-dependent constructions of reality rather than more or less mirror-like representations of it. Findings per se cannot resolve or close down debate precisely because they are inescapably dependent upon, and interpreted within, a *particular*, contestable theory. The dynamics of debate are a matter of politics (the capacity to frame and pursue a particular research agenda) as well as ethics (the value attributed to different agendas), and are not reducible to assessments of the reliability and/or validity of empirical evidence per se. Each perspective, or way of seeing, embeds a distinctive politico-ethical understanding. It is a matter of ethics because researchers exercise an existential responsibility when choosing between alternative research agendas. And it is a matter of politics because debate about the 'best theory' occurs within asymmetrical power relations that condition what is considered 'credible', 'coherent', 'justifiable', etc.

Conclusion

In this chapter, I have offered some reflections on the field of management studies and, more specifically, on organization theory. I have sought to explore, and hope to have exemplified to a degree, the role of reflexivity in problematizing the reliance of organization theory upon unscrutinized common-sense ideas about organization(s) and their analysis. By sharing how this practice entered into the production of my PhD and in making sense of how organization is theorized, I have endeavoured to flesh out some aspects of the 'broad argument' conveyed in this book that 'management research … pays insufficient attention to the practice of reflexivity' (Jeanes and Huzzard, 2011: 1).

In my career as a management researcher, reflexivity was initially prompted (or better, escalated) by a hiatus in producing an empirically based doctoral thesis. The impasse was unblocked by shifting its focus to consider more directly the role of theory – including the role of ontological and epistemological commitments – in the production of knowledge. In principle, distinctively 'critical' research pays attention to issues and concerns that tend to be submerged and marginalized in more mainstream accounts of the practicalities of research processes – issues that include consideration of the pressures that are influential in 'choosing'[14] the research topic and its methods of study. Undertaking critical research hinges upon exposure to heterodox theoretical traditions as well as encouragement to embrace their agenda(s). How such pressures are practically handled has consequences for every aspect and phase of the research process (see also Bristow, 2012; Prasad, 2013). I suspect that many researchers face crises of confidence in what they are doing, but such troubles are largely hidden. They leave a trace mainly in withdrawals from PhD programmes and in theses that are never completed. I was fortunate in being supported through the process of transforming my angst from a comparatively shadowy background resource into the focal topic of my dissertation.

---

[14]The quotation marks are intended to indicate how such 'choices' are historically and culturally conditioned within specific epistemic communities.

Established 'uncritical' (see Willmott, 2013) forms of theorizing affirm power-invested common sense in which, for example, 'organization' is assumed to be an entity, and to which actorhood is unproblematically ascribed. Such common-sense knowledge is contested inter alia through an appreciation of organization as a continuously emergent process; or, alternatively, by connecting the naturalization of organization to the operation of power relations to establish forms of domination through which material and symbolic resources are created and distributed. When conceived in these terms, the way in which 'organization(s)' is formulated is by no means a merely scholastic matter involving skirmishes among academics cloistered in ivory towers. It has implications for how everyday organizational life, including 'management', is practically interpreted and enacted, and potentially may be transformed.

References

Berger, P. and Luckmann, T. (1966) *The Social Construction of Reality.* Harmondsworth: Penguin.

Bittner, E. (1973) 'The concept of organization', in G. Salaman and K. Thompson, (eds), *People and Organisations.* London: Longman. Published originally in *Social Research*, 32(3): 239–255.

Blumer, H. (1969) *Symbolic Interactionism: Perspective and Method.* Englewood Cliffs, NJ: Prentice Hall.

Bohm, D. (1980) *Wholeness and the Implicate Order.* London: Routledge.

Bristow, A. (2012) 'On life, death and radical critique: A non-survival guide to the brave new higher education for the intellectually pregnant', *Scandinavian Journal of Management*, 28(3): 234–241.

Burrell, G. (1999) 'Normal science, paradigms, metaphors, discourses and genealogies of analysis' in S.R. Clegg and C. Hardy (eds), *Studying Organization: Theory and Method.* London: Sage.

Burrell, G. and Morgan, G. (1979) *Sociological Paradigms and Organizational Analysis.* London: Heinemann.

Chia, R. (2003) 'Organization as "world-making"', in R. Westwood and S. Clegg (eds), *Debating Organization: Point-Counterpoint in Organization Studies.* Oxford: Blackwell.

Delbridge, R. and Edwards, T. (2013) 'Inhabiting institutions: Critical realist refinements to understanding institutional complexity and change', *Organization Studies*, 34(7): 927–947.

Friedland, R. and Alford, R.R. (1991) 'Bringing society back in: Symbols, practices and institutional contradictions', in W.W. Powell and P.J. DiMaggio (eds), *The New Institutionalism in Organizational Analysis.* Chicago: Chicago University Press.

Giddens, A. (1979) *Central Problems of Social Theory.* London: Macmillan.

Giddens, A. (1987) *Social Theory and Modern Sociology.* Cambridge: Polity Press.

Jeanes, E. and Huzzard, T. (2011) 'Critical management research: Reflections from the field', mimeo circulated to contributing authors.

King, B.G., Felin, T. and Whetton, D.A. (2010) 'Finding the organization in organization theory: A meta-theory of the organization as a social actor', *Organization Science*, 21(1): 290–305.

Knights, D. and Willmott, H.C. (eds) (1990) *Labour Process Theory*. London: Macmillan.

Law, J. (1996) 'Organizing accountabilities: Ontology and the mode of accounting', in R. Munro and J. Mouritsen (eds), *Accountability: Power, Ethos and the Technologies of Managing*. London: International Thompson Business Press.

Learmonth, M. (2006) 'Is there such a thing as "evidence-based management"?: A Commentary on Rousseau's 2005 Presidential Address', *Academy of Management Review*, 31(4): 1089–1091.

Learmonth, M. (2008) 'Speaking out: Evidence-based management: A backlash against pluralism in organization studies', *Organization*, 15(2): 283–291.

Learmonth, M. and Harding, N. (2006) 'Evidence-based management: The very idea', *Public Administration*, 84(2): 245–266.

Nichols, T. and Beynon, H. (1977) *Living with Capitalism: Class Relations and the Modern Factory*. London: Routledge.

Prasad, A. (2013), 'Playing the game and trying not to lose myself: A doctoral student's perspective on the institutional pressures for research output', *Organization*, 20(6): 936–948.

Rousseau, D. (2006) 'Is there such and thing as "evidence-based management"?' *Academy of Management Review*, 31(2): 256–269.

Silverman, D. (1970) *The Theory of Organizations: A Sociological Framework*. London: Heinemann.

Taylor, I., Walton, P. and Young, J. (1973) *The New Criminology: For a Social Theory of Deviance*. London: Routledge.

Thornton, P.H., Ocasio, W. and Lounsbury, M. (2012) *The Institutional Logics Perspective: A New Approach to Culture, Structure and Process*. Oxford: Oxford University Press.

Tsoukas, H. and Knudsen, C. (2005) *The Oxford Handbook of Organization Theory*. Oxford: Oxford University Press.

Willmott, H.C. (1990) 'Beyond paradigmatic closure in organisational analysis', in J. Hassard and D. Pym (eds), *The Theory and Philosophy of Organizations*. London: Routledge, pp. 44–62.

Willmott, H.C. (1993a) 'Breaking the paradigm mentality', *Organization Studies*, 14(5): 681–720.

Willmott, H.C. (1993b) 'Paradigm gridlock', *Organization Studies*, 14(5): 727–730.

Willmott, H.C. (2013) 'Reflections on the darker side of conventional power analytics', *Academy of Management Perspectives*, 27(4): 281–286.

PART IV
REFLECTIONS ON THE FIELD

TWELVE

Writing: What can be said, by who, and where?

Martin Parker

Introduction

Writing is at the same time the most visible and the most invisible of academic practices.[1] We only know most academics through what they write, and so their words on screen and paper are the only traces of their presence that we have. Yet, despite this rather obvious point, there is relatively little attention paid to writing in the training of academics in the social sciences. There are some good practical and aesthetic guides, but if we compare them to the shelves full of books on methods, methodology and epistemology, we can see that the dominant assumption is that writing is what happens *after* all the interesting action has already taken place. Writing is dissemination, and is often barely worthy of comment. Indeed, for many, it *should* be invisible, merely a featureless conduit between brains, in which style is an interference to clear communication. This, it seems, is what distinguishes science from other forms of communication. It is also worth noting that most of the guides to writing well are written by people in the arts and humanities, perhaps locations where the question of writing is itself also problematized as a topic, both as source and cultural product. In the social sciences, then, and most particularly in the business school, writing often cannot be seen despite the fact that it is in front of our noses all the time.

[1]Thanks to Emma Jeanes and Hugh Willmott for comments on an earlier draft of this chapter.

Publishing is a different matter, of course, with an increasingly obsessive compulsive attempt to quantify and qualify the places where writing becomes classifiable as an 'output'. (In this way, an experience becomes a thing, a subject becomes an object, and a verb becomes a noun.) Journals are ranked, citations are measured, lists are compiled, and persons are ascribed E, G and H indices[2] or elevated to the pantheon of 'highly cited'. Yet again, the actual writing – the words, practices, techniques – seems almost irrelevant when so heavily processed by an institutional apparatus which is designed to weigh the virtues of employees, departments, institutions and even nations. It is precisely at this point, at the moment when the reverse alchemy of turning writing into output is happening, that we can see the questions of what can be said, by whom, and where, most clearly. For almost anyone can write, in the simplest meaning of that term. The difference between social network sites, private diaries, academic journals and best-selling books is not a matter of whether words are written, but how a ramified set of judgements is made about the techniques of dispersal which those words will be entered into. This means that we cannot ignore institutions and politics, because the arts of judgement which open the doors to dissemination are also the plays of power. Any critical academic cannot assume their writing is somehow innocent of the shadows of publishing and the rankings of output, unless they wish never to be read.[3]

This chapter is not a 'handy hints and tips' guide for readers who want to be published. There are already plenty of those (for example, Murray, 2005; Booth et al., 2008, Graff et al., 2008),[4] and journal editors have been doing the rounds of conferences for years impressing early-career staff with their wisdom as they tell them how to structure their article and write the revise and resubmit letter.[5] Neither is this a guide on how to write well, though this is an important issue (Williams, 1990) and one I will be touching on at various points in the chapter. Rather, I want to consider what has happened to writing in an institutional climate which makes writing into a means to an end, and hence as invisible as a keyboard or pen (see also Billig, 2013). I am imagining my reader as an early-career academic, but this chapter also aims to stimulate some thinking for the senior professors who edit the journals too. This is a chapter which tries to turn our critical attention onto the structures which turn 'writing' into 'output', and hence shape things like who gets invited to write for books like this. I also want to think about what might be done about this situation, and that involves thinking about how we write, who we write for, and how it gets

---

[2] Each being attempts to measure academic productivity and success by combinations of numbers of publications and numbers of citations.

[3] And they may not, because 'not writing' is a perfectly defensible position at a time when output is demanded so insistently.

[4] See the excellent blog by Thomas Basboll for very useful and well-written ruminations on writing and academic life (http://secondlanguage.blogspot.com/). Or for a novelist's view, see King (2000).

[5] Including the author, who smugly lectures others on what to do to be like him.

published. And, along the way, I want to use the style of this chapter to ensure that you always remember that it was written. It didn't just arrive here, in this book, with no struggle. Someone sat here, at this desk, where I am now, sighing and drinking cups of tea as they wrote about writing, whilst the rain fell outside in the English Midlands.

Writing down

At the present moment (because it hasn't always been so) the gold standard for academic output in business and management is an article in one of the small number of super-elite journals which are almost all US-dominated and have very high rejection and citation rates. We know that they are super-elite because there are a number of ranking organizations, such as the Web of Science, the *Financial Times*[6] and the UK Association of Business Schools, which produce data or lists which rank journals on the basis of their 'quality'. Note that they are not evaluating the papers, but the journals that they appear in, because it seems that if a paper appears in such a journal it must also be of high quality. In theory, it doesn't matter what the paper is about, what matters is the company that it keeps, and the fact that some of the most demanding gatekeepers in the discipline have judged the work meritorious enough to deserve inclusion. A paper in, say, the *Academy of Management Review* means that you are playing with the big boys (and girls), and will be rewarded with envious glances, promotion, and perhaps even a cash prize from your employer. The *AMR* offices are located in New York state, but it is at the top of a global hierarchy, and academics from Shanghai to São Paulo will be competing to be published there. It is a journal which in 2012 Roy Suddaby, the first non-US editor in the journal's history described as 'the preeminent repository of management thought' (2012: 6).

In 2009, the *Academy of Management Review* had an impact factor of 7.867, based on 14,649 citations.[7] That's just short of one citation an hour, for two years solid. The higher the number of citations, the better the journal is supposed to be, but better at what? Citations clearly mean something, but it is not clear what they mean. They could be an indicator of the power which certain journals have to define a field, and the consequent lack of pluralism or heterodoxy. It could mean that people read and cite only a very few journals, and that broader reading is discouraged. High citations could indicate something about the consensus over core problems and methods that exists in the centre of a discipline (and hence which mistakes parochialism for inclusiveness), or the sheer size of a particular national university system (which mistakes

---

[6]Owned by Thomson Reuters and Pearson PLC, respectively, with turnover of $13.8 billion and £5.8 billion in 2011.

[7]This paragraph has been stolen from Parker and Thomas (2011), and then slightly modified.

sheer scale for universality: Grey, 2010), or the dominance of a particular language (Meriläinen et al., 2008). They could tell us about the widespread acceptance of certain political assumptions, perhaps concerning the ways to imagine economies, organization and governance. They could even tell us about the way that books, chapters in books, reports, journalism and so on are being treated as superfluous forms of output in some disciplines even while they are perfectly acceptable in others. Or they could tell us that authors need publications so badly that they will follow the implicit rules on citation in order to get jobs, pay increases, permanent positions, and promotions. They could also tell us something about the remarkable effectiveness of interlocking forms of institutionalization to agree on what matters – making the simple matter of a reference in someone else's writing into a signal that produces all sorts of consequences. High citations could also suggest that the work was good and getting read, but that is only one possibility amongst many.

But what does it mean to say that a piece of writing is 'good'? It is important to remind ourselves that 'quality' is not an immanent feature of a text, despite the common assumption that it is. That is to say, I am here rejecting the idea that there are certain transcendental standards of value which can be found in some writing and not in others. This also means being suspicious of ideas about individual genius, and the idea of the writer-artist which we get from European romanticism – someone with inner qualities which make them capable of adding to the best that has been thought and said. It is rather an obvious point, but if we all knew what quality meant, and what quality work was, we wouldn't need an institutional apparatus to help us decide. It wouldn't matter where things were published, or in what format, or what the critics said, because the qualities of the text would be evident, and would be recognized as such by those who encountered it (Becker, 2007). So let's revise what we mean by the word 'quality' here, and say that what is really happening is an ascription of value, a determination which is not given by the text itself but by the way in which it is read. Good work is what most people say is good work, a collective judgement, a wisdom of the crowd. Every time we use a value term to describe a piece of writing, we should therefore silently preface it with 'what people believe to be'. This is really important, because it allows us not to be bewitched by the idea that if something is in *AMR* it must be good in some absolute sense, while at the same time acknowledging that *AMR* is a machine which makes judgements which are widely held to be important. In the process of turning writing into output, *AMR* matters, and it would be silly to say that it doesn't.

Following this sort of logic, let's also be clear about what sorts of judgements are fed into this institution. In saying that the definition of value that *AMR* generates is collective, we shouldn't fall into the trap of believing that everyone who wants to has a voice. This isn't the wisdom of an unruly crowd, but the assumptions of an extended family. And what do we find if we investigate who those few are? They are, by and large, the professoriate from the top North American business schools. Not all men, not all white, not all have English as their first language, not all are based in the US or Canada or were trained there, but the majority are. By definition, these are people who have done rather well from the publishing and ranking system, and are unlikely to feel highly motivated to deny its effectiveness at encouraging the best to rise the top. Those who occupy high-status positions are also often those who claim to believe in the meritocratic nature of existing hierarchies. We could describe these people as those who define the centre of the discipline, in the sense that they work in the most prestigious universities, sit on the boards of journals, occupy positions in professional associations, examine PhDs, sit on promotions committees and so on. The current editor of *AMR*, in an editorial which asks for the journal to become more global in its representation, notes that in 2010, 27 of the 136 editorial board members were based outside North America, and of the 62 authors that year, 14 worked outside North America (Suddaby, 2012: 7; see also Grey, 2010).

It would be surprising if these two ratios were not related. That is to say, if an editorial board is dominated by a set of people who work or were trained in a particular place, it is likely that the work that they will deem to be 'good' will be work which reflects the orientations of that place. Refereed journals are mechanisms which do precisely this by ensuring that there is a broad consensus among reviewers, associate editors and editors. The demand for agreement results in the likelihood that at least one link in this chain will object to work which is deemed to be risky. This often means that pieces which depart from the core assumptions in terms of epistemology, politics, problem definition or style will be winnowed out – either by being rejected, or by going through multiple revise and resubmits which ensure that all the sharp edges have been rounded off. The letters which authors send back explaining changes are now often as long as the papers themselves, such is the absolute pressure to submit to the will of reviewers and editors in order to get a publication. The contemporary elite academic journal is a mechanism which enables networks of powerful actors to discipline what gets said, and then to justify their interventions in terms of using putatively meritocratic mechanisms to guarantee quality. This is not, by and large, an intentional process – more the averaging effect of a series of small decisions which combine to exclude matters which don't fit. So the journal tends to produce what Thomas Kuhn called 'normal science' – the routine gap spotting and problem solving which occurs within the core of a discipline, and which is mostly unremarkable apart from its function in administering the glass bead game of academic hierarchy. Normal science, as Kuhn (1996: 52) reminds us, 'does not aim at novelties of fact or theory and, when successful, finds none'.

Using this description, we can further refine what it means to say that a piece of writing is good. It means that it is what the powerful at the centre of a discipline believe to be good, simply because these are the people who decide what sort of work gets into *AMR*. If a piece is published somewhere like that, it tends to suggest that this is work which doesn't offend the standards and sensibilities of the editorial board and reviewers. This is not necessarily a bad thing, because I am not assuming that there is a particular virtue in being offensive, but it seems pretty evident that highly ranked academic journals will tend to be sites for the reproduction of the status quo in terms of the problems, methods, styles which define what counts as knowledge within a particular field. This isn't a new insight (see Bourdieu, 1988, for example), but it's an important one, because it begins to show us that turning writing into output is a social question. It's not merely a matter of individual talent, or hard work (though these matter) but a question of shaping work so that it fits in to the spaces which are already prescribed for it. Of course the successful would rather stress the talent and the hard work, because an account which described them as merely conforming would not be terribly flattering. But let's be clear, if the best work is found in the best journals, presided over by the best academics who themselves publish in the best journals, then 'best' can never be defined in anything other than tautological terms.

If we are relatively skilled actors within a given social situation, we will anticipate the sorts of things that we need to do in order to be successful, to 'pass' as a member. We try to imagine what others might think of us and our actions, and adjust them accordingly. It is in this sense that academic writing is often shadowed by output, by the fear that reviewers and editors will find your work deficient and that you will be rejected. This is true of novelists and journalists too, of course, but there is something relentless in the frequency with which contemporary academics are held to judgement about their capacity to publish in the right places. Failure is endless, even among the supposedly successful, so no wonder that so much anxiety is generated, and so much need for the hints and tips sessions at conferences on how to get published in top journals, as well as so much dull resentment about the disciplining effects of having to submit to top journals. If the romantic writer is characterized as someone who expresses their inner passion or intellect because they can't help it, then the contemporary academic is a fearful clerk – always trying to please the boss in demeanour and attitude. They sullenly produce output.

What does output look like?

What I am here calling 'output' is writing that begins with a particular notion – the idea of publishing an article in a certain journal. The end then shapes pretty much everything about the project, because there are no specifications or restrictions other than those which help or hinder the process of achieving the golden prize. Virtually all aspects of output are shaped by the sorts of explicit demands and implicit prejudices of those who run journals, or rather, the interpretation of those demands and prejudices by anxious authors. The primary reason for output is career advancement, though there may well be other motives and factors which shape what sort of things get chosen as topics, methods and so on. Academics, like people in general, rarely only have one reason for doing things.

Journals almost always contain a series of very explicit instructions on what submissions should look like, sometimes called 'information for contributors', or 'style guides'. Oddly, they are actually instructions on how to make sure that various aspects of a paper are the same as every other paper in that journal. The *AMR* guide is a fairly typical one, with details of numbers of pages, title pages, the indentations for paragraphs, font size, spacing, abstract length, footnotes, acknowledgements, headings, tables and figures, appendices, referencing conventions and the format of the biographical sketch. It also contains a brief paragraph concerning the use of 'sexist and other biased language', and the following paragraph about style:

> Authors should use first person and active voice if they do not dominate the communication. **Authors should also avoid anthropomorphic language.** Vigorous, direct, clear and concise communication should be the objective of all articles in Academy journals. (*AMR*, 2012: 158; bold type in original)

What is interesting about these instructions is the extent to which they are deemed to be necessary in order to discipline the submissions to the journal. Stylistic standardization is simply assumed to be a prerequisite of submission, which in this sense should be understood to mean submitting to the will of the editors. New online submission systems allow even greater surveillance of some of these prescriptions, such that articles will be returned if they are one word over the, for example, 8,000 that a particular journal permits.

These kinds of instructions are deemed necessary in order to control what the journal looks like, which is a reasonable aim for any publication,[8] but they also have the effect of sending a message about the discipline which authors will be subject to. If we add to this the 'editorial statement', or 'information for contributors' which explains what topics the journal covers, and what sort of research the journal is (and is not) interested in publishing, then it is clear that the content of the journal has already been prefigured very explicitly. While there are huge variations in this structure (and *AMR*'s guidelines are by no means particularly oppressive when compared to Emerald Group Publishing's 'structured abstract' which has to make a claim about the 'originality/value' of a contribution), this is a general feature of the contemporary academic journal. It defines an area of knowledge, and hence what is not included in that area, and then determines the form which that knowledge must take if it is to be included. Any social process which begins with such prescription and proscription is clearly tightly controlled. Journals are like swimming pools, parks or libraries – locations where conformity is continually emphasized by the signage, and creativity or dissent discouraged.

Yet even when the editorial statement suggests that the journal welcomes scholars and ideas from outside the centre, it seems that they rarely manage to get in. In 2008, Stephen Dunne et al. published a survey conducted in 2006 which showed how a sample of management journals scored on ten different dimensions – having authors from outside the top 500 universities or who are located in the developing

---

[8]Though most articles in most journals are now downloaded as PDFs, and not read from a hard copy of the journal. This means a reader might not know what 'house style' the journal has because they only see one instance of it.

world, and publishing articles which engaged with feminism, sexuality, postcolonialism, war, the environment, workplace exploitation, collective representation and inequalities of wealth. It revealed some interesting distinctions between journals, but, most importantly for my argument here, it also revealed that most of these highly ranked journals publish very little work which is engaged with issues which are of central global importance. For example, there is no explicit instruction to authors to ignore 'the relationship between business/corporate practice and war, violence and/or the displacement of populations' (Dunne et al., 2008: 278), yet only 37 management articles out of over 2,300 surveyed mentioned it. Whether articles on these themes are being rejected, or whether they are never being written, the result is that the dominant academic journals publish on a narrow and predictable range of topics written by authors who work in a predictable set of countries and institutions. Another way of putting this is to say that, for an academic concerned to produce output, the best strategy is to look at what journals currently publish, and then try to write something pretty much the same. Obviously, it is much easier to do this is if you are already based in a university or country where there are scholars already doing this, can get easy access to the journals you want to publish in, and if you share the training, assumptions and professional networks of those who already publish in those journals. This is to say nothing of the language which, it goes without saying, is usually English (Steyaert and Janssens, 2013). Since most people on the globe don't speak English, this presents them with a problem in getting published in *AMR*.

Finally, there is there question of style itself, because output is almost always written in some quite specific ways. After describing (in a manner laced with the sexism of the 1950s) just what the good academic voice sounds like, C. Wright Mills, in the 'On Intellectual Craftsmanship' appendix to the 1959 book *The Sociological Imagination*, makes the following observations:

> The other way of presenting work does not use any voice of any man. Such writing is not a 'voice' at all. It is an autonomous sound. It is a prose manufactured by a machine. That it is full of jargon is not as noteworthy as that it is strongly mannered: it is not only impersonal; it is pretentiously impersonal. (1959: 220–221)

What Mills describes as the 'mannered' nature of social science, and evidences in his book with the example of Talcott Parsons, is not an absence of style, but a particular style. It is easy to spot in PhD students when they try to write in a particular way – using technical terms; polysyllabic words; long sentences, often with subordinate clauses; long paragraphs; and breaking up the flow of sentences with long lists of references. Not only does this produce text which is often ungainly and difficult to read, it is also exclusionary, in the sense that it is difficult to imagine someone outside the academic in-group having the patience or expertise to understand what might be meant. Grey and Sinclair go even further than this, suggesting that much writing in critical management studies is 'pretentious, obscurantist and dull ... a punitive, even sadistic, way of writing has been created that perpetuates the very problems that critical approaches ostensibly set out to critique and subvert' (2006: 445).

I'm uncertain whether critical management studies is worse than other areas of the social sciences, but Grey and Sinclair are absolutely right to draw attention to the exclusionary nature of this method of expression.

Now if what was being discussed was cosmology, or multi-dimensional mathematics, then it wouldn't be surprising if Jane and Joe Public couldn't read it, but these are descriptions of social life, which all humans know about. In principle, a motivated and reasonably educated person should be able to understand most of what is being argued over in the social sciences. Unless, of course, the genre of 'social science writing' is exclusionary precisely because it is a project which supports a particular identity claim, and in turn a set of institutions. Writing like an academic is a practice which performs the distinctiveness of academics as a professional or occupational group who deserve a particular kind of status and reward (Billig, 2013). Consider a counter-factual. If academics wrote like journalists, or like novelists, or like policy-makers, then how could they claim that what they did was different and special? This is particularly important in the social sciences, suspended as they are between the detailed unintelligibility of science and technology, and the cultural legitimacy of the arts and humanities. There is no reason not to write a history book or literary biography as a good story, but the collective insecurities of social scientists often mean that books on gender, organization or cities are incomprehensible to urban women and men who work as managers.

We can say, then, that 'output' is defined in particular ways. It is a piece of writing published in a narrow range of periodicals, and which submits to the instructions that pertain to those periodicals in terms of its structure and style. It is also likely, though not inevitable, that it will be a piece of writing which conforms to the dominant assumptions of a particular intellectual field, since those are the forms of thought which the key figures in a field feel comfortable with. 'Output', in other words, is a form of soft conformity, an agreement not to innovate too much, and to respect your elders and betters in manner and speech. The academic who commits herself to output, perhaps in the name of playing the game or paying the mortgage, is already ceding some of their intellectual autonomy. The game that will end up playing them is already constituted by some powerful forces, not least of which are the forms of capitalism which are manifest in the global publishing industry.

Money

So far, I have been concentrating on the example of the academic journal as disciplinary structure which tends to produce fearful clerks. This has meant concentrating on the ways in which certain institutions – universities as employers and journals as gatekeepers – operate to discipline what can be written, by whom, and where. This is not the whole story, however, because just as important is the academic publishing industry, a set of commercial concerns which are almost entirely parasitic on universities, but which have managed to insinuate themselves into the process of generating and disseminating academic writing to a remarkable extent. There are now a series of companies which trade in information – news, academic work, professional databases, etc. In 2011, for example, Wiley had a turnover of $1.7 billion, Reed Elsevier £6 billion, and Informa £1.275 billion. These are companies which now own many familiar publishers – such as Routledge, which is owned by Taylor and Francis, which in turn is owned by Informa. Cengage is privately held, but had an estimated turnover of £1.958 billion in 2009. Sage, the publisher of this volume, is also privately owned, but it's difficult to come to any figures on turnover. Large concentrated capitalist firms dominate this industry. They aren't the only academic publishers, because there are influential university presses and professional associations too, but the commercial sector is the biggest and fastest growing.

This is problematic enough, and there is increasing discussion of the ways in which library budgets are being sucked dry, academic labour being expropriated and costs externalized in order to support hyperprofitability (Lightfoot et al., 2012; Land et al., 2012). However, my focus here is on the ways in which this set of institutions is also disciplining intellectual production. The clearest example can be seen if we look at the other way in which academics publish – books. Though in large parts of the social sciences they are not as valued as they once were, books are still a significant form of output, particularly in the arts and humanities and some areas of the social sciences such as sociology and politics. It goes without saying that commercial publishers don't produce books solely for their cultural value, so they tend to be commissioned on the basis of likely profitability, and channelled into clear market segments. The most common form of production is the 'textbook', which is signalled as essential reading on large courses. There is one important feature of such a book – that it should be generic in order to fit as many courses as possible. This means that new or controversial ideas, as well as local and specific forms of thinking, will be discouraged in favour of reproducing the core assumptions and examples from a particular domain. Textbooks will tend to be conservative because they are designed to be marketed to lots of lecturers and students on lots of different courses in lots of different places. If they narrow their market, they will not make money for publishers.

The implication of this is that it is becoming harder to find publishers who are keen to take a book which does not already have evidence of customers already waiting in a particular market segment. The killer question for many book proposals, and presumably at commissioning meetings, is 'does anyone teach courses on this?' If the answer is no, and there aren't other compelling reasons to take the book on, then it will remain an imaginary project. While there are some specialist monographs and edited collections produced by academic publishers, this one being an example, they tend to be priced so that a short print run can cover costs, effectively meaning that even the author's mother would think twice about buying a copy for very limited hardback runs. The idea of the textbook (and associated supporting text) has come to dominate the academic publishing imagination, with its assumptions about the reproduction of authority, of sameness, of the established core of normal science. In this way, a business strategy translates into a political epistemology.

Big academic publishers have an imperative to make profits – they are commercial concerns – so unsurprisingly they seek high-value markets and predictable returns. Their heavy investment in journals since the 1990s reflects this imperative too, precisely because a successful journal externalizes the costs of authors and editors to universities, at the same time as it delivers continuing annual returns from library budgets. Even a textbook can't guarantee this, because its value decreases over time. The key question for publishers is what makes a successful academic journal that can justify a high subscription fee, and here we return to the entanglements of journal ranking systems, the imperatives of universities and academic careers (Parker and Thomas, 2011). Publishers have an interest in encouraging academics to care about the citations which lead into impact factors, the relative positions in lists, institutional affiliations, visibility in North America and so on. Their interest is in maximizing the income from a journal, but this interest also tends to reinforce the importance of the disciplinary core, because this is where the big numbers are found. Though *AMR* and other Academy journals are not owned by a publisher, all journal publishers in management would see theirs as an enviable market position, and seek to emulate it. This is rarely an explicit strategy, but rather to say that the financial incentives for large capitalist publishing firms reinforce the gravitational pull of the geographical and intellectual centre. They are more likely to reproduce the conditions for fearful clerks to produce output, than to (for example) challenge the Thomson Reuters system of ranking journals on the basis of two-year impact factors.

Money, in the sense of the huge profits which can be made by selling academic writing, is important here, but so too is it in a quantitatively smaller sense. If writing is a job, it is done for money, and is hence constrained in some way by the person who pays the money. This is as true for novelists and poets as it is for academics, and the enduring concern of the former about their royalties and advances once again questions an account which romantically elevates the writer-artist away from the ground (Holgate and Wilson-Fletcher, 1998). Academics work for money too, not just for noble vocational reasons, and if we look at salary levels, it's pretty clear that the closer you get to the centre, the higher they get. That is to say, in the countries of the global North, in the research elite universities which can charge the highest tuition fees, and in the 'best' business schools, we find the highest academic salaries, and often even payment systems which reward publication with cash prizes. Follow the money and it leads you once again to the core, in this case the US elite, together with a small number of other mostly English-speaking institutions in North West Europe. If you want to turn this into a piece of career advice, in order to maximize your salary, do everything you can to end up at Harvard Business School or similar, and hence produce forms of output that will maximize this possibility. Let's be clear, if you don't do this, you won't earn as much, and your rates per word will be lower. Decide how much you care about this.

Writing up

The tone of this chapter has been a little depressing so far. It seems to be an account of interlocking institutions which reproduce the same and mitigate against difference; of a series of processes and decisions which claim impartiality but end up reproducing work which is pretty much the same as everything else. It's a tale of conspiracy, but a vague and generalized one. It's not a story of how some evil straight patriarchs censor women and gays, or white people suppress black voices, or socialists are marginalized by neo-liberal editors – though I'm sure all these things happen. Instead this is a story of the way in which the solid inevitability of institutions makes things seem necessarily so. Most publishers, editors, reviewers, deans and authors are people with integrity who are kind to kittens; they do not intend to be or produce fearful clerks, but the collective consequence of their interactions is the dominance of output. But what is to be done about it?

It's easy enough to see that parts of the system can be unimagined. There is no reason why commercial publishers should continue to make gigantic profits by expropriating the labour of academics, particularly since it is often funded by taxpayers. In an age of open access, there are compelling policy reasons to make sure that the results of publicly funded research are available to the public, and not hidden behind paywalls or priced for libraries, and hence effectively inaccessible to those without access to money or a university. (And even the internet, outside the wealthier enclaves of the global North.) But taking back some of the tools of the trade won't solve lots of the other problems. The gravitational pull of the centre – in topic, epistemology, politics, language and style – will remain and continue to shape writing.

Merely kicking against the pricks won't make them go away, because power doesn't work like that. As any sociologist of knowledge will tell you, we can't collectively step outside the power of institutions to some place in which we are free to write whatever the fuck we want, whenever the fuck we want, and publish it on dried leaves which we will throw to the wind. However, understanding the spider's web of gentle constraints might help us think harder about writing itself, and make it visible in ways that it very often isn't. As I suggested at the start of this chapter, writing is often articulated as something that happens after the real work has been completed. As a result, we often don't see writing as important, and make it disappear into categories like 'dissemination', 'reach' and 'output'. Issues of audience and style are simply assumed, when perhaps they should always be questions. Making writing and the institutions of publication visible is hence the first step to avoiding it becoming output. The problem needs to be made present before we can do anything about it.

Once this has been done, there are two obvious things to think about. One is the joy and responsibility of writing as something that is worth doing, and worth doing well, for its own sake. The horror and anxiety that 'writing up' often provokes in academics, particularly younger ones who haven't yet managed to conceal their fear, is both sad and counter-productive. This is writing in the expectation of harsh judgement from those above you, those who 'supervise' you, and shaped by the straitjacket of expectation. It is writing which is closed, defensive and opaque because it reflects a fear of opening too much, and hence of being revealed to be insufficient. As Grey and Sinclair (2006: 452) put it, this is writing 'as a shriven, cowed and cowering path towards routinized, professionalized "publication"'. This is writing which is boring and painful to do, and so perhaps it's unsurprising that we tend not to talk about it very loudly, apart from complaining about how hard we have been working, and (like a petulant footballer) how we are misunderstood by stupid referees. But writing could be a pleasure, a form of self-expression which plays with language and ideas with a serious joy. In so many other contexts – conversations, emails, texts, messaging – we are capable of being witty and clever without it hurting too much, so why does academic writing weigh us down?

In practical terms, I think this means encouraging social science students to read and write in different genres, and to think about the qualities of the texts they read, and which make the discipline to which they wish to lend their labours (Geertz, 1988; Simons, 1998; Billig, 2013). It is likely that academic social science will have certain generic qualities, just as science fiction novels do, but that is no reason not to encourage play and bending with the genre, just as science fiction does. Judgements will still be made, of course, because we can't destroy the panopticon by willing it so, but if we begin from assumptions about pleasure and difference, then perhaps what we imagine to be constraints might subtly shift. Rather than writing being a weight and a duty, it might become an opportunity to play, and make something new. This will involve reflective training in writing, and critical education about publishing, as embedded parts of thinking about research training. The issues which I have discussed above are not epiphenomenal to research in management, they are central to its constitution and reproduction and need to be taught alongside epistemology and methods.

It is worth thinking about this in some quite personal ways too, particularly if you are a reader who feels that it's all very well for Professor Fattypants Parker to say these things, but entirely different for someone doing a PhD, or needing to get past probation. But the ideas I have played with above aren't really that outlandish. Indeed, they are commonly shared by writers and readers, supervisors and students, deans and professors, and one of the things that prevents a loosening of the cobwebs is a kind of collective but unvoiced sense that this is just the way things are, even if we don't like them very much. As with much of the social, we know it's stupid, but carry on doing it anyway, even when there are some splendid books that try to persuade us otherwise (Becker, 2007; Billig, 2013). That suggests that, if you do decide to stop writing output, you might find that readers of various kinds are actually rather more sympathetic than you thought they would be because they are sick of reading and writing output too. Not all the time, because you will get accused of 'journalism' (by people who don't know how difficult journalism is), or having an inappropriate 'style' (by reviewers who appear to have little style themselves). But sometimes readers won't cluck these clichés, and will actually let themselves enjoy what you have written, and the way that you have written it, and then your piece might be accepted.

It might, but there are no guarantees when you, or I, write for any reader, and the only way to stop writing output is to stop writing output. Just be prepared to be rejected. You will be rejected anyway, even if you try to write the most colourless, contentless and formulaic articles simply in order to get a paper in a 'top-ranked' journal (Alvesson and Gabriel, 2013). The rejections just happen and they will carry on happening as long as you write for editors and reviewers. (And they will continue to hurt, too.) So armour yourself, which is what all writers of all kinds do, and get rejected in style. At least you will then feel you have said what you wanted to say, written for people you care about, and perhaps even enjoyed the writing. You can also break out of the self-loathing and endless doubt that comes from believing that you must always satisfy the Big Other, even when the Big Other refuses to even give you a second glance. It's your choice, so if you care about this stuff, then take responsibility and don't blame someone else. Your words probably won't change the world, but at least they will feel like *your* words.

Just as important as this is the possibility of writing into different institutional fields or worlds altogether. The universe of academic books and journals is a tiny one, though it may seem big enough when you are positioned in the middle of it. Academics are rarely encouraged to write elsewhere, outside the charmed circle. Indeed, often enough other academics get rather sniffy, perhaps seeing mere journalism as a vulgar practice which should be discouraged. Yet it is obvious that there are plenty of other ways in which ideas can be communicated, and plenty of audiences who have no time or inclination to learn how to read an academic comic. All these other media have their own conventions, but there seems to me no intrinsic reason why an academic author would not be capable of moving between local newspapers, a blog, specialist magazines, professional newsletters, the national press and so on. None of this is easy. If you want to write for newspapers, you need to read newspapers and practice writing rapidly, in short sentences and paragraphs, with clear hooks to get the reader. If you write for a professional newsletter, you need to know what this audience cares about before you can get them to care about what you have to say. If you want to get ordinary people to care about what critical management studies means, you need to write in places where they might read it and in way that makes them want to read it. These are choices about styles and audiences, and they require an understanding of how not to write like an academic who needs their reader to know that they are an academic.

No form of writing is innocent, free of constraints and able to provide a wide open playing field for the ego and the imagination (Becker, 2007). Symmetrically, though, there is no form of writing that is inevitable, entirely determined by a set of parameters which are already established before the author switches the computer on. Some academic social science, and particularly some articles in *AMR*, might feel like that when you read them, but language is *parole* as well as *langue*, and hence there are huge combinatorial possibilities in even the simplest expression. If we add to that the complexities of meaning and context, then the prison bars become fairly bendy. For any academic who wants to write, to express their politics and their imagination in sentences that haven't been written before, merely producing career-enhancing output for top-ranked journals should not be enough. However, all knowledge has a politics, and any knowledge that pretends to be 'critical' has particular responsibilities to reflect on the institutions that structure us, and the audiences we write for, and not pretend that they are an individual genius who can make the world obey their pen. Writing is simultaneously individual (at this moment, now), and collective (as this piece will be edited, reviewed, published, discussed, cited and so on). It could not work without a set of institutions, but it could not exist unless the keys were tapped by someone.

The injunction of this book was to 'reflect from the field', and we are all fieldworkers when it comes to writing. The problem, in part, is that we don't realize it. We don't make the keystrokes audible, as they pitter-patter on the plastic; see the curve of a C, or the violence of a particular word; notice how a certain metaphor turns thought around; see how trying to sound clever can decorate common sense with pomposity (Billig, 2013); or see just how powerfully the centre gravitationally shapes our trajectories (Li and Parker, 2013). This is true of the PhD student, just as it is true of the most senior professor. The spectre of output will continue to haunt us, because we mostly work for money in institutions that endlessly judge us, but we should be careful not to let output dictate what we write, how we write, and where we write. Writing can be a joy, a form of play which allows us to be and make in remarkable ways, and which can be aimed at a wide variety of different audiences who might come to share our fascinations and concerns.[9] It might – but be careful here – even help bring about new worlds which at the moment we can only imagine on paper and screen. It is a practice which exists on the edge of possibilities, unless the only thing we want to do is to get to the centre as quickly as possible, like a burrowing maggot.

References

Alvesson, M. and Gabriel, Y. (2013) 'Beyond formulaic research', *Academy of Management Learning and Education*, 12(2): 245–263.

AMR (2012) 'Style guide for authors', *Academy of Management Review*, 37(1): 155–158.

Becker, H. (2007) *Telling about Society*. Chicago: Chicago University Press.

Billig, M. (2013) *Learn to Write Badly. How to Succeed in the Social Sciences*. Cambridge: Cambridge University Press.

Booth, W., Colomb, G. and Williams, J. (2008) *The Craft of Research* (3rd edn). Chicago: University of Chicago Press.

---

[9]The editors asked me to give some examples here, but I think it is better to ask my readers to do that. So, think of some authors who you really admire, and who you enjoy reading, and then try to write like them.

Bourdieu, P. (1988) *Homo Academicus*. Cambridge: Polity.

Dunne, S., Harney, S. and Parker, M. (2008) 'The responsibilities of management intellectuals: A survey', *Organization,* 15(2): 271–282.

Geertz, C. (1988) *Works and Lives: The Anthropologist as Author*. Oxford: Polity.

Graff, G., Birkenstein, C. and Durst, R. (2008) *They Say/I Say*. New York: W.W Norton.

Grey, C. (2010) 'Organizing studies', *Organization Studies,* 31(6): 677–694.

Grey, C. and Sinclair, A. (2006) 'Writing differently', *Organization,* 13(3): 443–453.

Holgate, A. and Wilson-Fletcher, H. (eds) (1998) *The Cost of Letters*. Brentford: Waterstones.

King, S. (2000) *On Writing*. New York: Scribner.

Kuhn, T. (1996) *The Structure of Scientific Revolutions* (3rd edn). Chicago: Chicago University Press.

Land, C., Beverungen, A. and Boehm, S. (2012) 'The poverty of journal publishing', *Organization,* 19(6): 929–938.

Li, E. and Parker, M. (2013) 'Citation patterns in organization and management journals: Margins and centres', *Organization,* 20(2): 299–322.

Lightfoot, G., Harvie, D., Lilley, S. and Weir, K. (2012) 'What are we to do with feral publishers?' *Organization,* 19(6): 905–914.

Meriläinen, S., Tienari, J., Thomas, R. and Davies, A. (2008) 'Hegemonic academic practices: Experiences of publishing from the periphery', *Organization,* 15(4): 584–597.

Mills, C.W. (1959) *The Sociological Imagination*. New York: Oxford University Press.

Murray, R. (2005) *Writing for Academic Journals*. Buckingham: Open University Press.

Parker, M. and Thomas, R. (2011) 'What is a critical journal?', *Organization* 18(4): 419–427.

Simons, H. (ed.) (1988) *Rhetoric in the Human Sciences*. London: Sage.

Steyaert, C. and Janssens, M. (2013) 'Multilingual scholarship and the politics of translation in management and organization studies', *Organization* 20(1): 131–142.

Suddaby, R. (2012) 'Editor's comments', *Academy of Management Review,* 37(1): 6–9.

Williams, J. (1990) *Style. Towards Clarity and Grace*. Chicago: University of Chicago Press.

THIRTEEN

Conclusion: Reflexivity, ethics and the researcher

Emma Jeanes and Tony Huzzard

In this book we have tried to present a range of tales from the field that reflect the various 'stages' of the research process (a formulaic notion we challenge, but which we recognize as having an important resonance, especially for those embarking on research for the first time). In doing so, we have brought together a collection of reflections on the research process, capturing the nature of and challenges faced in engaging in critical research. We have also presented examples of how reflexive and ethical research can be conducted and the challenges in trying to achieve that in (critical) research. The book has not sought to be normative or prescriptive (though Chapter 9, which looks at methods, goes some way towards offering the reader a more practical introduction) but illustrative and reflective: a basis for discussion rather than a toolkit.

In this conclusion we explore three interrelated themes of reflexivity, ethics and the researcher identity which are recurrent throughout many of the book's contributions and thus worthy of closer attention in this conclusion. Reflexivity has been positioned as a core concern of CMS (Fournier and Grey, 2000) and thus being reflexive has become a hallmark of being a critical researcher (though it is not exclusive to this community). While we agree with the importance of reflexivity to critical research, we suggest that it also raises some concerns, such as researchers using it as a rhetorical device to signify a certain identity or ambition for the research, rather than actually engaging in reflexive *practice* (ironically, becoming a box that has to be ticked leading to superficial engagement or gratifying the idiosyncrasies of thesis examiners or journal referees). Furthermore, reflexivity has become the marker of a good, and one might assume ethical, researcher (Alvesson et al., 2008). In this sense it appears that reflexivity has become the substitute for formal ethics, not least in light of the limitations of formal or procedural ethics when conducting research. This may be fruitful, but it is also crucial that ethics is not lost in the discourse or practice of reflexivity, which might otherwise be focused on theoretical (ontological and epistemological) rather than ethical concerns. Therefore questions of how, when and why researchers engage in reflexivity and its links with ethics are crucial. Lastly, we explore these issues in relation to researcher identity. Who we are, our background, experiences, values, perceptions, judgements, influences and so on are crucial to our reflexivity. By focusing on researcher identity we seek to understand the interplay between reflexivity and ethics from the perspective of the community or communities in which we want to be recognized, and the researcher we want to become. Understanding the research process as part of an identity project highlights the situated nature of research in the context of researcher's communities, personal ambitions, institutional environment and so on – all matters that are typically disconnected from the research process despite, as reflexivity reminds us, being fundamental to it. Understanding research from the perspective of the researcher's identity, particularly in the context of critical management research, and what constitutes reflexive, ethical research within that academy, encourages a more critical take on our own research, its ethics and reflexivity.

Reflexivity in critical management research

Reflexivity has been described as the 'new sensibility' (Willmott, 1998) and is typically related to our intellectual responsibility to examine our metatheoretical commitments and predispositions, in order to appreciate how they impact on scholarly outcomes (and, in doing so, understand how management knowledge is produced, organized and legitimized). Reflexivity is discussed in a growing literature (Alvesson et al., 2008; Cunliffe, 2003), and can be linked closely to ethics, not least because our ethical standpoints shape our accounts of our research (see Chapter 9, on accounting for our methods). Alvesson and Sköldberg (2000: 5) focus on 'the way different kinds of linguistic, social, political and theoretical elements are woven together in the process of knowledge development, during which empirical material is constructed, interpreted and written'. Gill and Johnson (2010: 242) contrast situational reflexivity ('the monitoring by an ethnographer of his or her impact upon the social situation under investigation'), with epistemological reflexivity ('where the observer attempts hermeneutically to reflect upon and articulate the assumptions he or she deploys in apprehending and interpreting his or her own observations'). Johnson and Duberley (2003) differentiate between methodological reflexivity, deconstructive reflexivity, and epistemic reflexivity (monitoring the impact of the researcher on the research setting and addressing impact in writing, problematizing the researcher's own voice in favour of polyvocality, and participatory approaches to the co-creation of knowledge, respectively). Whilst all broadly engaging with the same themes, their different hues highlight the challenges facing the aspiring reflexive researcher, as well as the ability to select certain 'aspects' of reflexivity and ignore others.

In this text we have tried to demonstrate that reflexivity should not just be seen as a marker of critical management studies, or critical research – an end in itself, signifying the identity of the researcher or the research project as 'critical' – but as an ongoing process. This may appear to be somewhat nonsensical – how can one be unreflexively reflexive? We argue that this is possible by partial, contained or moments of reflexivity in research, rather than sustained and wide-reaching endeavours. Just as ethics may be partial and contested (even research celebrated for its ethical concerns – such as Laud Humphrey's (1970) *Tearoom Trade* – is not uniformly considered to be unethical, even by some of its critics), so reflexivity can be partial – in terms of scope (selecting certain aspects) and temporality (the length of time in which we engage in this reflexive practice). Given that reflexivity, following Fournier and Grey (2000), is often seen to be one of the hallmarks of critical research, there is the risk that 'some' reflexivity will be seen as an end in itself: an indication of the brand of research or as a marker of trustworthiness. The relative newness of reflexivity in discussions of research practice (see Chapter 11) also raises questions about reflexivity as a fad – a currently fashionable way to demonstrate the scholarly nature of our research (see Abrahamson, 1996).

Instead we argue that reflexivity should be seen as a means to creating scholarly research (and in turn becoming a scholarly, ethical researcher). Reflexivity is a key element of the means by which we challenge current research and dominant ideas (see the discussion of Alvesson and Sandberg in Chapter 2 on how we shape our research questions) and deconstruct so called 'common sense' (see also Willmott, Chapter 11, in which he explores how certain concepts – such as organization – become taken for granted). It is also central to how we consider our role as a researcher in the field, and the impact this has on our research, the research participants and the broader field of study, notably in ethnography as discussed by Nyberg and Delaney in Chapter 4, and particularly in the intensive, often intimate moments in which we engage directly with research participants (see Ekman's discussion of this in relation to interviewing in Chapter 7). Reflexivity can also be used to inform our decisions in the field, in ethnographic research (Chapter 4), and participatory research in which closeness and distance from the field must be constantly negotiated and cannot be prescribed (or proscribed) in advance. This aspect was emphasized, for example, in action research by Huzzard and Johansson in Chapter 5 and in the negotiations involved when researching the internet as described by Bertilsson in Chapter 8.

What becomes clear is that reflexivity is important not only in writing research, or accounts of how we went about the research (such as the methods section; see Chapter 9), but also in the moment of data collection, analysis, reflection and the development of ourselves as (critical) researchers (and which can be evidenced through our autobiography, as exemplified by Hugh Willmott in Chapter 11). In this regard such reflexivity informs not only our own sense of researcher identity, but also the community as a whole, as a means of exposing inequalities in researcher collaboration as well as recognizing our own role in shaping research teams, projects and the broader community. This is well illustrated by Jeanes, Loacker and Śliwa in Chapter 3, who highlight, for example, that despite claims of reflexivity such an endeavour is not always evident in practice. This chapter also draws attention to the need for a broad scope for reflexivity, which is otherwise often focused on the outputs of research, particularly written work. As Ashcraft and Ashcraft highlight in Chapter 9, reflexivity is not just a performance in order to make the research (and by implication the researcher) trustworthy, but a means by which we can move the field forward, in terms of how we research, analyse and theorize.

Whilst reflexivity has become cited as marker for critical research, in practice there is often more limited engagement with it, or explicit expectation demand for it. As Van Maanen (1996) notes, writing is framework- or paradigm-dependent, crafted within the rules and conventions of a particular community or journal. Increasingly journals specify research process-based criteria for submissions, such as confirming that ethical guidelines have been followed. Yet if we look at critically leaning journals such as *Organization* and *ephemera*, for example, there is a focus on the theoretical developments, but no specification for reflexivity in this process. *ephemera* seeks papers that 'counter the current hegemonization of social theory' and encourages 'the amplification of the political problematics of organization'. *Organization* 'promotes an ethos which is explicitly: theory-driven, international in scope and vision, open, reflective, imaginative and critical, interdisciplinary, facilitating exchange amongst scholars from a wide range of current disciplinary bases and perspectives'.[1] Reflexivity is implied in *Organization*, though not explicitly stated. Instead the emphasis in both is on (denaturalizing) theorization with, in the case of *ephemera*, a more explicit political ambition. In practice, therefore, engagement with reflexivity can be token, to signify an identity, or the validity of the research as critical, and there is little to compel us to be more reflexive in our research. Practical challenges also affect this, such as the limited journal article word limit in which we can evidence our reflexivity (but see Ashcraft and Ashcraft, in Chapter 9).

In this book we have sought to demonstrate that reflexivity needs to be embedded in the everyday of research practice – how we problematize and develop our research questions, how we approach and engage with the field, and account for it afterwards, as well as how we negotiate these relationships with our colleagues. We have also sought to evidence, by drawing on reflections from the field, the limits of this practice. We anticipate that readers will observe the limitations of the reflexivity presented in what might be seen as 'confessional tales' (Van Maanen, 1988. Reflexivity is challenging, confusing (Brannick and Coghlan, 2006) and never complete. To what extent, for example, do the chapters retain polyvocality, keeping the

---

[1]Taken respectively from the journal websites http://www.ephemerajournal.org/what-ephemera and http://org.sagepub.com/.

many stories rather than imposing an authorial voice (Lincoln and Denzin, 1994)? Or provide autobiographical accounts of research practice (Czarniawska, 1998), commenting systematically on their role (Easterby-Smith et al., 2008)? At the same time, to what extent can we or would we want to prescribe the exact nature and extent of reflexivity required? As Kunda (1992: 229) notes: 'Fieldwork, as all who have engaged in it will testify, is an intensely personal and subjective process, and there are probably at least as many "methods" as there are fieldworkers'.

However, whilst emphasizing the centrality of reflexivity in CMS research, it is important not to take things too far. As we have argued, although reflexivity can be an important means for questioning knowledge and denaturalization (Fournier and Grey, 2000), there is a danger that the apparent abandonment of any referential basis for anchoring our truth claims can lead to intellectual chaos (Brannick and Coghlan, 2006; Cunliffe, 2003). Moreover, to do so risks the rendering of critical research as little more than navel gazing. The danger here is that the researcher self takes over as the core research object or, put differently, reflexivity becomes the ends rather than the means.

Ethics in critical management research

Reflexivity has become a core means by which critical research engages with ethics. Eschewing more formal, often bureaucratic means of aspiring to ethical practice, reflexivity calls upon the researcher to be mindful and reflective of the impact of their research throughout the research process. Further, by identifying different aspects of reflexivity (see, for example, Johnson and Duberley, 2003), the otherwise abstract notion of reflexivity is given more concrete dimensions, which in turn suggests a guiding rationale or recognized praxis hinting at trustworthiness, in terms of both the ethics of the process and the quality of the research (Lincoln and Guba, 1985).

It is therefore perhaps no surprise that the chapters of this book engage more explicitly with reflexivity than with ethics. That said, these chapters also reflect the ethical concerns faced in the field, such as what Guillemin and Gillam (2004) have described as ethically important moments (see the discussion in Chapter 4 on critical ethnography), the inherently ethically questionable forms of research such as covert research (Chapter 6) and the challenge of seeking 'informed consent' (among other ethical concerns) in public arenas such as online (Chapter 8), and in contrast the challenges of open, negotiated research contracts in which ethics is – at least to some extent – made explicit (as explored in Chapter 5 on critical action research). As Chapter 5 demonstrates, a critical approach highlights the inherently power-laden nature of collaboration and construction of knowledge in which the researcher participates.

In action research, the movement between distance and closeness is more explicit, but all researchers face the challenge of balancing distance from the field (with overtones of a scientific 'objectivity') and a desire to become embedded or immersed in the field of study, or developing intimacy with respondents. In Chapter 7, Ekman explores the possibility of engaging with compassion as a means to navigate between the ethics of sensitivity and distance in research (and how they can assist each other) when interviewing. A Levinasian approach is explored which recognizes the essentially unknowable nature of others and the compassion inherent in recognizing and respecting this Otherness to ourselves (in accepting that they are not the same as me). This approach contrasts significantly with the traditional and institutionalized approach to ethics in which ethical research is accomplished through the following of rules and procedures, and often requiring ratification of the research design in advance, based on an assumption of a generic, typical or knowable researcher subject whose interests can be presumed in advance. The problems with and limitations of formal ethics are well documented, particularly for those engaged in qualitative research (Boden et al., 2009; Guillemin and Gillam, 2004). Typically the critique focuses on the impossibility of being able to foresee all the ethical challenges, and account for them in advance of entering the field, given the open and unfolding nature of qualitative research. Not only is formal ethics argued to be incapable of capturing this aspect of research, it is also seen to risk suggesting that research is ethical when no such claim can be made. The mere process of having received approval can mean that researchers fail to appreciate the ongoing negotiation of ethics in their research in the face of the unknowable Other. Levinas (1969) reminds us of the inherently unknowable nature of our responsibility to our research subject(s); that we know we have a responsibility to them does not mean we are able to deduce the precise nature of our responsibility and how we can or should respond to that demand (Jeanes and Muhr, 2010).

Ultimately we are left with the sense that ethical research is in some ways impossible. We can never know precisely the impact of our presence in the field, and the effect of our research. This, of course, does not negate the importance of understanding ethics and ethical practice in our research, as evidenced by a number of texts (Hammersley and Traianou, 2012; Israel and Hay, 2006; Mertens and Ginsberg, 2009; Miller et al., 2012; and the journal *Research Ethics*, among others). Primary ethical concerns, such as avoiding harm to research participants, ensuring participants give their informed consent, respecting the privacy of participants, and, where possible, avoiding deception remain important considerations. Related concerns focus on the relationship with funders, self-protection, and professional integrity as it relates to one's profession (Warwick, 1973), and (as demonstrated by Chapter 3, which explores researcher collaboration) how we engage with each other within our research community.

Formal ethics may be critiqued, not least for being seen to be focused on avoiding litigation, or creating the impression of quality and legitimacy (Rossman and Rallis, 2010), or as a managerial device to limit academic freedom (Graffigna et al., 2009; Lewis, 2008), particularly for qualitative research, where it is harder to anticipate the details of the research process in advance, which may preclude such research being approved (Boden et al., 2009; Guillemin and Gillam, 2004). The role of ethical codes and ethics committees has also been challenged for inviting a mechanistic approach to research ethics (Halse and Honey, 2007), removing individual responsibility once ethical approval has been awarded (Boden et al., 2009), or an unreflective application of guidelines (Cannella and Lincoln, 2007) and for being abstracted from the practice of undertaking research (Calvey, 2008). Critics of formal ethics point to the need for an ongoing consideration and negotiation of ethics (Boden et al., 2009; Hardy et al., 2001), and also the challenges in trying to prescribe how 'best' to manage ethics – a moralism that Hammersley and Traianou (2012) suggest underpins much of the current emphasis on formal ethics (codes, committees and so on; see also Chapter 7 on critical and compassionate interviewing). A different approach to ethics appears called for in which ethical guidelines are considered in a more reflexive, unfolding manner.

A reflexive approach, for example, calls upon us to consider potential harm to our research participants in a broader sense, and on an ongoing basis. As critical researchers we must ask ourselves what our critical standpoint brings to the way in which we engage within the field, and theorize without (Ford et al., 2010). For example, how does our critical stance influence our approach to ethics, and how do the negotiations between individual and collective concerns shape our framing of what constitutes harm? Similarly, from whom do we seek informed consent, and to what extent is there an openness in our ambitions such that consent can be considered to be fully informed? It is unlikely that managerial-level gatekeepers would be as willing to permit access to organizations if a full account of the critical ambitions or concerns of the project was revealed, or likewise the critical standpoint of the researcher (notwithstanding the fact that critical management research is not anti-managerial per se (Alvesson and Willmott, 1996; but see also Parker, 2002, 2006; Clegg et al., 2006, Willmott, 2006, for a discussion). Nonetheless, it is precisely these sites that critical researchers need to access in order to understand, critique and theorize organizing and organizations (and thus capitalism and its associated structures of domination: see Adler et al., 2007). However, reticence for full disclosure should also be a site for personal reflection and consideration. On what basis do we as critical researchers make these ethical judgements?

Not all of these are concerns exclusive to the critical researcher, but the particular ambitions of critical research (eschewing, or at least challenging, dominant managerial ambitions and denaturalizing common assumptions, perhaps with emancipatory goals: see Kelemen and Rumens, 2008) need to be reflected not only in our (critical) theorizing, but also by being critical of *how* we theorize and, prior to that, how our theoretical and political agendas (and ultimately the means by which we create our identity within the critical community) shape the way in which we engage with our field of study.

Concluding thoughts: The critical management researcher

What does it mean to be a critical management researcher? Who are we? What do we do? As put succinctly by one scholar: 'The selection of a research topic and a corresponding method are in many ways also a life choice. They are indicative of that which the researcher believes is important to "see" in the world, to investigate and how' (Rosen, 1991: 21). These questions, of course, are matters of identity, and it seems pertinent now in the final part of this book to reflect on this, as all the chapters in the book can be seen as narratives of the self authored by our contributors. As noted elsewhere, how we construct our sense of self is in effect a matter of identity (Gabriel, 2000; Giddens, 1991; Holstein and Gubrium, 2000). Theorists of identity have also insisted that selfhood is constructed intersubjectively, that is, with and through others (see Ricoeur, 1992). Being (or becoming) a critical management scholar is an exemplification of this in that we see ourselves as *critical* as a means of defining ourselves against the 'other', where the 'other' is something we generally understand as the 'mainstream' in management research and the assumptions and ideologies that this presupposes. This positioning against the other is something that we argue can be seen in the contributions to this volume.

However, as we highlighted in our introduction, the broad domain of critical management studies, although seemingly united against a clearly understood other, is nevertheless a contested terrain. Within CMS there are debates, positions, preferences of a paradigmatic nature. No consensus exists within CMS on ontology and epistemology; indeed, such differences may well prompt different methodological choices. The other also exists internally within CMS such that members of the CMS community seemingly need, when reading the work of others, to ask the question 'yes, but in what way is it critical?' This question will be familiar to those, for example, who have had papers questioned by fellow CMS scholars at seminars or conferences. It is a question that was also posed to us by our reviewers when initially receiving feedback on our publishing proposal. It has even been a question that we as editors have posed to each other on our various readings of the material from our authors. Accordingly, our identities not only inform our choice of research paradigm, but also are informed by the choice of paradigm. Furthermore, particular views as to what constitutes critical research (and what does not) can lead to critiques based on whether a critical researcher conforms to a certain norm that can, ironically, foreclose its critical possibilities.

However, as is well documented in the literature on researcher identity, our identities as researchers are multiple and fragmented (Davidson, 2012). This would also appear to be consistent with observations that there is increasing ambiguity concerning the sense of belonging of researchers (seen in general terms) and their affinity or identification. Hakala (2009), for example, has argued that there has been a recent shift from identification with one's discipline or field towards identification with a particular institution, which may have something to do with the way in which the academy has become increasingly marketized (Smith, 2012). Academic labour – CMS scholars included – has been increasingly subject to strict funding regimes, quality assessments, accreditation exercises and other forms of control. In turn, these have generally ushered in concomitant forms of identity regulation: one's identity becomes subject to being a reliable supplier of deliverables to funding bodies, one becomes a regular publisher in three- or four-star journals according to the ABS journal ranking system; one becomes an active player at one's own business school in the EQUIS accreditation merry-go-round. Let us not forget as well that being or becoming a CMS scholar – buying into the CMS brand (Thompson, 2004) or joining the CMS community of practice – also entails inevitable processes of identity regulation (see Chapter 12 in this volume, by Parker).

Most of us invest our selfhood in a particular paradigm as a means of finding some sort of anchoring for our identities as (critical) scholars. In many ways this is no different than subjectivities at work in any profession. Yet if there is one characteristic that marks critical scholars of management out from others it is a belief in the need for reflexivity. This is a core statement about critical scholarship as underscored in Fournier and Grey's (2000) article and indeed by critical scholars of management of a rather different paradigmatic persuasion (see Thompson and McHugh, 2009: 13–14). Essentially, reflexivity is about being constantly aware of our paradigmatic preferences and how these might bias, compromise and perhaps unduly influence our scientific endeavours, and how we might account for this (see Chapters 9, 11 and 12 on methods, analysis and writing, respectively).

Yet we contend that what it means to be a critical researcher is often focused on the non-performative intent and denaturalization (often with emancipatory intentions) at the expense of reflexivity. Put another way, the broader goals of critical management research have become more important than the means by which we achieve them (see also Wray-Bliss, 2003). This comparative lack of reflexivity affects not only the process of research, but also by definition its outcomes. As was reflected in Chapter 9, on methods, the identity of a project matters, and shapes the process and product of research, as does the way in which we go about researching it (see Chapter 3 on collaborative research). Similarly, the identity of the researcher shapes the process of research, as can be reflected in an autobiographical approach to one's research career, as presented by Willmott in Chapter 11.

In their blending of the methodologies of problematization and mystery creation in Chapter 2, Alvesson and Sandberg argue that these both imply a different identity than is normally presupposed in social science. The methodologies call for a broader set of theories and vocabularies for challenging dominant assumptions and more emphasis on self-critical hermeneutic interpretations. Members of the CMS community, like all scholars, have their own comfort zone within which identity is reasonably secure – yet venturing outside this is what the demand for reflexivity essentially entails. Stepping outside one's comfort zone is what the authors call making a transition from 'cultivating an incremental gap-spotting research identity to [becoming] a reflexive and path-(up)setting scholar, with some preferences for irony and promiscuity over a fixed, programmatic position'. This is a matter of critically investigating and perhaps redefining one's own assumptions as well as those of the research field and paradigm in which we have invested our scholarly identities.

But there are several different forms of reflexive practice that we as critical scholars might undertake. For example, Alvesson et al. (2008) propose multi-perspectives, multi-voicing, positioning and destabilizing. They also argue that each of these entails a rather different researcher identity, namely traveller, builder or bricoleur (multi-perspective practices), participant, confessor or artist (multi-voicing practices), networker, politician or adventurer-explorer (positioning practices) and trouble-maker, infiltrator or insurgent (destabilizing practices). Huzzard and Johansson show, in their illustration of critical action research in Chapter 5, how the identity of the researcher changed as the reflexive practice in their case study iterated between multi-voicing and positioning. In this case this entailed a concomitant oscillation between the researcher as intimately related co-constructor of knowledge and distanced, dispassionate critic.

This apparent duality of researcher identity was also evident in Skrutkowski's account of doing covert ethnography in Chapter 6. The tension here was between maintaining the mask of having a corporate persona as an insider, on the one hand, and being an authentic covert ethnographer, on the other. This account also illustrates well how identity and reflexivity become inevitably intertwined in what he describes as a triple hermeneutic process, whereby raw data is first digested into a meaningful account, then attempts are made to investigate why this account might be better understood through the lens of critical theory, and finally the researcher's own constructive role is scrutinized critically. Interestingly, the author maintains that it was only after the third of these stages that his own identity struggles were brought to bear, prompting a deep reflection on what he saw as the fakeness of the company's project to repair its tarnished image as well as his own role in such a project.

As discussed elsewhere in this volume and in the CMS literature more broadly (see Alvesson et al., 2009), some sort of sympathetic attachment to the plight of the underdog in organizational life and thereby to the aim of emancipation is generally seen as a core characteristic of CMS. However, in Chapter 7, Ekman warns us against going too far with taking on an identity of being emancipators. Her complaint here is that such a position can easily end in a tendency towards suspicion of and moral superiority to actors in the field. In essence the CMS researcher, in his or her eagerness to 'emancipate', can easily end up defining the interests and even identities of those who are seen to be suffering the effects of power or domination. The danger here is that the power asymmetries of organizational life are augmented or even replaced by a new asymmetry between researcher and researched. In the context of interviewing she proposes, as a means of escaping these potential dilemmas, what she calls a compassionate approach that retains the ambition to point out suffering yet also insists on an extensive attempt to make sense of every subject in the research process. This sensitivity to the many others may be all the more worthwhile highlighting, given the findings presented in Jeanes, Loacker and Śliwa's chapter that researchers in the critical tradition may not be as reflexive in their practice as one might be led to assume.

We believe this book raises questions about why we undertake reflexive practice. Is it an end in itself, and if so, whose? Alternatively, is it a means to an end, and if so, to what end? We get the sense that reflexivity, or at least claiming to have been reflexive (as an add-on piece of supplementary text), in research accounts may in practice simply be an example of playing the research game, a box-ticking exercise to get published or to support claims to being 'critical' in order to gain legitimacy within a particular community (see also Brewis and Wray-Bliss, 2008). In this sense, the claim that one is engaging in reflexive practice is little more than undertaking some rather cynical identity work. Alternatively, accounts of reflexivity can be earnest attempts to lend trustworthiness to a piece of research, particularly within more interpretivist approaches. Whilst this is certainly more defensible, we see merit in going further with reflexive practice by using it, as suggested by Ashcraft and Ashcraft in Chapter 9, to move the field forward rather than simply using it as a defensive device for legitimacy within a given set of paradigmatic rules (for doing research). Perhaps, however, in our endeavours to pin down our selfhood as researchers we need to go beyond reflexive tales and, as Pullen (2007: 316) observes, question how 'rewriting the self … involves challenging authoritative frameworks which suppress difference and multiplicity and encourage writing multiplicity'. The concern with the practices of writing (and the performativity of 'critical writing') echoes the concerns expressed in this volume by Parker, in Chapter 12.

As this book has shown, we do believe that there are certain aspects of doing critical management research that differentiate themselves from doing 'mainstream' management research (Alvesson and Deetz, 2000). Perhaps, however, the dividing line is not always that clear-cut. It is now more than two decades since the publication of Alvesson and Willmott's *Critical Management Studies* anthology (1992), and, as we have argued in the introduction, the critical study of management has a far greater history than that publication which is often seen as the initiation of CMS (Fournier and Grey, 2000). But although we feel that CMS has now become a relatively mature sub-domain within the broad management field that offers many a meaningful sense of identity and mission within the business school, its adherents nevertheless cannot easily escape the processes of identity regulation exerted by CMS itself.

References

Abrahamson, E. (1996) 'Management fashion', *Academy of Management Review*, 21(1): 254–285.

Adler, P.S., Forbes, L.C. and Willmott, H. (2007) 'Critical management studies', *Academy of Management Annals*, 1(1): 119–179.

Alvesson, M., Bridgman, T. and Willmott, H. (2009) 'Introduction' in M. Alvesson, T. Bridgman and H. Willmott (eds), *The Oxford Handbook of Critical Management Studies*. Oxford: Oxford University Press.

Alvesson, M. and Deetz, S.A. (2000) *Doing Critical Management Research*. London: Sage.

Alvesson, M., Hardy, C. and Harley, B. (2008) 'Reflecting on reflexivity: Reflexive textual practices in organization and management theory', *Journal of Management Studies*, 45(3): 480–501.

Alvesson, M. and Sköldberg, K. (2000) *Reflexive Methodology: New Vistas for Qualitative Research towards a Reflexive Methodology*. London: Sage.

Alvesson, M. and Willmott, H. (1992) *Critical Management Studies*. London: Sage.

Alvesson, M. and Willmott, H. (1996) *Making Sense of Management: A Critical Introduction*. London: Sage.

Boden, R., Epstein, D. and Latimer, J. (2009) 'Accounting for ethos or programmes for conduct? The brave new world of research ethics committees', *Sociological Review*, 57(4): 727–749.

Brannick, T. and Coghlan, D. (2006) 'Reflexivity in management and business research: What do we mean?', *Irish Journal of Management*, 27(2): 143–160.

Brewis, J. and Wray-Bliss, E. (2008) 'Re-searching ethics: Towards a more reflexive critical management studies', *Organization Studies*, 29(12): 1521–1540.

Calvey, D. (2008) 'The art and politics of covert research: Doing "situated ethics" in the field', *Sociology*, 42(5): 905–918.

Cannella, G.S. and Lincoln, Y.S. (2007) 'Predatory vs. dialogic ethics: Constructing an illusion or ethical practice as the core of research methods', *Qualitative Inquiry*, 13(3): 315–335.

Clegg, S., Kornberger, M., Carter, M. and Rhodes, C. (2006) 'For management?', *Management Learning*, 37(1): 7–27.

Cunliffe, A.L. (2003) 'Reflexive inquiry in organizational research: Questions and possibilities', *Human Relations*, 56(8): 983–1003.

Czarniawska, B. (1998) *A Narrative Approach to Organization Studies*. London: Sage.

Davidson, J. (2012) 'The Journal Project and the I in qualitative research: Three theoretical lenses on subjectivity and self', *The Qualitative Report*, 17, Article 63.

Easterby-Smith, M., Thorpe, R. and Jackson, P.R. (2008) *Management Research*. London: Sage.

Ford, J., Harding, N. and Learmonth, M. (2010) 'Who is it that would make business schools more critical? Critical reflections on critical management studies', *British Journal of Management*, 21(S1): S71–S81.

Fournier, V. and Grey, C. (2000) 'At the critical moment: Conditions and prospects for critical management studies', *Human Relations*, 53(1): 7–31.

Gabriel, Y. (2000) *Storytelling. The Poetics of Organizational Life*. Oxford: Oxford University Press.

Giddens, A. (1991) *Modernity and Self-Identity: Self and Society in the Late Modern Age*. Cambridge: Polity Press.

Gill, J. and Johnson, P. (2010) *Research Methods for Managers*. London: Sage.

Guillemin, M. and Gillam, L. (2004) 'Ethics, reflexivity, and "ethically important moments" in research', *Qualitative Inquiry*, 10(2): 261–280.

Graffigna, G., Bosio, A.C. and Olson, K. (2009) 'How do ethics assessments frame results of comparative qualitative research? A theory of technique approach', *International Journal of Social Research Methodology*, 13(4): 341–355.

Hakala J. (2009) 'The future of the academic calling? Junior researchers in the entrepreneurial university', *Higher Education*, 57: 173–190.

Halse, C. and Honey, A. (2007) 'Rethinking ethics review as institutional discourse', *Qualitative Inquiry*, 13(3): 336–352.

Hammersley, M. and Traianou, A. (2012) *Ethics in Qualitative Research: Controversies and Contexts*. London: Sage.

Hardy, C., Phillips, N. and Clegg, S. (2001) 'Reflexivity in organization and management theory: A study of the production of the research "subject"', *Human Relations*, 54(5): 531–560.

Holstein, J.A. and Gubrium, J.F. (2000) *The Self We Live By. Narrative Identity in the Postmodern World*. New York: Oxford University Press.

Humphreys, L. (1970) *Tearoom Trade: Impersonal Sex in Public Places*. Chicago: Aldine.

Israel, M. and Hay, I. (2006) *Research Ethics for Social Scientists*. London: Sage.

Jeanes, E.L. and Muhr, S.L. (2010) 'The impossibility of guidance – a Levinasian critique of business ethics', in S.L. Muhr, B.M. Sørensen and S. Vallentin (eds), *Ethics and Organizational Practice – Questioning the Moral Foundations of Management*. Cheltenham: Edward Elgar.

Johnson, P. and Duberley, J. (2003) 'Reflexivity in management research', *Journal of Management Studies*, 40(5): 1279–1303.

Kelemen, M. and Rumens, N. (2008) *An Introduction to Critical Management Research*. London: Sage.

Kunda, G. (1992) *Engineering Culture: Control and Commitment in a High-tech Corporation*. Philadelphia: Temple University Press.

Levinas, E. (1969) *Totality and Infinity. An Essay on Exteriority*, trans A. Lingis. Pittsburgh: Duquesne University Press.

Lewis, M. (2008) 'New strategies of control: Academic freedom and research ethics boards', *Qualitative Inquiry*, 14(5): 684–699.

Lincoln, Y.S. and Guba, E.G. (1985) *Naturalistic Inquiry*. Thousand Oaks, CA: Sage.

Lincoln, Y.S. and Denzin, N.K. (1994) *Handbook of Qualitative Research*. Thousand Oaks, CA: Sage.

Mertens, D.M. and Ginsberg, P.E. (2009) *The Handbook of Social Research Ethics*. London: Sage.

Miller, T., Birch, M., Mauthner, M. and Jessop, J. (2012) *Ethics in Qualitative Research* (2nd edn). London: Sage.

Parker, M. (2002) *Against Management: Organization in the Age of Managerialism*. Cambridge: Polity.

Parker, M. (2006) 'Stockholm syndrome', *Management Learning*, 37(1): 39–41.

Pullen, A. (2009) 'Becoming a researcher: Gendering the research self', in A. Pullen, N. Beech and D. Sims (eds), *Exploring Identity*. Basingstoke: Palgrave.

Ricoeur, P. (1992) *Oneself as Another*. Chicago: University of Chicago Press.

Rosen, M. (1991) 'Coming to terms with the field: Understanding and doing organizational ethnography', *Journal of Management Studies*, 28(1): 1–24.

Rossman, G.B. and Rallis, S.F. (2010) 'Everyday ethics: Reflections on practice', *International Journal of Qualitative Studies in Education*, 23(4): 379–391.

Smith, K. (2012) 'Fools, facilitators and flexians: Academic identities in marketised environments', *Higher Education Quarterly,* 66(2): 155–173.

Thompson, P. (2004) 'Brands, boundaries and bandwagons: A critical reflection on critical management studies', in S. Fleetwood and S. Ackroyd (eds), *Critical Realist Applications in Organisation and Management Studies.* London: Routledge, pp. 51–66.

Thompson, P. and McHugh, D. (2009) *Work Organizations: A Critical Approach* (4th edn). Basingstoke: Palgrave Macmillan.

Van Maanen, J. (1988) *Tales of the Field: On Writing Ethnography.* Chicago: University of Chicago Press.

Van Maanen, J. (1996) 'On the matter of voice', *Journal of Management Inquiry,* 5(4): 375–381.

Warwick, D.P. (1973) 'Tearoom trade: Means and ends in social research', *Hastings Center Studies,* 1(1): 27–38.

Willmott, H. (1998) 'Re-cognizing the other: Reflections on a "new sensibility" in social and organization studies', in R. Chia (ed.), *In the Realm of Organization: Essays for Robert Cooper.* London: Routledge, pp. 217–246.

Willmott, H. (2006) 'Pushing at an open door: Mystifying the CMS manifesto', *Management Learning,* 37(1): 33–37.

Wray-Bliss, E. (2003) 'Research subjects/research subjections: Exploring the ethics and politics of critical research', *Organization,* 10(2): 307–325.

Index

Figures and Tables are indicated by page numbers in bold.